THE COUNTRY LIFE BOOK OF BOOK COLLECTING

The
Country Life
Book of

BOOK
COLLECTING

Edited by
Richard Booth

Country Life Books

© 1976 Carter Nash Cameron Limited

Published for Country Life Books by
The Hamlyn Publishing Group Limited
London · New York · Sydney · Toronto
Astronaut House, Feltham, Middlesex, England

ISBN 0 600 31378 6

Produced by Carter Nash Cameron Limited
25 Lloyd Baker Street, London WC1X 9AT

Designed by Tom Carter

Set by SX Composing Ltd.,
61 Oakwood Avenue, Leigh-on-Sea, Essex
Printed and bound by
Waterlow (Dunstable) Ltd
George Street, Dunstable, Bedfordshire
Printed and Bound in Great Britain

Contents

Acknowledgments

Collection William Allan; photo Ian Cameron: 133, 137, 138a,b,c,d, 140, 141a,b,c,d,e,f, 142a, 145, 149, 159a & b, colour plate facing p. 113

By kind permission of Professor Quentin Bell & The Hogarth Press 162a

Biblioteca Apostolica Vaticana 22a

Bibliotheque National, Paris 22c

By courtesy of the Bodley Head 156b & c, 157a, 167

British Library: photo Ray Gardner 22b, 24b, 26a & b, 29, 30b, 31a & b, 35, 40, 42a & b, 44a, 45, 46, 47b, 82, 99, 100a & b, 101a,b,c, 102, 112b, 114b & c

By courtesy of the Trustees of the British Museum 21, colour plates facing pp. 48, 112

By kind permission of Chatto & Windus 152b & c

By kind permission of the Council of the Linnaean Society of London 64, 65a,b,c, 66, 67, 70a & b, 72, 73, 74a,b,c, 76, 78, colour plates facing pp. 64,65

By kind permission of Mr Peter Dickinson 158a

By kind permission of Mrs Barbara Edwards & Hodder & Stoughton Children's Books Ltd. 122b

William Heinemann Ltd. 59c, 161b, 166b

Photo Oliver Gamgee; Paneikon 59c

By kind permission of the Hogarth Press 169a,b

Raymond Mander & Joe Mitchenson Theatre Collection 59b

The Mansell Collection 30a, 33, 34a, 86, 89a & b, 90a & b, 91

Line illustrations by Ernest H. Sheperd from *Winnie The Pooh* by A.A. Milne. Copyright under the Berne Convention. Copyright in the United States 1926 by E.P. Dutton & Co., Inc. Copyright renewal 1954 by A.A. Milne: 123

By kind permission of the Owen Estate & Chatto & Windus 157b

Piccadilly Rare Books; photo Rodney Todd-White jacket illustration

By courtesy of Bertram Rota Ltd; photo Ian Cameron 146b, 151a & b, 152a,b,c, 153, 154a & b, 155a & b, 156a,b,c, 157a & b, 158a,b,c, 159a,b,c, 160, 161a & b, 162a,b,c,d, 164, 165a & b, 166, 167, 168, 169a & b

Victoria & Albert Museum; photo Sally Chappell 51a,b,c, 114a

Victoria & Albert Museum; photo Angelo Hornak colour plates facing pp. 128, 129

By kind permission of Frederick Warne & Co. 122a

With kind permission of the Executors of the Estate of Mrs George Bambridge 119b & c

The editors would like to express their gratitude to all those who made it possible to assemble the pictures for this book. While every attempt has been made to trace the holders of copyright, inevitably there will be some omissions for which we apologise.

Note
The opinions expressed by the various authors of the chapters in this book do not necessarily reflect the views of other contributors or of those individuals and organisations who have made illustrations available. Where prices are quoted they are intended as a guide only and should not be understood to be exact valuations.

Introduction

In the last ten years I have handled several million books—probably more than anyone in the history of the world. Unfortunately this has made me a very bad book collector. I have been distracted by a thousand different interests. One day I look at the first novel written around a dog—*Snarlegrow* by Captain Marryat: on the next I talk to a scholar from Oklahoma whose sole interest is the illustrators of the Wild West, and on the third a collection comes in on the revival on monasticism in the Anglican Church. The day after that all my attention is concentrated on a student from Oxford in a navy blue velvet cloak who is attempting to live in the 1890s. The succession of book collectors and their interests is endless. Innumerable times I have been inspired to commence collecting, but still my own library represents a hopeless jumble of interests. I have a fine copy of Felix on the Bat, the most aesthetic book on cricket ever written, a copy of White's *History of Selborne* because it is a landmark in the literature of natural history and a small group of books illustrated by Bewick, the most influential English book illustrator of the 19th century. I have several books in English published in the 18th century by Tourneisen of Basle because I felt I would be interested in discovering the influence of England on 18th century Switzerland. The five thousand books in my library, however, do not form a reasonable collection: there are, indeed, the nuclei of several hundred collections, but none has been developed or fulfilled. I am a hopeless eclectic. My catholic tastes rather than my individual ability to establish a collection are my qualifications for writing the introduction to this book. My enthusiasm for books is diverse but passionate. I am afraid that this is often the fate of the general secondhand bookseller. How can the unlucky fellow be expected to build the world's finest collection of several thousand books, articles, tape recordings etc. on Sussex when, just after he has decided to do this, his resolve is torpedoed by a superb collection of writings on Abyssinnia coming into stock.

My first enthusiasm for books was kindled by an ex-First World War guardsman who had started bookselling in Guildford in 1923—cycling round the area to acquire his purchases. After the Second World War, Guildford was to become a centre for the secondhand book trade but he by then had moved to Woking. I was grateful for this because while his colleagues were purchasing expensive books in sales and supplying universities, he had time to talk lengthily with a twelve year old boy and thus to kindle my enthusiasm for books. He prophesied that I should become a secondhand bookseller but at that time going to Oxford and becoming an accountant was about the only socially acceptable career in Woking. I therefore regarded myself as superior to his advice. It was permissible to read the whole of Gibbon because Macaulay had done it, but the retailing of secondhand books was not part of the social system. Congreve, the early 18th century dramatist, who thought it more desirable to be a gentleman than to write plays might, paradoxically, have been rather admired in Woking.

I lasted three years at Oxford and three weeks as an accountant. After that I moved to Hay-on-Wye, which is a remote town on the Welsh Border and from where I now sell books. The town's chief claim to fame is that it is the only town in the world whose main industry is books (the bookshops are bigger than the supermarkets), and my own boast is that I own the only secondhand bookshop with three full-time gardeners. In twelve years there have been enormous changes in the collecting and selling of secondhand books, some of which have been commented on but many of which have been unnoticed. The theory that the removal from the market of antiquarian books to institutions would kill the trade has been conclusively exploded. True, several thousand 16th century books have vanished but several million late 19th century novels (some of which fetch several hundred pounds each) have entered the realms of the collectable and the valuable. Treasures are waiting to be discovered as never before—even the first ten issues of Private Eye or Playboy can be worth £80 to £100.

The opportunities for the collector are limitless—the collector of Kennedy or Churchill before the market value of their work soared astronomically would have made thousands. Even the purchaser who bought the early and rare issues of paperback and science fiction could now sell for fifty times the price paid. Australiana, which once only justified perhaps fifty items in a London bookseller's catalogue is now worth a five-day sale in Sydney. Inevitably because the collector is working on a narrow and more specialized field than a dealer, he knows more, can pick up bargains and make a unit which is worth several times the separate parts. The other and less satisfactory side of the picture is that the secondhand book trade throughout the world is declining. Fourth Avenue in New York and Cecil Court and Charing Cross Road in London were both intended to be centres of the trade for their respective countries, but in the last ten years they have declined rapidly. Towns with populations of half a million now do not support a secondhand bookshop. John Carter, Ben Weinreb and many others—all eminent figures of the English book world—recently published letters in *The Times* suggesting that secondhand booksellers should be subsidized, but it is unlikely that a private or a public patron will be found; and the owners of secondhand bookshops are more often book enthusiasts rather than businessmen. The problems of the trade have furthermore not generally been of much concern to the Antiquarian Booksellers Association, which tends to be more concerned with organizing book fairs in Tokyo than with how to keep alive the unpretentious merchandisers of secondhand books who do far more to support them.

In 1961, however, I naively commenced business in Hay—a small Welsh town on the Herefordshire border with a population of 1,200. In the first few years of operation virtually every bookseller of note in Wales went out of business. They retired or died and nobody replaced them. Thus the prosperous days when Kyrle Fletcher sold books to the Marquess of Bute, when Williams of Carmarthen supplied the Carmarthen gentry, and when Galloway and Porter of Aberyswyth prospered with its concentration of intellectuals, were all finished. Only Ralph of Swansea, a close friend of Dylan Thomas, who steadfastly refused either to send books through the post or sell them expensively, continued to prosper; and even he moved from his shop by the station to a less expensive site further from the centre of the city. Although this situation presented me with the opportunity to buy large quantities of books, I did not realize that I was a witness to the greatest change in secondhand bookselling since Lackington.

In effect general secondhand bookselling was a craft which was disappearing. There were many reasons for this. The motorcar meant that the booksellers were unable to buy books at sales in the face of more specialized and metropolitan competition. Television impeded the sale of their more ordinary merchandise. The money which had been pouring into universities meant that the more adaptable and commercial members of the trade saw the advantage of supplying these unprecedentedly large customers without the impediment of a shop. Due to commercial pressure thousands of small shops vanished in Wales in the period 1945 to 1961 and the secondhand bookshop was just a minute part of the statistic. What was happening in Wales was also happening throughout the rest of the British Isles and America. My survival in Hay was due to the fact that it was the only town in the world where secondhand books were viable as the main industry. Bristol, South Wales and the Midlands were all within easy reach of Hay and therefore it was possible to make a town of books. This was luck rather than calculation. In 1961 I started precarious journeys round the book trade in the British Isles. As I had never really travelled outside the British Isles, I did not really realize what treasures I was seeing. Whatever the faults of the British Empire, its wealth meant that in the 19th century and early 20th century, its books were the finest and most handsomely produced. Yet in the 1960s bound volumes of *Punch* and *Cornhill,* full of first editions of Thackeray, George Eliot etc. were still being thrown away: so were innumerable Victorian novels which shortly afterwards were to become collectors' items. I did not realise that the fashion in books was a rapidly changing scene and so I despised them myself. This I see as one of the major problems of the collector—how to dissociate himself from the prejudices of experts. The antiquarian and secondhand book trade throughout the world has been and still is responsible for the destruction of millions of pounds worth of books a week. Let me give one example. About five years ago I visited a customer in Santa Cruz, California who like many others throughout the world was beginning to become interested in the fairy tales and occult stories of George Macdonald, whose children, incidentally, had been responsible for Lewis Carroll publishing *Alice in Wonderland*. As my customer's interest was fairly serious, he was anxious to read all of Macdonald's works. Macdonald had been a Methodist Minister and published three volumes of sermons. My customer was unable to locate a copy in the Library of Congress, any of the large Californian libraries, and indeed in any major American Library. Eventually he was able to locate a copy in Cleveland, but since the owners were not prepared to have it photocopied, he was never able to read the sermons. The reason for the scarcity of this book, which had been common in Victorian times, was undoubtedly that, before the author had become known or famous, every provincial bookseller had seen Macdonald's Sermons as a totally uncommercial piece of Victorian piety and thrown it away. *Alice in Wonderland* itself, of which a good copy of the first edition would now fetch 5,000 dollars, although of course largely destroyed by the infant readers, probably had a few copies destroyed in an earlier generation as an unmarketable children's book. The destruction of books, which takes place because of the pressure of space, is probably therefore an increasing rather than a decreasing trend.

This, however, I only discovered later. I started in business with no commercial experience and simply purchased every book haphazardly that I could find. On one occasion four twenty-ton lorryloads came into Hay from the widow of a dealer in Bradford who had assembled a phenomenal collection of Victoriana—like most of the book compilers in the pre 1961 period, he had died without seeing again innumerable books he had purchased twenty years earlier. Throughout the country I came upon what I can only describe as the Philips syndrome. Sir Thomas Philips was an early 19th century baronet who purchased books and manuscripts, which would now be worth hundreds of millions of dollars. As he was a rich man and bought before the value was generally appreciated, he assembled a collection which was the finest in the world. However, he

quarrelled with the British Museum, St David's College, his son-in-law and anyone who was prepared to look after his books after his death. His passion nearly bankrupted him and he cannot have had time to look at many of the extraordinary treasures he purchased. He has been studied as an isolated eccentric but I can remember at least ten Englishmen, and have heard of several more Americans, who with more limited means filled their houses with tens of thousands of books now worth a fortune, but which brought them no personal benefit. In Scotland, particularly, where Non-Conformist tradition believes it is ridiculous to buy a new edition when a secondhand book costs less, there were people observed who had this passion. In a granite house near Aberdeen I met a Scotsman whose house was full of books. Even the kitchen walls were two-thirds covered with books. He proudly proclaimed that there was no fiction there and, as I later discovered, was only selling his books because he was dying. He was working on the technology of papermaking and from all the places in the world that he had visited he had posted books back to himself. Like Sir Thomas Philips he was a man of a certain vision and only the acquisition of an object he personally adored was important. Loving books myself I did not find it surprising that men should want to do this.

Unlike the rest of the English and American book trade who were finding specialization and dealing without a shop profitable, I continued to buy enormous quantities of books. I bought everything from large country house libraries, to the libraries of schoolmasters who had collected everything on socialism in the thirties, to the libraries of Welsh Non-Conformist ministers. Some were disastrous. A Welsh Non-Conformist minister's library, for example, might have about two thousand books in it, only 5 per cent of which are saleable. There would be innumerable "Parch y Pergetha"—biographies and prayers of Welsh ministers of the late 19th century with a photograph of the author in the front—for which the only useful purpose I ever heard suggested was that it would be possible to write a complete history of later 19th century hairstyles from them. Sometimes the libraries would be macabre—as when I bought the library of a vet who had everything ever written on euthanasia as applied to small animals. Sometimes they were valuable beyond my wildest dreams as when I purchased the library of a Welsh country house whose owners had tolerated Swinburne's homosexuality to the outrage of their neighbours. As a bookseller, I would have to try to imagine on one day who would be interested in Zameroff and the beginnings of Esperanto and the following day it would be the Dead Sea Scrolls. Above all, I found that I could have all the pleasure of handling books without the responsibility of keeping them.

Two years after moving to Hay, I bought the castle. I have subsequently added several shops and filled the cinema, previously closed down, with shelves. I acquired books and property to the limit of my capacity and very often beyond it. When Major Egginton, my first director, joined me after three years, he saw the possibility of a very prosperous small business, but we have nevertheless continued to expand as a less prosperous large one. Personally I have been dominated by the idea of a logical bookshop which would comprise many millions of books and be larger than the largest library in the world. This may be lunacy, but I think the use of books is more important than the storage of books and therefore deserves a larger monument. Practically, it is certainly possible because a bookseller can buy 10,000 books with less bureaucracy than a library can buy one. This enables the book trade to be far more international. Thus, logically, a customer who is interested in such a subject as needlework would like to visit a bookshop which contained hundreds of books from America, Britain, the Continent and anywhere in the world on this subject. This is true of tens of thousands of subjects. Although the realization of this idea is many years away for me and in many subjects I do not even hold a single book in stock—when I buy 50,000 Spanish American books I touch only one per cent of the interests of that area—I nevertheless feel I can still progress a long way.

I do not distinguish, furthermore, between the new and the secondhand book. Oxford University Press had the original 18th century printing of Bishop Wilkins Greek Testament in stock for over two hundred years and I, as essentially a secondhand dealer, have not infrequently bought from reviews and sales representatives books several months before they have been published. The distinction cannot be made chronologically. From the customer's viewpoint, he is simply interested in his subject and he would be lucky if the ordinary provincial new or secondhand book shop were to have anything on it. For this reason, the bookseller I most admire in the past was James Lackington whose memoirs, written in 1797, went into many subsequent editions. As far as I know he is the only bookseller whose books did so. The reminiscences of most members of the new and secondhand trade have been single editions composed largely of anecdotes and stores of amazing bargains. Lackington, however, was different. Unlike nearly all secondhand booksellers he had a passionate interest in the problems of shopkeeping. He used his supply of secondhand books to beat fixed price agreements among new booksellers and in Letter 26 he more or less explains how he was the pioneer of the modern remainder system. Previously it had been the custom to destroy publishers' stocks of unwanted books in order to keep the price up. Furthermore, he invented a coin to be used as a token which was perhaps the origin of the book token as it is now known. His memoirs are anyway very illustrative of his period in which he calculated that reading perhaps increased twentyfold. He had a hatred of the Wesleyans and quotes with pride a statement of John Wesley that he could never keep a bookseller in his flock for six months—booksellers were far too rational to become fanatics. He had the occasional prejudice and in fact actually destroyed all books by freethinkers. My admiration for him, however, is based on the fact that he seems to have been the last bookseller really to unite new with secondhand bookselling on a large scale. In the Victorian times both became largely specialist occupations and the new book business became a question of hunting the bestseller and the secondhand book business became a question of finding or creating the expensive book. The two trades became remoter and remoter from each other. Now the new book trade is suffering the same kind of decline as the secondhand. In most provincial towns they cannot afford to stock any but the most popular titles which are the least likely to interest the collector.

A revival can come either through specialist shops, serving large areas, or through the centralisation of the book trade in one town, as has, to some extent, happened in Hay. In the first few years of trading we ran into many problems associated with handling huge numbers of books, and the result, predictably enough, was chaos. With several hundred thousand books each requiring a separate decision as to its price and proper category, the investment in time and money was enormous. We are far from having beaten these problems today, but as a book lover I am convinced that what I am doing is the only way to preserve as much as possible against the day when sufficient numbers of collectors can emerge to order and make understandable what will otherwise be destroyed.

Thus, by a very roundabout way we come to the purpose of this book. In no way can it hope to compete with the many distinguished works produced by scholars and bibliiphiles which so brilliantly adorn the history of book collecting. we have attempted to do is to provide a number of signposts to kindle the enthusiasm of readers who are book lovers but not yet book collectors. The categories we have included are,

of necessity, only a tiny proportion of what can be collected—but at the same time we have tried to suggest along the way some indication of the vast range of possibilities open to everybody. The simple thesis of this book is that there is no subject, attitude, idea or area of knowledge which cannot be represented by a collection of books. Moreover, unless such collections are assembled, by great numbers of individuals, the world resource of printed matter, which I regard as just as important as North Sea Oil, will be wastefully scattered and destroyed. Far too many people, in my opinion, have too long believed that book collecting is the expensive hobby of the rich. In fact, we have shown in this book, it is within the pocket of everybody.

How and What to Collect

IN 1824 the Reverend J. F. Dibdin published *The Library Companion or the Young Man's Guide and the Old Man's Comfort in the Choice of a Library*. His attempt to prescribe the requirements of a well-balanced library was crucial in the history of book collecting. No similar synthesis had been tried before, and, naive as he was, Dibdin stands as a landmark between the amateur collectors of the eighteenth century and the professionals of the nineteenth. The appearance thirty years later of Brunet's eight-volume *Manuel de l'Amateur des Livres*, with its detailed analysis of thousands of examples, reduced Dibdin's work to the status of a curiosity. None the less he was right at the time to claim of his book: 'No single volume in our language contains such a record of so many rare, precious and instructive volumes'. In the context of the eighteenth century he was a pioneer. Yet by the end of the nineteenth century bibliomania had reached such proportions that the American H. B. Wheatley devoted to it a series of twenty-five books and innumerable periodicals were started—including three concerned simply with the collecting of book plates. At the same time the genius of William Morris ensured the survival of the finest traditions of the past.

Dibdin's authorship of the first widely read books on the subject, his assessment of the merits of various editors and his invention of the very word 'bibliomania', surely mark him as the father of book collecting. He sees enormous advantages in his pursuit: complaining that only half the applicants to universities are accepted, he considers the use of a private library of new and secondhand books, selected for intellectual quality and beauty, as an alternative form of education. He also suggests it as a counter to the 'mischievous application of superfluous wealth'. Furthermore, 'religion, patriotism, public and private happiness, *more* and fixed principles of taste, intellectual refinement of the most exalted kind in its present and future results, are all involved in a sedulous and straightforward cultivation of the pursuits in question'. For Dibdin book collecting was the salvation of mankind.

The Victorian era, however, saw a considerable increase in publishing activity, and the specialist skills of the antiquarian dealer became separated from the commercial techniques of the new bookseller. The concerns of morality and education led to the production of cheap books for a general readership, and the antiquarian trade became the indulgence of booklovers. Most collectors of the time almost certainly began at their local secondhand bookshop: handling books and talking with a knowledgeable proprietor would always have been of more use than reading Dibdin. Within five years, his book was largely out of date, and the books he recommended were available only to the rich. He thought that a well balanced library should cover most of the whole body of knowledge, but was not to know that his were the last few years in which that aim could even be approached. Patterns of book collecting change radically every few years, and each generation regards the previous decade or two as a period of great riches. It appears that virtually none of the items discussed in *Book Collecting*, published by the Antiquarian Booksellers Association in 1947, is obtainable now. In my own twelve years of experience many books have moved from the inexpensive towards the unobtainable category: for instance three-volume novels by G. A. Henty have risen in price from £16 to £600 and Roberts' *Holy Land* from £10 to £100. The collector, therefore, can never follow the example of his predecessors, but must always be a pioneer. The expansion of knowledge since the time of Dibdin means that, far from being confident of covering the most important books on a subject, he can concentrate on only one small aspect of it. Dibdin suggested the most valuable books about Africa: ten years ago, it might have been possible to acquire most of the key books about Kenya;

in the 1970s it might be wise to specialise in Kenya since independence; in ten years time there will undoubtedly be collectors looking for one Kenyan writer.

A specialised illustrative collection may reach beyond the established categories of book collecting to include significant information published in other forms. Theoretically, perhaps, the most valuable collection ever possible might have been made by a contemporary of Shakespeare who had amassed not only all the printed books but also the playbills and other material relating to the dramatist. If a great modern playwright were to receive such devoted treatment, especially if his work were being produced in several countries, the collector of his writings, together with newspaper cuttings and playbills, might find himself the owner of the finest collection on his subject in the world. This raises such questions as whether a fine edition is more important than the cheap reprint which brought the book to the majority of its readers, or whether a newspaper review of the first publication might be more important than either. New books and ephemera are as relevant to modern book collecting as the old, and with tens of thousands published every year, a book which appeared in 1970 may be more difficult to obtain than one dating from 1870. Furthermore, the later publications are likely to appreciate faster. *Early English Watercolours* by Iolo Williams, published in 1961 for $14 and then sold at half price, had risen in value within ten years to £95 ($220). In my last chapter I shall talk of new books as an investment, but it is important to realise that any new book which fits into a coherent collection may within a short time be as difficult to obtain as an old one.

The justification for including any item must always be its relevance to a theme, and only by acquaintance with as many books as possible can a collector recognise instinctively what may be a useful addition. The actual handling of books has an educative value which may in some cases surpass the benefit of reading them. Once, when sorting a miscellaneous accretion of about 200,000 paperbacks, I was immediately presented with a view of the reading habits of the past twenty years. I saw the development of high historical fiction, the gradual detachment of war reminiscences from reality and the growing influence of James Bond and the Agatha Christie novels. Reading back copies of *Paperbacks in Print* would not have been a tenth as interesting

as handling the books themselves. At that time I was interested in starting a collection to show how spy stories were replacing detective fiction through their closer relevance to modern attitudes, but I am sure that this one source held material to illustrate many other themes. So many titles now appear in paperback form only, where the destruction rate is high, that this is a field to which collectors will undoubtedly turn their attention. Finding books is, moreover, often a matter of discovering categories which have simply dropped out of public consciousness. Succeeding generations become interested in what previous ages have discarded, and it is possible that in fifty years time every clothbound book will be sought after.

The influence of changing fashion is especially marked in the genre of the novel. Dibdin failed to note its existence, and classics, to which he devoted a long chapter, seemed much more worthy of the collector's attention. Lately, however, a first edition of Fielding's *Tom Jones* may fetch £1,000, while eighteenth-century versions of the classics are available for £10. Throughout the history of book collecting, whole classes of novels have achieved enormous popularity, only to fall into obscurity and become extraordinarily rare. Even a first novel by a living writer, like Graham Greene's *Bubbling April*, can fetch £150. To my regret, I have thrown away many English novels of the period from 1880 to 1920, which would since have become valuable. There are no reference books to guide the way through the uncharted terrain of the English novel or the English paperback. The true collector has his own belief in a theme which will ultimately produce a collection of quality, often inventing his own subject and using his acquisitions to illustrate it. One of the most famous collections of recent years was compiled by the late A. N. L. Munby, Librarian of King's College, Cambridge, and contains several hundred English and American books published between 1800 and 1920 on ballroom etiquette and social behaviour. Many were acquired from Goodspeeds Bookshop in Boston, but a large number was added in England. While the proper behaviour of a lady in 1900 may be interesting in itself, a substantial body of books on the same subject and from the same period forms a vivid record of the development of manners on both sides of the Atlantic, and is an indispensable source for many other aspects of social history. None of the books cost more than a few shillings, yet, like all others, the collection is unique, and its contribution to the store of knowledge is more nearly complete than anything an institutional library can offer in the same field. To make a collection is to achieve an original work of research which may demonstrate a thesis in a more concrete way than a single book, and this sophistication of approach is something which a large library cannot rival. Much of the value of Munby's collection lies in the fact that it contains many books which neither bookseller nor librarian considered worthy of shelf space. I do not believe that there is a finer model for the potential collector. Any enthusiast can start with the assumption that, at the very least, he will create a unique library, which could easily become pre-eminent in its field throughout the world.

The psychological and aesthetic appeal of books deserves the collector's attention. Political leaders often appear on television against a background of books (by implication their own), with the result that books have been advertised more widely than cornflakes. Designers in television and film studios invest a set with dignity by introducing several bookcases. Apart from such commercial uses, however, there is a growing tendency on both sides of the Atlantic to buy books for social or decorative purposes: the Square Orange bookshop in Pimlico Road, London, trades in books chosen more for their cover than their content, and the main business of the 'antique book' departments in many large American stores such as Macy's or Bloomingdales is of a similar nature. There are many people who criticize the practice on the grounds that books should be appreciated for what they contain, yet for the last five hundred years their survival has often been due solely to their decorative value. Even if the large aristocratic library was unread, its handsome appearance prevented its destruction, and the founder of any library, while perhaps not primarily interested in the information which it contains, may provide a source of especial value to the next generation.

The mechanics of book collecting are secondary to the urge to gather books. Many fine collections have been made without any background of bibliographical knowledge, and, in most modern fields, bibliographical aids will be few. Although I may conflict with much that is said elsewhere in this book, I feel that the acquisition of a quantity of books by anyone has the right to be called a collection. Bookselling should not degenerate into the purveying of fine objects to persons of good taste—a bourgeois activity on a level with antique dealing. Even an apparently miscellaneous accumulation of books may have a theme of enormous importance to the owner, and in the end the only authority a collector stands by is himself. Bibliographical knowledge becomes more significant after the acquiring of books than before, and, in any case, the majority of collectors, whether they are enthusiasts for the Tubingen School of Theology or the early novels of P. G. Wodehouse, will come over a period of a few years to rely largely on their own experience and the discrimination gained by the physical handling of many volumes.

Books cannot be judged quickly: it is possible to examine a shelf several times without being fully aware of what it contains. An ordinary bookshop may contain twenty to thirty thousand items, each of which will take a minute or two to investigate. Obviously it is possible to go again and again to the same shop and still make interesting discoveries on the same shelves. Intrinsic quality and interest, rather than preconceptions of price, should govern a purchase. There are many cases of dealers throwing out books which later became collector's items. Quaritch, the London firm, are reputed to have thrown away seventeenth-century theological pamphlets for which they would now pay considerable sums, and even today some dealers discard late nineteenth-century textbooks while others treasure them as representing the extraordinary attitudes of the superior Christian Boy in charge of an Empire. Do not be surprised, then, at under- or overpricing in a secondhand bookshop. The proprietor has to make hundreds or thousands of arbitrary decisions in a day and, after a time, 'book exhaustion' may make the process more or less automatic. Certainly, most booksellers have favourite prices and consistently mark their books at 65p or £1.85, but, if a book is unpriced, they may be embarrassed to seem small-minded and will instead ask 50p or £1.50. The difficulties of pricing in a secondhand shop demand an amount of charity in a purchaser not called for in a new bookshop. Librarians and prospective customers often make very naive demands on the secondhand bookseller. They ask him to obtain a few books published twenty or thirty years ago without seeming to realize that they are asking him to do on his own what the British Museum does with a staff of a few hundred. Even for a specialist dealer to supply a book in his particular subject may be unprofitable. It costs an ordinary American library about $10 to process a book into stock, but unfortunately no secondhand bookseller's customers would be prepared to pay a similar premium over the cost of a book. Librarians are professionals, while secondhand booksellers are often amateurs, many of whom have come to the trade from other careers. The skills of accountancy and efficient cost analysis are rarely applied, and this is reflected in the service available. Hence the collector gets his opportunities, but also needs to be tolerant.

Throughout this chapter, I have ignored conventional approaches to book collecting in favour of a looser, open ended strategy. My primary concern has been to encourage those who may never before have considered collecting, and to convince them that collecting books is neither a mystical experience, nor the slightly comic pursuit of antique first editions by even more antique bibliophiles that generally occupies the popular imagination when the subject is mentioned. Quite simply, a collection represents an individual's interest in the world around him. The more clearly defined the interest, and the more fully illustrated, the more valuable the collection is likely to be, whether its subject is needlework or the Theory of Relativity. Clearly, from this perspective, the distinctions between old and new books, or books proper and, say, pamphlets and periodicals, become subordinate to their relevance to a theme. Newspaper cuttings, reviews, even photograph albums, may all have a part to play. The raw material for such collections is piled high on the shelves of bookshops, in junk shops, jumble sales and street seller's barrows, the vast mass of printed material that may be worthless until someone undertakes to provide the context in which it can be made to yield its value. In this situation, no expert advice can be a substitute for the collector's own enthusiasm: in the end, he must follow his intuition and collect whatever gives him the greatest pleasure. There is no mystique in the acquisition of books, and it can be done in any way by anyone.

□ □ □

The following section is devoted to an outline of the mechanics of collecting. They are generally a matter of common sense and can be rapidly acquired through experience.

Before starting your collection, the most important thing to do is to visit as many book shops as possible. If it is not practicable then read every bookseller's catalogue you can get your hands on. While your subject will obviously reflect your interest, the success of your collection will be strongly influenced by availability. Some experience of what is available is therefore essential. The three established sources are secondhand booksellers, catalogues and auctions.

Secondhand booksellers can be eccentric, superior, busy, pleasant, chatty, or downright rude. This unpredictability is one of their attractions. They may trade anywhere, from the High Street to a garden shed and may be extraordinarily well-informed or profoundly ignorant. Whatever they are, they should be treated with a certain respect, and it is always wise to assume that they know something, if not a lot, about what they are selling.

It follows that one should first attempt to establish some sort of relationship with the bookseller himself, a simple strategy which may well produce useful information and lead to the discovery of books that might otherwise be unknown to you. A word of warning, some booksellers tend to be very possessive of their stock, and it is always wise to ask permission before browsing.

When making a purchase from a bookseller with whom you have not previously dealt, respect the price that he has chosen to ask. As I have already indicated, booksellers have to make arbitrary decisions about their stock and are likely to have favourite prices which, generally speaking, represent their last word on the subject. Contrary to popular opinion, most secondhand booksellers resent haggling. Indeed, any attempt to do so may well antagonise them and prevent them from offering you material in the future.

It is a good idea to select a few bookshops for regular visits and to inform the proprietors of your interests. If you buy a book without referring to a catalogue, you should check that it is complete, as guarantees that normally apply to catalogued books do not always cover stock from the shelf. Many booksellers have a place reserved for rare and valuable stock, and it is often necessary to make special enquiries, or to establish some confidence, before gaining access. Provided that you are reasonably treated by a bookseller, it always pays to foster your relationship with him. If you know of collections coming on the market, tell him, on the principle that one good turn deserves another. Booksellers often have private collections of their own and are delighted when customers show interest.

There are several directories of booksellers. The Shepherd's Press produces one for North America and Great Britain, but there are also one or two international directories. All can usually be ordered through your local new bookseller. Compiled from questionnaires filled in by the booksellers themselves, they are often unreliable, but nonetheless essential.

Most secondhand booksellers produce some form of catalogue. It may be anything from an elaborate, glossy piece of high-powered salesmanship to a rather scruffy mimeographed sheet. However, reliability in terms of the description of books can vary just as widely as the catalogues and bears no relationship to their physical appearance.

In the majority of cases, a postcard indicating your interests and asking to be placed on a mailing list is sufficient to ensure that you will receive the bookseller's catalogue, although some booksellers are efficient enough to strike your name off their list if you have not purchased a book after receiving a certain number of catalogues. Other booksellers feel, sometimes rightly, that the erudition or splendour of their catalogues justifies charging a subscription. The guiding principle should be to receive as many catalogues as possible. They make excellent bedtime reading —often more interesting than the books they describe—and a collection of booksellers' catalogues might be a worthy goal. To make a purchase from a bookseller's catalogue, you need only to follow the instructions given, usually at the front or back. They vary according to the bookseller. The laws governing trade descriptions apply to secondhand books, but if you are unfamiliar with the bookseller, or if he is of dubious repute, it does not harm to state with your order that you purchase a book on the basis of his description and any significant faults which are not mentioned will justify your returning the book. There is a very complex language of description used in catalogues, most of which will be explained in the glossary of this book. The most important abbreviation to watch for is w.a.f. (with all faults). This may mean that the book is so complicated that the cataloguer has not been able to check it thoroughly, but usually indicates that it is imperfect and not subject to return. Remember that a book advertised in the catalogue is likely to be the only copy held in stock and that if you live some distance away, or the catalogue is likely to take some time to reach you, you should check promising catalogues as soon as they arrive and telephone to ask that anything you require be reserved, pending your written confirmation.

Apart from shops and catalogues, the other main point of sale for the acquisition of books is the auction. The conduct of auctions is a fit subject for at least a dozen doctorates in Behavioural Science, and perhaps one or two in Criminology. It is always difficult to keep yourself fully informed about the time and place of auctions. Auctioneers who frequently hold book auctions advertise in directories of booksellers and will send circulars and catalogues. Again, for this information, it is sometimes necessary to subscribe to the more substantial catalogues. Smaller, occasional book auctions are usually advertised in the classified columns of both local and national newspapers.

Having obtained your catalogue, you should attend the viewing to inspect the books themselves. General auctioneers often produce very inaccurate catalogues and seldom make any guarantees. It is therefore necessary to satisfy yourself about the identity and condition of the book or books you are interested in. Some of the specialist auctioneers do research the books they are selling very thoroughly and provide some form of guarantee; it is worth finding out who they are. Decide the price that you are prepared to pay when you actually examine the books at the public view. You can then mark your catalogue for use as a guide during the sale, or make note of the lot numbers and a maximum price and ask the auctioneer or his staff to bid for you. It is also possible to commission a friendly bookseller to buy a book for you. If, however, you remain undaunted by the prospect of fighting it out at a sale, then you should observe the general rule that prevails at most auctions, not to engage in animated conversation with your neighbour lest your nodding be taken as a bid. If you find yourself in an auction room with a great many people who seem to know one another, and are perhaps known to the auctioneer, it is reasonable to assume that they are booksellers. Very occasionally it happens that they have formed a ring, contriving not to compete with one another at the sale, but hold their own private auction later. This is illegal, but very difficult to prove. Experience will tell you if it is taking place, and it should not greatly affect your ability to purchase books. It may, however, be a good idea not to patronise dealers whom you may recognise as having taken part. Again, it is necessary to point out that such recognition is possible only with a great deal of experience.

When your lot number is called, the auctioneer will start the bidding by asking for a particular price—do not bid. He will then lower his price in stages which generally indicate the average progression of bids. At a certain point, the book will achieve a fairly low price, and the actual bidding will begin. It is sometimes possible to make a quick, successful bid just before this low is reached, but usually you will encounter some sort of competition. Bids should be made clearly and definitely, ideally by raising your hand so that it is clearly visible to the auctioneer. It is seldom necessary to speak. In the heat of the moment, it is very easy to get carried away by the excitement of competition, but unless you have badly misjudged prices at the view, it is advisable to stick to the figures you marked.

If the item is knocked down to you, you will need to give the auctioneer your name and address. It is a good idea to write it clearly on a card beforehand and keep it ready to hand to one of the porters. It is usually unnecessary to do this more than once during an auction. At the end of the sale, you must pay the auctioneer's clerk who will give you a slip entitling you to claim the lots which you have purchased. Unless you are known to the auctioneer, or have made previous arrangements, you will be required to pay in cash. Having paid your money and collected your slip, you are then directed to a porter who will collect your lots. Before removing them, ensure that they are correct. It often happens, particularly with assorted lots, that a volume goes astray, and while you have no guarantee that the books are perfect, it is up to you to see that you do collect what you have paid for. Most auctioneers expect books to be removed from the rooms on the day of sale. There are sometimes lots described as various books, various books of a particular type, or one specific book with a number of others. They do, on occasions, contain sought-after gems and are well worth examining carefully.

As well as investigating the many other sources, such as jumble sales, junk shops, street barrows, houses under demolition, attics and charity shops, a resourceful collector might try trading with other collectors or buying discarded duplicates from libraries. Try to make the acquaintance of your local public librarian, who is in an excellent position to advise you on the availability of books, as well as on the books already in your collection. In return, he (or she) is likely to be grateful for any information you may pick up about local book sales, collections, or private libraries.

The two topics most commonly discussed in connection with collectable books can be summarised in two words: condition and edition. The specific chapters here mention condition where necessary. There are few infallible rules and, generally, the collector should decide his own criteria of condition. Obviously books should be complete, but in certain areas, for example incunabula, it may only be possible to acquire part of a leaf from the work of a particular printer. The best rule is one of common sense: try to check that all the plates and errata, advertisements and so on, are present, but where a book is known to be rare, settle for a reasonable copy. Fine bindings and mint copies are luxuries which may come later or appear along the way as a bonus. There is no reason, of course, why you should not set the highest standards possible—providing you have large quantities of time and money. As to edition, more nonsense is talked about this subject than any other aspect of book collecting. First editions are often inferior to later ones both in production and content. The collector, as in many other questions, must decide for himself where he stands on this controversial issue. It is safe to say that the collecting of first editions in certain areas is, and will undoubtedly continue to be, very useful, but at its worst it is particularly insidious, drawing attention away from the book itself to minor questions, such as the spelling of a particular word on a particular page. Clearly, there is a great deal to be said for having the first edition of an important book, but to make this an overriding concern may often be counter-productive. In some cases it is very interesting to compare the first with a subsequent corrected edition, for example in circumstances where the first edition may be completely insignificant, while a later one may be of great importance. In 1660, Robert Boyle published his *New Experiments Physicomechanical Touching the Spring of Air and Its Effects*. The second edition was much revised as a result of criticism by Franciscus Linus and incorporates what is now known as 'Boyle's Law'. Consequently, it is considerably more important and valuable than the first edition.

The best advice concerning edition is that it is better to start with a later edition than do without the book in the hope of obtaining the first. As your collection develops you may decide to collect the most important editions or, perhaps, the most attractive ones. The bibliography at the end of this book gives a reasonably comprehensive list of reference works which may help in deciding whether you actually possess a rare first edition or provide you with points to look for if you are seeking one, but these reference works are seldom to be regarded as the final authority, and in many fields it is not uncommon to discover variant editions and even unrecorded firsts.

Finally, I want to deal with the problem of cost. This often confusing subject can be expressed very simply by stating that there is no established scale of prices. Book values are governed by innumerable factors and, in the last analysis, the laws of supply and demand are probably more effective in the secondhand book trade than any other market. However, it is possible to acquire a fair idea of the broad limits of prices by reading catalogues, since many booksellers normally base their prices on auction records. These are published in the United States under the title *American Book Prices—Current*, and in Great Britain under the title *Book Auction Records*. These expensive reference works may be consulted in most libraries, and it is probably not worthwhile for private collectors to buy them. Above all, they should be used with discretion—prices are not only highly variable in one country, but may also differ considerably from one country to another.

▢ ▢ ▢

When handling books in a book shop, never open them while wearing gloves, which are often clammy, and dirtier than you realise. Always hold the top of a book when removing it from the shelf; do not grip the spine.

Even if the room in which books are kept is normally a dry one, the wall behind the shelves may become damp because it is sheltered by the books from the heating in the room. If any part of the wall appears damp, move the books from shelf to shelf at regular intervals to ensure that none of them stays in a damp place long enough to suffer any damage. When being stored, books should always stand upright on the shelf.

Books are subject to attack by insects, as well as conditions that are damp or too dry. Silver fish, which like damp conditions, eat old glues, pastes, and size in the paper, as does the fire brat, lover of a warm environment. Book lice eat fungi and leather bindings, and woodworm may also cause problems. Cleanliness will prevent all these insects from thriving. Keeping books behind glass makes an enormous difference to their condition, although it is not always feasible.

Books are very sensitive to being moved. If moving is necessary, they should be laid *horizontally* in a large carton, wrapped in corrugated paper. Even two or three moves can take as much as ten per cent off their value.

Many books carry marks of ownership or marginal annotation. Unless these are particularly crudely executed, or scurrilous, they should not be regarded as a blemish. They may even add to the value. A book which has been annotated by anyone, however insignificant, is unique.

Dusty pages can be cleaned with a soft brush and careful use of a soft indiarubber. Never repair a torn page with adhesive tape. Scotch tape or Sellotape, if already used, should be removed with a careful application of benzene or lighter fuel. The mending of tears with tissue and flour paste should only be attempted by a qualified binder. Foxing—brown stains on pages, caused either by damp or a fungus—may be removed by washing, another job for the qualified binder. To remove grease marks from pages, place an unsoiled sheet of brown paper above and below the page you wish to clean. Then, carefully apply a cool iron until the grease is absorbed by the brown paper.

Modern first editions are often described as 'uncut'. Strictly speaking, this means that the pages have not been cut down from their original size during binding, and is a decided advantage. However, books that are described as 'unopened' —those with the pages still joined together at the top or forward edge—are probably of interest in this state only to the dilettante collector. If you want to read the book, by all means cut the pages carefully, using a letter opener.

Libraries often dispose of duplicate or otherwise unwanted stock. The more organised among them use a cancellation stamp. The issue stamp or its envelope, when still present, may be dampened and gently prized off as the adhesive softens; to do this, start at a corner and work across. If your conscience is troubled by an uncancelled library stamp, you can check with the library, of course.

Until the development of cloth case binding, pioneered by the firm, Pickerings, in the second quarter of the nineteenth century, books were issued and often sold in boards. The preliminary stages of binding had been carried out, and the whole book, or in some cases only the spine, covered with paper. Provided that they are in good condition, books in this original state are more highly valued than those which have been completely bound, unless the binding is of particular significance. For example, if you were to find a first edition of one of Byron's works in this state, it would be a mistake to have it rebound. It is a long time since books were commonly found in boards, and most books on the market today have been rebound at some stage. Those with damaged leather bindings should, whenever possible, be repaired rather than rebound. A leather-bound book with a broken spine should have the back replaced rather than the entire cover. Original bindings are almost invariably of some interest; a modern binding tends to detract from the value of an antiquarian book.

Nevertheless, in a large number of cases, rebinding or extensive repairs are necessary. This is always expensive, and good binders are very hard to find. The book's value and any loss incurred by the operation should always be weighed carefully against the cost of binding. If the decision is taken to go ahead, a binder should be given clear instructions about what is expected of him. It is still necessary to stress that pages should not be cut down. A particularly valuable or interesting book can be taken completely to pieces, washed where necessary, and resewn. Tears may be repaired and, if it is unavoidable, the title page, etc., may be mounted on fine tissue. Such extensive operations are justified only when the collector feels strongly about the book concerned. Many binders operate on contract to libraries and can put a 'library' binding on a book rather more cheaply than an individual binding. Library bindings have the advantages of strength and convenience, but are seldom attractive.

If dirty, cloth-bound books should be dusted with a soft brush. To restore the lustre of the cloth, use one of the several proprietary brands of cloth book solutions that are available. Cloth bindings should never be washed. Warping of the boards can be corrected by *gentle* pressure in a binder's or letter press.

A very dry atmosphere is as detrimental to a leather binding as it is to antique furniture. Central heating and high temperatures should be avoided, or mitigated with the use of humidifiers. In a dry atmosphere, the leather will dry out and the boards warp. If a leather binding is dry, British Museum Leather Dressing may be applied. The formula—$\frac{1}{2}$ oz. beeswax dissolved in 11 ozs Hexane, to which are added 7 ozs anhydrous lanolin and 1 oz. cedarwood oil—should be mixed by a chemist rather than the individual at home. When using the mixture, always remember that it is inflammable. Before application of the dressing, the book should be cleaned with a soft duster or, if it is very dirty, with a lightly moistened cloth and a piece of toilet soap. The formula should be applied sparingly, rubbed well into the leather and left for forty-eight hours before it is polished. It should not be used if the leather binding is suède, or is crumbling badly. A point worth noting is that good, sound leather bindings, dated between 1880 and 1900, are exceptionally rare. A chemical tanning process developed and used at that period was found, after some time, to cause deterioration and crumbling of the leather.

Vellum—calfskin, not tanned but de-greased —is used either limp or over boards in the binding of books. The material is sensitive to changes in humidity and, by contracting, may bend boards outwards. You can correct this by placing the book carefully in a press, first protecting it with sheets of paper. Be careful not to wind up the press too tightly. If this fails, the book should be taken to a binder, who can correct the bending by pasting down a paper lining under the endpapers.

Limp vellum bindings have a distinct tendency to cockle. Unless this is very bad, it should not be regarded as a blemish. However, a good binder can correct cockling without altering the binding in any way. Note that no attempt should be made to smooth a limp vellum binding with an iron (it has been known!). If vellum-covered books are dirty, they can be cleaned with the use of a slightly dampened cloth and a piece of toilet soap, or wiped gently with milk, and left to dry at room temperature. On no account should vellum actually be washed. It can be polished with a good white furniture cream.

The History of the Book

NOTHING has been as influential in shaping men and events as the printed book. Despite enormous technological advances in other means of communication, the printed word remains the most powerful of all. Books have not only influenced everything we think, but also our way of thinking. Many of the finest and the most shameful events in human history can be ascribed to the influence of the Bible alone. This survey of the development of the book is the briefest of glimpses at the subject. A list of more detailed works is given in the bibliography.

A book is a portable object which spreads and communicates a substantial message. The first books were those of the early civilisations of the Middle East, in a tradition begun by the Sumerians in the third millennium B.C. and carried on by the Hittites, Babylonians and Assyrians. Tablets of washed clay were inscribed

The epic of Gilgamesh: a seventh-century BC *cuneiform tablet from Nineveh.*

while moist with a stylus to produce the characteristic wedge-shaped indentations of the cuneiform script. The tablets were dried in the sun or, if particularly important, baked in a kiln. In the seventh century B.C. the Assyrian king and antiquary Assurbanipal constructed a library in his palace at Nineveh and from this and other sources as many as 700,000 tablets are known to have survived. Most were intended to preserve accounts, legal codes and other commercial and governmental records.

Almost parallel with the development of the clay tablet was that of the papyrus roll. First used in Egypt, papyrus is a paper-like substance made from strips of pith from the papyrus reed laid in two layers at right angles to each other, usually in sheets about six inches wide. The horizontally-laid strips formed the writing surface, and the papyrus was rolled up with the text on the inside. The Egyptians applied inks of various colours in one of three scripts: the formal hieroglyphic which, though decorative was better suited to inscriptions; the hieratic or religious script, and the demotic, used for commercial records. The earliest surviving example of papyrus dates from 2,500 B.C., but there is evidence that it was in use before that date. Many of the surviving rolls are mortuary texts buried with the dead. Others include scientific records, law, myths and legends.

The Chinese were approximately five hundred years later in their development of primitive books. At first, strips of wood or bamboo were linked together with cords. Few early examples survive. The damp climate and the attempt in 213 B.C. by the emperor Shih Huang Ti to burn all books destroyed much of a very strong literary tradition. The surviving books were the subject of the first national bibliography, produced in the first century B.C. and listing 677 titles in science, astronomy, philosophy, poetry and theology.

The Greeks and Romans adopted the papyrus roll. The Greeks probably had books as early as

A late fourth-century manuscript of Virgil's Aeneid *on vellum.*

libraries like that at Alexandria, with as many as 650,000 rolls, grew up. Most Greek literature, however, perished. What survives is the result of a tradition of manuscript copying.

In Rome, most early patricians had large private libraries of rolls. Scriptoria, where as many as fifty copyists were at work producing books, meant that books became relatively cheap. The Romans introduced another important early development. Papyrus rolls had obvious disadvantages; they were cumbersome to read and not very durable. Parchment and vellum made from calf skin lasted longer and, unlike papyrus, did not have to be brought from the Nile delta. Their use as writing materials stems from an early rivalry between bibliomaniacs. Ptolemy V of Egypt, fearing that his rival, Eumenes II of Pergamum, might actually succeed in his intention to build a greater library than his own, cut off the supply of papyrus. Eumenes' answer to this unethical embargo was to make use of

the sixth century B.C. although their earliest surviving rolls date from 400 B.C. Somewhere in the region of 30,000 papyri are known to have survived, although it seems that the Greeks preferred verbal communication as a means of instruction. Indeed, much surviving Greek literature is in the form of dialogue. After the time of Alexander the Great, as Greece became more aware of the outside world, the expansion of knowledge favoured the development of books. The trade became lucrative and great

Right: *a folio from the fourth-century* Codex Sinaiticus. Below: *from the* Codex Theodosianus, *written in the sixth century, probably at Lyons.*

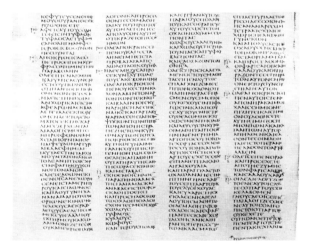

parchment. The words for it in both Latin and Greek mean 'material from Pergamum'. Parchment rolls, however, though wide, were still somewhat difficult to use, particularly when reference was necessary to earlier parts of the text. The change from rolls to the *codex* form which we use today was a natural and obvious development. It was made popular by the advent of a new force, Christianity, which derived much of its influence from the realisation by its perceptive advocates that the written word would give their beliefs an advantage over those of the traditionally oral religions. The *codex,* where sheets of parchment or the finer vellum were bound together at one edge, was ideally suited to the study of the gospels. The form became known as the 'Christian book' and, by A.D. 400, had superseded the pagan rolls.

The barbarian invasions which led to the fall of the western Roman Empire also threatened the survival of the book. The monasteries, and particularly the monks of the Irish Church, deserve much of the credit for preserving a literate culture. Thanks to isolation, Christianity in Ireland had developed in a vital and independent manner. While Europe was plunged in darkness, Ireland entered the greatest period in her history. The monks, who gradually spread to Britain and then throughout Europe, disseminated their own particular brand of Christianity and kept alive the practice of literacy. One of these early missionary monks, St Columba, left home because of a battle fought in 561, appropriately over a book. With others, he fostered the traditions of the celtic manuscript which produced such great books as those of Kells, Lindisfarne and Durrow. The influence of these monks extended, and can still be seen, throughout Europe, but their greatest achievement was a pattern of book production which led to the most important development of all, printing with movable type.

The Advent of Printing

Important and effective as they were, these early books had an extremely small distribution and the scribes who made them often produced errors in transcription. The real impact of the book began to be felt in the fifteenth century. An enormous amount of scholastic energy, thousands of tons of paper and many years of printers' time have been expended on the question of who actually invented printing with movable type.

In fact, it makes little difference: it was not, strictly speaking, an invention but a natural and inevitable development.

The first obvious advance was the discovery of a material on which books could be produced cheaply. Paper is reputed to have been the invention of a Chinese, Ts'ai Lun. In A.D. 105 he reported to the emperor that he had manufactured paper using tree-bark, hemp, rags, and fish nets. Again, this was probably not an invention but a development, although the oldest surviving piece of paper certainly dates from the time of Ts'ai Lun. It was discovered in 1931 by the Swedish archaeologist, Folke Bergman, near Kharakhoto. The Chinese also take credit for the earliest surviving printed book. This was found in 1907 by the explorer Sir Aurel Stein. It bears the imprint 'printed on 11th May 868 by Wang Chien' and is in the form of a roll sixteen feet long by twelve inches wide. It is made up of seven sheets printed from wooden blocks and pasted together. It demonstrates a degree of sophistication which indicates that the art was already well-established. Also in China, sometime between 1040 and 1048, Pi Sheng made movable printing type from baked clay. It is difficult to understand why he did so. A Chinese printer using movable type would need several thousand pieces, as Chinese scripts are ideographic rather than alphabetic. Whatever the reason for Pi Sheng's experiment, it was significant only in so far as it seems to have spread to Korea. The earliest Korean book extant is block-printed and dated 1361. Early in the fifteenth century, the Koreans began printing from movable type. A set of 100,000 copper types, cast by royal command, was used to produce a number of books until 1544.

It seems unlikely that these eastern developments went unnoticed in Europe, particularly in view of the extent of travel to the lands of spices. However, the earliest surviving example of European printing dates from 1423. This is a wood block print of St Christopher, now in the John Rylands Library, Manchester. A print in the Royal Library at Brussels, dated 1418, is almost certainly an impression made about 1450 from an earlier block. It is possible that a number of block prints and crude block books were produced during the second quarter of the fifteenth century, but the technique was ill-suited to the reproduction of script because of the difficulty in cutting characters accurately. In the 1430s, Johann Gensfleisch zur Laden, known as Johann Gutenberg, began experiments in the art of printing.

Above: a wood block print of St Christopher, dating from 1423, said to be the earliest dated woodcut. Below: the opening page, 'In hoc volumine haec continentur', of Aelius Donatus, De Barbarismo et de Octo Partibus Orationis.

Records are sketchy and those that do exist are guarded in their reference to Gutenberg's experiments. However, it is clear that he spent and borrowed heavily. The lawsuits in which he became involved are as frustrating for the historian as they must have been for him, since the legal records, while preserving valuable information, complicate the question of who did what. However, the earliest and first dated specimens of European printing from movable type appeared in 1454. These were two issues of a thirty-line indulgence granted by Pope Nicholas V to contributors of funds for the war against the Turks. These are attributed to the press of Gutenberg and his partners, Fust and Schöffer.

Next came an early version of the '36-line Bible', so-called from the number of lines per page. The printer is not identified and no date is given but the bible was probably printed in 1454. This and an edition of Donatus' Latin Grammar, *De Octo Partibus Orationis,* also probably produced in Mainz in 1454, are attributed to Guten-

berg, perhaps working independently. The famous 'Gutenberg' or '42-line Bible' was probably started in 1453, and completed in 1455. It bears no printer's name, but there is no good reason for not ascribing it to the press of Gutenberg and his two partners. A survey privately issued in 1951 by Edward Lazare records forty-six copies of this book, twelve of which are on vellum, and thirty-four on paper. Of these, four on vellum and seventeen on paper are complete. A copy exhibited at the New York Antiquarian Book Fair in 1973 was priced at one million dollars; it was probably cheap at the price. Gutenberg, however, earned little from his labours. On 6th November 1455, his partner, Johann Fust, brought a lawsuit against him to recover money he had lent. Practically all Gutenberg's equipment passed to Fust. Gutenberg's achievement in bringing together a series of separate developments and evolving a practical application for them seems to have brought him little reward. His synthesis of existing techniques, the development of printing ink and the invention of a consistent and convenient method of casting type from lead were to remain unchanged for centuries. Doubtless he continued to print, but after 1455 Fust and Schöffer stole the show. In August 1457, they completed the *Psalterium Latinum* at Mainz. This was the first printed book to bear the name of the printers, and the date of printing. This is a truly magnificent book, printed in three colours which were applied simultaneously. Ten copies are known, all on vellum, five with 143 leaves and five with 175. Henceforth, the history of printing is one of refinement, design and the spread of printing presses. No great technical advances took place, nor indeed were necessary, for over two hundred years.

When two rival Archbishops caused the sack of Mainz in 1462, commerce in the city was brought almost to a standstill. Then began the extraordinarily rapid spread of printing. In Germany, it had already spread to Bamberg, Strasbourg and Cologne. After the sack of Mainz, German printers moved to important commercial centres throughout Europe, seeking patronage. Italy was the second country to receive printing and, for a while, became the most important. Two Germans, Sweynheym and Pannartz, began printing in Subiaco. In 1467, they moved to Rome and adopted the Roman style of letter instead of the Gothic style used in

The first ornamented title page printed by Erhard Ratdolt in Venice, 1476.

Germany. Venice rapidly became a major centre and, after the arrival of a French printer, Nicolas Jenson, in 1470, Roman type became firmly established. Indeed, the types designed by Jenson remain unsurpassed in their clarity and beauty. The Italian presses produced some ten thousand books before the close of the century.

The first press in Switzerland was probably established in 1468. In France, two professors at the Sorbonne established the first university press by inviting three printers to work in the university in 1470. The venture was short-lived, but produced important work. Printers were also active in the Netherlands from 1470, and there is some reason to suppose that the Dutch were printing even earlier. It is sometimes suggested that a Dutch innkeeper, Lourens Coster of Haarlem, was printing with movable wooden type before Gutenberg, although there is not a great deal of evidence to support this. It was in Flanders, at Bruges, that William Caxton, the first English printer, learned the art. Caxton, born in Kent in the early 1420s, had spent some thirty years as a businessman in Bruges, and was the equivalent of a modern consul. His literary activities qualify him for a place in history greater than that of being the first English printer.

Caxton for some reason relinquished his office, and, still at Bruges, translated the romance of Raoul Lefevre, *Recueil des hystoires de Troye.* He went to Cologne in 1471 to learn the art of printing from Jan Veldener, so that he could publish his book to his own requirements. He set up his press in Bruges in 1473, and in the following year finished his *Recuyell of the Histories of Troye.* This was followed by a translation from the Latin of Jacobus de Cessolis, the very popular *Game and Playe of the Chesse.* Caxton printed at least three other books in Bruges. Everything he printed there was, in the past, ascribed to Colard Mansion, a calligrapher and printer, but it is now clear that the work came from Caxton's press, where Mansion was learning the art before setting up independently in 1474. Caxton returned to England in 1476 and set up his press in the precinct of Westminster Abbey. Here he carried on business until 1491, printing some ninety books. The first was *Dictes and Sayengis of the Philosophres,* published in November 1477. Seventy four of his books were printed in English, twenty two translated by Caxton himself. These translations are Caxton's chief contribution. They are remarkable not only because of their literary excellence, but also be-

cause they were significant in establishing the tradition of popular literature in contrast with the academic, Latin literary tradition. After Caxton's death, his business went to his assistant, Wynkyn de Worde. His standards were not as high as his master's but he was extraordinarily energetic, producing some eight hundred items before his death in 1535.

A period of intense creative activity ending early in the sixteenth century produced approximately forty thousand editions, many still unequalled as examples of fine craftsmanship and typographic design. The unfortunate tendency of historians, amongst others, to invent categories, has encouraged the belief that the infancy of printing ended abruptly at midnight on the last day of December 1499. If it is necessary to fix a date for the end of the first era of printing, then 1525 is still arbitrary, but slightly more logical. However, books printed before 1500 are traditionally termed *incunabula,* the Latin word for swaddling-clothes. The word has been corrupted so that any book printed in the fifteenth century is now an 'incunable', and its use can increase the value of a relatively poor and uninteresting book at the expense of a slightly later but better one. In fact, the infancy of printing comes to an end with the gradual growth of specialist functions

Above left: *from* Le Recueil des hystoires de Troye, *'le tout composé par excellent hystoriographe vénerable homme Raoul Le Fevre prefetre et chapellain de treshault et puissant seigneur Monseigneur Philippe duc de Bourgoigne. Nouvellement imprimé à Lyon'*: Above: *from* Game and Playe of Chesse, *dedicated to 'The righte noble right excellent and vertuous prince George duc of Clarence Erle of Warwyck and of Salisbury, grete Chamberlayn of England and leutenant of Ireland . . . Your most humble servant William Caxton, amongst other of your servants sends unto you peas, helthe, joye and victorye upon your Enemyes'. Translated from the latin of Jacobus de Cessolis (c1475).*

in the mid sixteenth century. The printers of *incunabula* varied widely in nationality, quality, scope and quantity of work, but most of them had a common bond in operating with less specialisation than printers as we know them today. They often translated or edited the works they printed, designed and cut punches and struck matrices for their type, cast the type, printed and bound their books, then published and retailed them. In many cases, like Caxton, they also imported books from foreign printers. The sixteenth century saw the rise of specialists.

ALDVS·PIVS·MANVTIVS·R·

Portrait of Aldus Pius Manutius, with his device of an anchor entwined by a dolphin.

Aldus Manutius, one of the greatest of all printers, embodied the best qualities of the scholar craftsman, but he also employed Francesco Griffo of Bologna to design and cut his types. Manutius had spent much of his early life studying the Greek classics. Those which had survived at that time were the result of innumerable transcriptions; seldom were two copies identical. Manutius spent years comparing manuscripts and editing before he entered the overcrowded printing business of Venice, where there were then as many as 160 printers. His first book, a Greek grammar, was published in 1495 and in the following year he published Piertro Bembo's *De Aetna*, using a new Roman type designed by Griffo. This was a milestone in book production; it was beautifully printed in a type which, with slight modifications, is still in use for book work. But Manutius' chief contribution was his series of pocket-sized editions of the classics. Competition in Venice was acute and the first productions of the Aldine press, finely produced as they were, failed to sell particularly well. They were in the large folio and quarto formats which were then general. Manutius changed his tactics.

Using a new type by Griffo which was designed for the task, he produced the first of a series of small octavo editions of the classics. The first book in the new italic type, as it came to be known, was an edition of Virgil printed in 1501. The tradition of scholarship and fine printing remained in the Manutius family for three generations, and over eight hundred books were printed on the Aldine press. Many of them are the finest prizes of book collecting. Aldine books can still be purchased at fairly reasonable prices, some for as little as $100, and they can be recognised by the famous printer's device of an anchor entwined by a dolphin.

The list of great printers of this early period is very long. Among them, Johannes Froben (1460–1527), friend and publisher to Erasmus, Henri Estienne (1460–1520), who founded a dynasty of fine printers, and Geoffroy Tory (1480–1533), who set the pattern for decorative printing with his books of hours, were a few of the great names during the latter half of the first era of printing.

□ □ □

Printing began to settle down towards the middle of the sixteenth century. Although developments were still being made the grand flourish of the early years was lost. Beautiful books were still being published but there was a great deal of competition and the emphasis was on low cost. The activities of book production were becoming more specialised. The master-printer was becoming a publisher employing specialist editors, printers and binders. Small quartos, octavos and even smaller books on thinner papers, were being bound in card rather than wooden boards. Lavish margins and extravagant typography were becoming less common. As the publishers began to dominate and the number of journeymen printers grew very large, the economics of the book business became very complex. When Aldus Manutius began to produce his small editions of the classics in Venice, they sold well because of their size and low price. As soon as their success was apparent, printers in Lyons quickly copied them. Manutius did all the work and, indeed, sold the books, but the copies printed in Lyons were cheaper and sold much more quickly. Printers and publishers responded to this problem of piracy by attempting to acquire patents or privileges for the exclusive publication of books in certain fields, such as law, liturgy, school text books, and Bibles. Official printers were appointed and protection was granted to particular books. Nevertheless, towards the end of the century, the general standard of book production suffered from overcrowding in the printing industry. The struggle to reduce publishers' risks is perhaps best illustrated by the early history of printing privileges in England. Fifteenth-century statutes limiting the number of foreigners entering the country had granted exemption to those skilled in the valuable art of printing. Early in the sixteenth century, the number of printers had grown to such a degree that the question of privileges was of prime importance. In 1503, Richard Pynson and William Faques were given royal authority to print statutes. This, in effect, established the important post of royal printer. A sermon by Richard Pace was granted a two-year privilege in 1518. The sole privilege to print all Bibles in English, given to Richard Marler in 1542, was followed by a number of privileges for other books. However, publishers eventually realised that effective protection was not to be achieved by royal authority. The Stationers' Company of London was chartered in 1557 to supervise the administration of commercial privileges, and also to restrict the content of books. A register, in which publishers might enter the titles of works in preparation in order to secure protection, failed to eliminate the problem of piracy.

Even so, the most important factor in the sixteenth century was neither the proliferation of printers, nor the struggle for privilege, but the realisation that the printing of books was not simply a quicker, cheaper and more accurate way of reproducing manuscripts. When the strength of the new medium was finally demonstrated, it was world-shaking. In 1517, Martin Luther challenged the theologians to oral debate. If the event had taken place a century earlier, it might have resulted in a few heresy trials and a burning or two at the stake, but the oral debate went into print. A wave of tracts and treatises swept over Europe, changing the course of civilisation. The printed debate took off in 1520, when Pope Leo X issued a Bull which excommunicated Luther and forbade the printing, distribution of ownership of his writings. A quick response came from Wittenberg, which rapidly became the centre of Lutheran printing. There, in 1520, Melchior Lotter printed Luther's tract *An den Christlichen adel deutscher Nation: von des Christlichen Standes Besserung,* which called for the renunciation of

A seventeenth-century ordinance regulating the printing of books.

the temporal power of the Pope. Perhaps one of the most important little books ever published, it set the Reformation in motion. Four thousand copies were sold within a few days, and seventeen further editions were published before the end of the century. Among the many books published in answer to Luther was another equally significant one, *Assertio Septem Sacramentorum,* printed by Richard Pynson in London in 1521. Its authorship earned Henry VIII the title of Defender of the Faith. Had Henry not made such an absolute assertion of papal authority, he might not have been so offended at the lack of Papal co-operation in his divorce proceedings and might, therefore, have felt less compelled to establish the reformed church. The religious controversy placed the Bible in demand. Martin Luther's translation of the New Testament in a middle German vernacular (Wittenberg, 1522) effectively created the literate German language. Previously, German had been a large number of different dialects. The same process was taking place in other countries. Language was being moulded and standardised through the printing of books. A direct consequence of the increased importance of books was a growth of interest in education. The classical languages of the scholar gradually began to lose ground to the vernacular. The reformers urged their followers to promote reading. Luther wrote a tract setting forth an educational programme. English priests were ordered to teach their parishioners to read the Creed, the Lord's Prayer and the Ten Commandments. The establishment of parish schools began throughout England. While existing records of book ownership at this period are rare and contain information about clergymen and scholars only, there are indications that literacy was growing rapidly. Many of the proscriptions issued in the religious controversy concerned books published in the vernacular. In refuting Tyndale's argument for an English Bible, Thomas More wrote in 1528 that forty per cent of the people 'could never read English yet', which might be taken to imply that as many as sixty per cent of the population were literate. This is unlikely, but reflects the intense literary activity of the time.

The great crisis in the church led to a renewed questioning of old values in all areas of knowledge. Well-worn assumptions were questioned and the excitement of reform spilled over into science and politics. The rebirth or renaissance of intellectual activity which was initiated by books is perhaps epitomised by the life of the great Desiderius Erasmus. His *Colloquia* (Basle, 1524) typifies the questioning that was taking place in all areas of knowledge. A series of dialogues on all the great issues of the day, it not only stimulated contemporary thought but laid foundations for the rationalist movement of the eighteenth century. The science of medicine, which had sunk into superstition, was revitalised and placed on an empirical footing with the publication of works by Hippocrates at Rome in 1525. The first scientific approach to language was demonstrated by Robert Estienne in his *Dictionarius sive Latinae Linguae Thesaurus* (Paris, 1531). Estienne was a noted member of one of the most accomplished families of scholar-printers. His dictionary has not yet been superseded. In politics, one of the most influential works of this period was the *Il Principe* of Niccolo Machiavelli (Rome, 1532), which firmly established a doctrine of pragmatism. In *De*

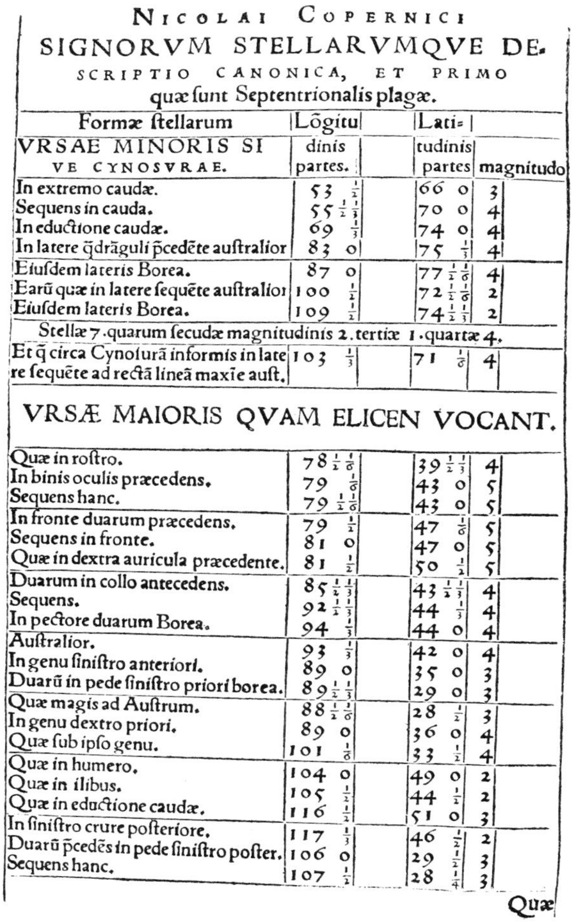
NICOLAI COPERNICI

SIGNORVM STELLARVMQVE DESCRIPTIO CANONICA, ET PRIMO quæ ſunt Septentrionalis plagæ.

Formæ ſtellarum	Lōgitudinis partes.	Latitudinis partes	magnitudo
VRSAE MINORIS SIVE CYNOSVRAE.			
In extremo caudæ.	53 1/2	66 0	3
Sequens in cauda.	55 1/2 1/3	70 0	4
In eductione caudæ.	69 1/3	74 0	4
In latere q̄drāguli p̄cedēte auſtralior	83 0	75 1/3	4
Eiuſdem lateris Borea.	87 0	77 1/2 1/6	4
Earū quæ in latere ſequēte auſtralior	100 1/2	72 1/2 1/6	2
Eiuſdem lateris Borea.	109 1/2	74 1/2 1/3	2
Stellæ 7. quarum ſecudæ magnitudinis 2. tertiæ 1. quartæ 4.			
Et q̄ circa Cynoſurā informis in latere ſequēte ad rectā lineā maxīe auſt.	103 1/3	71 1/6	4
VRSÆ MAIORIS QVAM ELICEN VOCANT.			
Quæ in roſtro.	78 1/2 1/6	39 1/2 1/3	4
In binis oculis præcedens.	79 1/6	43 0	5
Sequens hanc.	79 1/2 1/6	43 0	5
In fronte duarum præcedens.	79 1/2	47 1/6	5
Sequens in fronte.	81 0	47 0	5
Quæ in dextra auricula præcedente.	81 1/2	50 1/2	5
Duarum in collo antecedens.	85 1/2 1/3	43 1/2 1/3	4
Sequens.	92 1/2 1/3	44 1/3	4
In pectore duarum Borea.	94 1/3	44 0	4
Auſtralior.	93 1/3	42 0	4
In genu ſiniſtro anteriori.	89 0	35 0	3
Duarū in pede ſiniſtro priori borea.	89 1/2 1/3	29 0	3
Quæ magis ad Auſtrum.	88 1/2 1/6	28 1/2	3
In genu dextro priori.	89 0	36 0	4
Quæ ſub ipſo genu.	101 1/6	33 1/2	4
Quæ in humero.	104 0	49 0	2
Quæ in ilibus.	105 1/2	44 1/2	2
Quæ in eductione caudæ.	116 1/2	51 0	3
In ſiniſtro crure poſteriore.	117 1/3	46 1/2	2
Duarū p̄cedēs in pede ſiniſtro poſter.	106 0	29 1/2	3
Sequens hanc.	107 1/2	28 1/4	3

Quæ

A page from Nicolaus Copernicus' De Revolutionibus Orbium Coelestium *(1543).*

Revolutionibus Orbium Coelestium (1543), Nicolaus Copernicus was the first to question the anthropocentric view of the universe, a concept that was to be further shaken by Newton in the seventeenth century and, finally, demolished by Darwin in the nineteenth. Many of the modern sciences have their beginnings in great books of the sixteenth century. As well as Copernicus, there was Vesalius, whose *De Humani Corporis Fabrica* (Basle, 1543) started off the study of anatomy. Working from clinical observation and dissection, he broke away from the largely speculative postulations of Aristotle and Galen, and prepared the way for the discoveries of Harvey. The Spaniard, Martin Cortes, took the new spirit of investigation into the science of navigation and was the first to point to the discrepancy between the true and the magnetic poles in *Breve Compendio de la Sphere y de l'Arte de*

EL INGENIO
SO HIDALGO DON
QVIXOTE DE LA
MANCHA.

Compuesto por Miguel de Cer
uantes Saauedra.

IVAN MAVREZIO.

Con licencia de la S. Inquisicion.
EN LISBOA:
Impresso por Pedro Crasbeeck,
Año M. DCV.

Navegar (Seville, 1551). In zoology, Conrad Gesner's *Historia Animalium* (Zurich, 1551–87) may be regarded as the starting point of a scientific approach to the subject. One of the first technological works, and the first work in modern geology, was *De Re Metallica* by Georgius Agricola (Basle, 1556).

As time went on, the catalogue of great books, all revising the cherished tenets of the pre-Gutenberg world, grew. This was a century in which man's most cherished beliefs were constantly threatened and, though *Index Librorum Prohibitorum* (Rome, 1559) was only one of the many attempts to arrest that threat through censorship, the power of books was then too firmly established for progress to be stopped. By the end of the century, a firm tradition of discovery and investigation had begun.

In the following century, books continued and enlarged this tradition. Printing itself had become largely utilitarian. Few books of the seventeenth century can be described as objects of art. However, their content compensates for their

Left: *woodcut of a pump in a mine from a 1580 edition of Agricola's* De Re Metallica.
Above: *title page of Cervantes'* El Ingenioso Hidalgo Don Quixote de la Mancha.

undistinguished appearance. It was a century in which the collection and classification of existing information became as important as the extension of knowledge; bibliographies, biographies, practical dictionaries, encyclopaedias and critical histories had their real beginnings then. Scientific, literary and news journals were also started. Printing arrived in North America and probably rendered inevitable the birth of the United States, which followed in the next century. Altogether, the century produced about one and a quarter million different books. Literature reached a high peak, and scholarship became less closely tied to Latin as scientific and philosophic controversy touched more and more people.

A brief survey of the great books of this

period provides some indication of the tremendous advances made in all directions. In the realm of imaginative literature, one of the greatest works was Miguel de Cervantes Saavedra's *Don Quixote de la Mancha* (Madrid, 1605). This satire on contemporary literature inspired a tradition which is perhaps stronger than that established by Shakespeare whose much sought, and now ridiculously expensive, *Comedies, Histories and Tragedies* was first published in London seven years after his death in 1623.

Great scientific books proliferated. Kepler's *Astronomia Nova Aitologetos* (Prague, 1609) revealed the laws of planetary motion. Galileo Galilei published a series of works. The most famous, *Dialogo* was printed at Florence in 1632. The heretical statement that the earth moved around the sun placed its author in the position of defendant at one of the most famous trials in history. Robert Boyle's incredibly versatile mind generated a series of scientific works. He laid the foundations of modern chemistry with *The Sceptical Chymist* (London, 1661) and contributed to physics what came to be known as Boyle's Law, in *New Experiments Physico-mechanical Touching the Spring of the Air* (Oxford, 1662). Another important scientific work was Sir Isaac Newton's *Philosophiae Naturalis Principia Mathematica* (London, 1687) which establishes the principle of universal gravitation and the motion of the planets.

The knowledge boom had begun with a vengeance. The problem of collecting all this knowledge was quickly appreciated. In 1627, Gabriel Naudé published a tract advising Cardinal Mazarin on the formation of a library in which, he said, all publications should be preserved, even those which might be considered trivial or erroneous. He argued the importance of all books in illustrating different aspects of human thought. Naudé (1600–53) was librarian to Cardinal Richelieu and, later, to Mazarin and Queen Christina of Sweden. His *Advis pour*

Above right: *end-of-preface page of* The Sceptical Chymist *(or,* The chymico-physical doubts and Paradoxes, touching the Sphagyrist's Principles commonly call'd Hypostatical, as they are wont to be Propos'd and defended by the Generality of Alchymists', *by Robert Boyle.*
Right: *a page from Section II of Book I of Isaac Newton's* Philosophiae Naturalis Principia Mathematica.

lia in $\frac{S\,P\ quad.}{Q\,R}$, & punctis P & Q coeuntibus, scribatur S P pro R L

Sic fiet $\frac{S\,P\,qc}{S\,Aq}$ æquale $\frac{Q\,Tq \times S\,P\,q.}{Q\,R}$. Ergo (per Corol. Theor. V.)

vis centripeta reciproce est ut $\frac{S\,P\,qc}{S\,Aq}$, id est (ob datum $S\,A\ quad$)

ut quadrato-cubus distantiæ S P. Quod erat inveniendum.

Prop. VIII. Prob. III.

Moveatur corpus in circulo P Q A: ad hunc effectum requiritur lex vis centripetæ tendentis ad punctum adeo longinquum, ut lineæ omnes PS, RS *ad id ductæ, pro parallelis haberi possint.*

A circuli centro C agatur semidiameter C A parallelas istas perpendiculariter secans in M & N, & jungantur C P. Ob similia triangula C P M, & T P Z, vel (per Lem. VIII.) T P ad C P q. ad P M q. ut P Q q. vel (per Lem. VII.) P R q. ad Q T q. & ex natura circuli rectangulum Q R x R N + Q N æquale est P R quadrato. Coeuntibus autem punctis P, Q fit R N + Q N æqualis 2 P M. Ergo est C P quad. ad P M quad, ut Q R x 2 P M ad Q T quad. adeoq; $\frac{Q\,T\ quad.}{Q\,R}$ æquale $\frac{2\,P\,M\ cub.}{C\,P\ quad.}$ & $\frac{Q\,T\ quad. \times S\,P\ quad.}{Q\,R}$ æquale $\frac{2\,P\,M\ cub. \times S\,P\ quad.}{C\,P\ quad.}$. Est ergo (per Corol. Theor. V.) vis centripeta reciproce ut $\frac{2\,P\,M\ cub. \times S\,P\ quad.}{C\,P\ quad.}$ hoc est (neglecta ratione determinata $\frac{2\,S\,P\ quad.}{C\,P\ quad.}$) reciproce ut P M cub. Q. E. J.

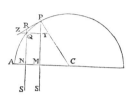

ADVIS
POVR DRESSER
VNE
BIBLIOTHEQVE.

Presenté à Monseigneur le
Président de MESME.

Par G. NAVDE' P.

Omnia quæ magna funt atque admirabilia,
tempus aliquod quo primum efficerentur
habuerunt.   *Quintil. lib.* 12.

A PARIS,
Chez FRANÇOIS TARGA, au premier
pillier de la grand' Salle du Palais,
deuant les Confultations.

M. DC. XXVII.

Title page of Naude's Advis pour dresser une
Bibliothèque.

Dresser une Bibliothèque remains tremendously
important. Its message is of considerable consequence today in the selection of books, where the
usual criteria will inevitably lead to a great many
identically bad libraries. Obviously to collect
all books is now impossible but to collect all
books on a selected subject, including what is
trivial and erroneous, must be the only way of
building a library worthy of the name.

The founders of the great early libraries
worked on the principle of comprehensive collection, but the main impetus came from the
publishers and booksellers. Although the Bodleian library in Oxford obviously owes some of
its greatness to its founder, Sir Thomas Bodley, a
large share of the credit must lie with the publishers and booksellers from whom Sir Thomas
reluctantly agreed to accept deposit copies of
licensed publications. One of the outstanding
examples of comprehensive collecting was that
set by a London bookseller, George Thomason,
who collected over twenty thousand tracts and
pamphlets published during the civil war period
in order to preserve them for posterity.

Books in America

The Spanish colonists are believed to have begun
printing in Mexico in 1535, but the first surviving
Mexican imprint is *Manual de Adultos,* printed by
Juan Pablos in Mexico City in 1540. It is possible,
also, that printing was practised in the Spanish
colony of St Augustin in Florida in the sixteenth
century, but nothing is known to have survived.
Indeed, the discovery of a sixteenth-century
book from Florida would cause considerable
excitement and enable its owner to retire very
comfortably.

The first recorded book to have been printed
in the United States, the *Bay Psalm Book,* was
published in Cambridge, Massachusetts in 1640,
ten years after the establishment of the colony.
It was printed on the press of Stephen Daye, who
had set up a printing workshop in 1638, and
edited by Richard Mather. It is probable that the
actual printing was carried out by Stephen
Daye's son, Matthew. Only five perfect copies
are known, and the most recent copy to come
on the market to my knowledge was sold at
auction in 1947 for $151,000.

The spread of printing in Colonial America
was rapid, despite the difficulties of communication. Four English colonies had presses before
1700 and the thirteenth, and last, of the original
colonies, Georgia, gained its first press in 1762.
Altogether, an estimated 88,000 publications
were produced in Colonial America. Most of
them came from the great centres of Boston,
New York and Philadelphia. An analysis of these
publications shows that by far the largest category was Theology (about forty per cent), with
Literature and Law (twenty per cent each) in
second place. The concern with freedom of expression on political subjects was characteristic.
It reached an important stage at the trial of Peter
Zenger for libel in 1735. Zenger, a printer, had
been very critical, in print, of the Governor of
New York. Despite direction to the contrary by
the judge, the jury acquitted Zenger on the
grounds that his criticisms had been based on
fact, thus establishing an important precedent in
the law of libel.

The eighteenth century saw only one significant change in book production, the invention
of stereotyping. However, this was not fully
exploited until the nineteenth century. In
America and in Europe the number of publications increased to a total of two million issues
and editions. The general standards of production

improved and many beautiful examples of printing and binding from the second half of the century can still be bought at under $100. The most important aspects of the eighteenth century are probably the growth of literacy and the profound influence gained by books in all areas of human activity. Of prime importance was increasing literacy among women. Its contribution to the long process of creating equality of opportunity between the sexes was limited, in certain types of literature, by the persistence of the view that women were intellectually inferior. Girls had increasingly attended schools from the sixteenth century. Indeed, in the seventeenth century, it was possible for a woman, Aphra Behn, to reach a position of literary eminence as a novelist and dramatist. During the eighteenth century, literacy among women was firmly established and a great many ladies' journals, novels and magazines were produced, as well as numerous awesome sermons pointing to the evils of reading light novels.

This growth in literacy was obviously catered for by publishers, who produced the eighteenth-century equivalents of *Woman's Own* and *Vogue*, sometimes with superb coloured fashion plates. However, there was also a rise in a new kind of book. Self-education was very fashionable in the eighteenth century. The man who educated himself through reading and consequently rose from his humble station was not uncommon, witness the cases of Robert Burns and Benjamin Franklin. The great encyclopaedias were an expression of this belief in self-education. The most famous were, of course, those by Diderot and the French Encyclopaedists, but other great national encyclopaedias, such as the German *Brockhaus* and the *Encyclopaedia Britannica* date from this century. The subscription libraries were another manifestation of the same movement. They enabled readers who could not afford all the books they needed to own them on a co-operative basis. The level of book prices was not particularly high; in fact, if allowance is made for changes in the value of currency, prices were much the same as they are today. In America, a volume of poetry cost, on average, about 25 cents, and a large folio could be bought for $2.75.

The foundations of modern philosophy and agriculture, the beginnings of the fight for women's rights and the great revolutions of France and North America all stem from books of the eighteenth century. The Irishman, George

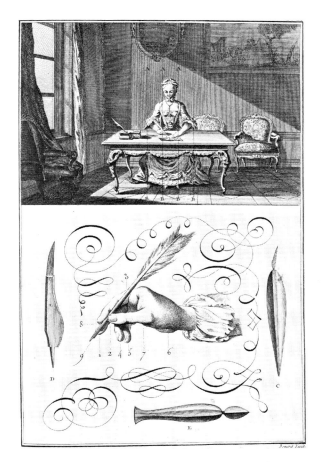

Illustration to the article Art d'Ecrire *in the* Encyclopédie, ou Dictionnaire raisoné des Sciences, des Arts et des Metiers, *by Denis Diderot with Jean Le Rond D'Alembert, initially published in 20 volumes in Paris in 1772, but increased by six volumes since it was 'a work of practical value'.*

Berkeley, in *Principles of Human Knowledge* (Dublin, 1710) pointed to the major points upon which later philosophical thought was to turn. The German, Leibniz, in *Monadologie* (1714) laid the basis for mathematical philosophy. Leibniz also proposed a universal language and a universal encyclopaedia which would contain all human knowledge on a systematic basis. Later in the century, Immanuel Kant published the most influential of all philosophical books, *Kritik der reinen Vernunft* (Riga, 1781). Among the body of great literature, Daniel Defoe's three-volume novel *The Life and Strange Surprizing Adventures of Robinson Crusoe* (London, 1719–20) has to be mentioned for its influence on literature and social ideas. Even the London in which Defoe worked as a prolific journalist and pamphleteer must have been difficult enough to live in, but

Above: *frontispiece to the first edition of Daniel Defoe's* The Life and Strange Surprizing Adventures of Robinson Crusoe.
Below: *part of a page from Arthur Young's agricultural report* A Six Weeks Tour through the Southern Counties of England and Wales.

In all this country, the method of separating the chaff from the corn in dressing it, is by means of turning an engine over it; of which I took the following draft:

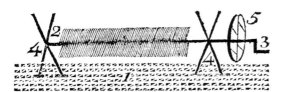

1. The corn. 2. The flyers, consisting of pieces of cloth, which are nailed by the edge to the center turning-piece 3. 4. 4. The supporters. 5. A kind of ballance-wheel, as I suppose, at least, for I could see no other use in it.

4   Around

Defoe could hardly have realised that his imagination of life on a desert island was to create a myth which today influences a whole range of aspirations and activities, from the travel industry to comic-strips. Modern agriculture has its foundations in the works of Jethro Tull, *Horse-hoeing Husbandry* (London, 1733), and Arthur Young, whose series of agricultural reports and tours include *A Six Weeks Tour through the Southern Counties of England and Wales* (London, 1768). His work was translated into Russian, French, German and Danish. In Science, there were such fundamental works as Linnaeus's *Systema Naturae* (Leiden, 1735) which established the binomial system of plant classification still in use today, and Boscovich's *Philosophiae Naturalis Theoria* (Venice, 1758), which laid the basis for atomic physics. Two of the most influential political works were Rousseau's *Principes de Droit Politique* (Amsterdam, 1762), which paved the way for the French Revolution, and Paine's *The Rights of Man* (London, 1791), which probably remains the clearest exposition of the elementary principles of democracy. Another work of tremendous, and now very topical, significance to come from this important century was *An Essay on the Principle of Population* by Thomas Malthus (London, 1798).

Towards the end of the eighteenth century the spread of ideas, made possible through books, had led to the mechanisation of manufacturing processes. The industrial revolution generated factories, and around the factories grew cities. Through the rapid growth of literacy, the spread of books created a demand for more. Some printers began to experiment with the mechanisation of their craft. Others strongly resisted change and continued to champion a technology that had remained essentially unchanged for three hundred and fifty years. After a number of experiments and suggestions, the first successful mechanised press, like the first successful movable-type press, was made in Germany. The printing machine was the invention of Frederick Koenig, who set out originally to improve the method of inking. Since Gutenberg's time, ink had been applied by hand to the type with balls or pads of leather. In 1803, Koenig, with a mechanic called Kummer, prepared designs for a power-driven press with leather-covered rollers which inked the type forme as it passed to the platen. It is not known whether the design, known as the 'Suhl Press' was ever completed. In 1806, Koenig went to London, where

AN

ESSAY

ON THE

PRINCIPLE OF POPULATION.

CHAPTER I.

Question stated.—Little prospect of a determination of it, from the enmity of the opposing parties.—The principal argument against the perfectibility of man and of society has never been fairly answered.—Nature of the difficulty arising from population.—Outline of the principal argument of the essay.

THE great and unlooked for discoveries that have taken place of late years in natural philosophy; the increasing diffusion of general knowledge from the extension of the art of printing; the ardent and unshackled spirit of inquiry that prevails throughout the lettered, and even unlettered world; the new and extraordinary

B   lights

Thomas Malthus, An Essay on the Principle of Population *'as it affects the Future Improvement of Society with remarks on the speculations of Mr Goodwin, M. Condorcet, and other writers. London, printed for J. Johnson in St Paul's Churchyard, 1798'.*

he formed a partnership with a printer, Thomas Bensley, and continued his experiments until 1810, when he obtained a patent for his printing machine. This was a steam-driven modification of his Suhl Press. It was fully automatic, although the paper had to be fed and removed by hand. While some work was produced on the new machine, it was not successful, and Koenig continued his experiments. Collectors of examples of printing history may be unable to obtain genuine Gutenberg material, but the first example of mechanised printing from Koenig's press, produced in Thomas Bensley's workshop, was section H of the *Annual Register* for 1810. Koenig achieved success with a rotary cylinder press in 1812, and a double-cylinder version of his machine was installed with great secrecy in the offices of *The Times* where its first production was the issue of 29th November 1814. The printing machine, as opposed to the old hand press, continued to improve steadily throughout the nineteenth century and is of course still doing so. The new machines, together with the huge upsurge in demand for books, magazines and newspapers, shifted book production into a much higher gear. Over eight million different issues and editions were produced before the end of the century, four times the production of the previous century. Books were cheap, literacy was increasing very rapidly, and publishers embarked on extensive programmes of cheap uniform editions. The Tauchnitz editions of paper-bound standard works were a prime example. Started in Leipzig in 1837, the Tauchnitz programme produced over five thousand separate English-language titles by 1935. The nineteenth century saw the foundation of great publishing empires. The most prominent and valuable was the firm of John Murray, which must have been responsible for publishing a very high proportion of the significant English language books of the century. Among the many ambitious popular-education publishing programmes were those of the Religious Tract Society and the Society for the Promotion of Christian Knowledge, which produced hundreds of fascinating and readily collectable books. Many fine colour-plate books were produced and are now very expensive. The great literary and popular periodicals advanced, and a huge boom occurred in the production of novels. School text books and children's books began to be produced in huge numbers, and the emergence of an independent and prosperous middle class led to a growth in the numbers of books concerned with travel and other leisure pursuits.

The mechanisation of the printing press was a very influential factor in the book boom. Equally so were mechanised type composition, the development of lithography and the Education Act of 1872. Even after Koenig's advance with the mechanised press, type still had to be cast and the individual letters composed into words and lines by hand. The process of mechanising the casting and setting of type began in 1822, when Dr William Church patented a design for a casting and a composing machine. There is no evidence that Church's machines were built. Another American, Brandt, produced a typecasting machine in 1845. Continued experimentation culminated in the production of the linotype composing machine, in 1890, and the monotype composing machine, in 1897. These two machines are still in use today. Along with their predecessors, they made possible the rapid production of books and newspapers.

Illustration from Antiquities of Westminster; The Old Palace; St Stephen's Chapel &c &c, *'containing two hundred and forty-six engravings of topographical objects of which one hundred and twenty-two no longer remain. By John Thomas Smith. London, printed by T. Bensley, Bolt Court, For J. T. Smith, 31 Castle Street East, Oxford Street and sold by R. Ryan, 353 Oxford Street, near the Pantheon and J. Manson, 10 Gerrard Street, Soho, June 9th, 1807'.*

Also of considerable technical significance was the development of lithography. This process works on the principle that the oil-based printing ink will not mix with water. The process was patented by Senefelder in Munich in 1798, and originally the image to be reproduced was drawn on a stone with a wax crayon. The stone was then moistened with water, which remained on the actual stone surface but flowed off the wax. Ink applied with a roller adhered only to the wax-drawn image and was then transferred to the paper. In 1807, Thomas Bensley used the new process to produce the first recorded lithographic book illustration, a plate in John Smith's *Antiquities of Westminster*. As the stone was broken during printing, only the first three hundred copies contain the illustration. Lithography developed slowly during the nineteenth century and the first commercial offset litho press, using metal printing plates was developed by Ira Rubel in New York in 1904. The process is now used in the production of large numbers of colour-illustrated books.

The invention of photography led to experiments in the application of photographic illustration to printing. Joseph Niepce developed the intaglio process and, in 1826, produced a portrait of Cardinal D'Amboise, the first known image reproduced by a photo-mechanical process. The first half-tone reproduction of a photograph, the type of illustration in use today, was made by Frederick von Egloffstein in 1865. The process was changed and developed by Frederick Ives of Philadelphia in 1885.

The growth of mechanisation, together with huge demand for books, led to a marked decline in standards of production and design. Quaint as mass-produced books may have been in the nineteenth century, they were nonetheless made hard to read by the style of production, if not by the style of writing. The publisher had become completely isolated from the printer, who was left to produce the books as cheaply and quickly as possible. Paper was machine-made by a process patented by John Gamble in England in 1801 and developed by the Fourdrinier brothers. Later applications of this process using wood pulp produced poor paper that deteriorated rapidly. Mechanisation of book binding also led to an initial decline in standards.

The natural reaction against shoddy production was started by the American typographer Theodore de Vinne, who attempted to re-establish standards of good design. The improvement in standards, however, owes most to the work of William Morris and his Kelmscott press. Morris, father of the private press movement, reverted almost fanatically to the traditional methods of the hand press. With Emery Walker, he designed new types and began to produce very small and expensive books. The Kelmscott *Chaucer* has been described as the most beautiful book ever produced. However, like most Kelmscott books, it is more pleasing to the eye than easy to read. But Morris's influence over the numerous private presses which flourished from the late nineteenth century until the end of the 1930s was undoubtedly responsible for the revival of craftsmanship and design in printing.

The nineteenth century produced many great books, some of which have not yet attained full recognition. Tremendous advances were made in science. Michael Faraday's *Experimental Researches in Electricity* (London, 1831) laid the groundwork for modern electrical engineering. Charles Darwin changed the concept of the origins of the world with two great works: *On the Tendency of Species to form Varieties* (London, 1858), written with Alfred Russell Wallace, and *On the Origin of Species* (London, 1859). Marconi's *Provisional Specification* (London, 1896) and *Notice sur le Cinématographe* by Auguste and Louis Lumière (Lyons, 1897) initiated a revolution in communications. In politics, two books, *Manifest der Kommunistischen Partei* by Marx and Engels (London, 1848) and Marx's *Das Kapital,* the first volume of which appeared in Hamburg in 1867, were to become the basis for a completely new political division of the world.

The production of books continued at a steady rate during the first quarter of the twentieth century. Quality was affected by the two world wars, and demand was changed by the competition from radio and cinema. The major change occurred after recovery from World War II. The gradual economic recovery which began in the 1950s and the great emphasis laid on social programmes, particularly education, combined with increasing leisure time and sophistication to create a publishing boom. In the nineteenth century, the great book collector, Sir Thomas Phillips, had set out to own a copy of every book ever printed. He came nearer to achieving his aim, despite constant financial problems, than any other individual. Today, his ambition would be completely impossible. It has been estimated that more books have been

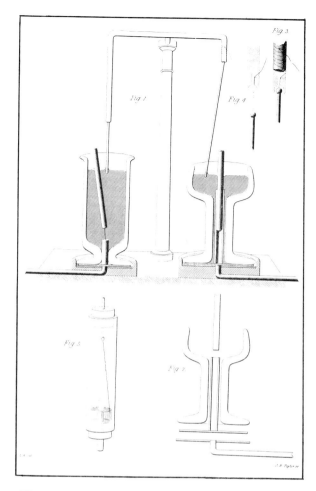

Illustration page from Experimental Researches in Electricity *by Michael Faraday, DCL, FRS. Richard, John and Edward Taylor, printers and publishers to the University of London, 1844. Reprinted from the* Philosophical Transactions *of 1838–43.*

produced since 1950 than in the previous five centuries of printing. Whether more great books have been produced, or whether many of the books are necessary or useful, remains to be seen. Modern methods of photographic and computer composition combined with the ultra high speed offset presses almost make it possible to achieve the instant book. Books are written about books about books about books and the world groans under the weight of questionable scholarship. Books decorate coffee tables, and magazines and weekly encyclopaedias dull anxiety while waiting to see the dentist. But, among all the bright, shiny, coloured publications, some are still in the true tradition of disseminating ideas which change the world. Ray Bradbury's science

Cover of the Corgi paperback edition of Ray Bradbury's Fahrenheit 451, *first published by Hart-Davis, London 1954.*

fiction novel, *Fahrenheit 451,* deals with a world where fires no longer occur and firemen are occupied solely with the burning of all books. A senior fireman explains that books have sunk to such a low intellectual standard on the one hand and, on the other, merely cause confusion by having degenerated simply into a medium for obscure academic squabbles. There is undoubtedly an element of prophecy in this. Many books have attempted to compete with such media as television and cinema rather than complement them. Many, too, are purely commercial commodities which, if they survive, will make interesting items of social history.

There are still many publishers who operate in the traditions of Aldus or, perhaps, John Murray. They have to balance their publications or charge high prices for their less popular but important books in order to survive. It seems likely, however, that the power of the printed word and the relative ease with which it can be printed will protect us from the dreadful situation in which publishers are guided entirely by numerical accountants.

Books have been among the greatest forces for change in the world. The force, being self-feeding, is unlikely to be stopped unless, perhaps, it chokes itself. It has often been predicted that new media such as television, film, cassettes, or the science fiction concept of a radio-transmitted newspaper printed out in each home, will render the book obsolete. It has also been predicted that the fragmentation of language through extremes of specialisation will reduce the currency of the book. All of these things are possible but unlikely. Nothing can replace a printed book that can be owned, admired as a work of craftsmanship, read, studied and used for reference. The last word probably lies with the author of a number of controversial and incisive books, Marshall McLuhan. He has argued that books, by presenting ideas or events in a logical left to right sequence, have shaped the manner in which men think. This is undoubtedly an oversimplification, both of McLuhan's thesis and of the modification of human thought processes. However, without books, our civilisation as such would not exist, and without the continued reliance on books its faults would stand little chance of being corrected.

The Book before 1800

ANTIQUARIAN books are now generally understood to be those printed before 1800. Although the examples in this chapter are drawn mainly from English literature, most of the technical questions which arise apply equally to pre-1800 books in other fields. Generally, the points under consideration derive more from a literary interest in the completeness of the text and a historical interest in the circumstances of publication than from a purely aesthetic concern. The difficulties—always somewhat technical—which are connected with the early methods of book production, and the factors affecting the survival of books, should not discourage collectors.

In most fields an arbitrary age, usually one hundred years, is taken as a measure of antiquity, but in bibliography the approximate date of 1800 has a particular and permanent significance as it divides the mechanized era from the earlier period when all processes were carried out by hand. Mechanization covers a number of different developments, including printing from stereotype or electrotype plates, the use of power presses and large rolls of paper instead of single sheets, and, eventually, typesetting by linotype or monotype. These processes were not adopted simultaneously, nor were any of them used consistently for some time after their first introduction, but in general the developments at the beginning of the nineteenth century provide a convenient dividing point in the technological history of printing.

The revolution in book production followed a period of some three hundred years during which methods of printing had changed extraordinarily little, whatever variations there might have been in standards of craftsmanship or the quality of the finished book. A printer of the early sixteenth century would not have felt completely at sea if he had been set down in William Strahan's printing-shop, where Adam Smith's *Wealth of Nations* was first printed in 1776. This constancy enabled R. B. McKerrow, whose practical knowledge of printing history was augmented by a study of books from the Elizabethan period, to consider the whole era from the start of the sixteenth century to the end of the nineteenth, in his monumental *Introduction to Bibliography* (1927), without feeling impelled to make too many historical qualifications. This assumption of historical continuity has been increasingly questioned by later scholars, especially in the light of the business records of some eighteenth-century printing firms. For instance, four ledgers recently lent to the Bodleian Library, Oxford, by the Grolier Club of New York record in varying degrees of detail, the printing operations of the William Bowyers, father and son. The records of William Strahan, clear, exact and comprehensive, are now in the British Museum. They present a fascinating picture of Strahan's personal and professional life and the workings of his printing house from 1739 to about 1780. J. A. Cochrane in *Dr Johnson's Printer: the Life of William Strahan* describes the information contained in these ledgers. The records of the activity of the Cambridge University Press around the beginning of the eighteenth century are fully exploited by D. F. McKenzie in *The Cambridge University Press 1696–1712: a Bibliographical Study*. These documents have formed the basis for much recent research, and draw attention to the growing complexities of procedure used in the eighteenth century. Printing was then one of the most efficient of industries, and a degree of what would now be recognised as mass-production was the rule in many large firms.

Like all hand-made artefacts, books from the era of hand printing are distinguished by the fact that no two are identical—although the differences become less obvious as the period advances: this indeed constitutes one of the attractions of collecting. Variations do not in themselves affect the value of books, but they make the study of them more complex. The unique significance of each copy has been appreciated since at least the early years of the twentieth century in the case of important books from the first two hundred years of printing. The American collector Henry Clay Folger, whose books were to form the nucleus of the Folger Shakespeare Library in Washington, D.C., collected nearly eighty copies of the Shakespeare first folio of 1623. But the same perception has not been applied to lesser works, and some odd prejudices have prevailed. Two or three generations ago it was fashionable to collect works from the presses of the seventeenth-century Dutch Elzevir family, whose books are notable for their small size. An eager collector would measure a new-found copy to see whether an extra millimetre in height or width would justify its purchase. The concept of the perfect copy, the finest that can be found, dies hard. Relatively few collectors consider the unique, perhaps barely perceptible, characteristic which may distinguish one copy from another, superficially more attractive. Obviously the pursuit of a fresh copy in its original binding, and without excessive trimming of the margins, is perfectly legitimate, but standards are sometimes applied too fastidiously. Many a collector might pass over a re-bound copy of Johnson's *Journey to the Western Islands of Scotland* (1775) in favour of a copy in crisp original binding, without checking for the uncancelled leaf D8 containing Johnson's invective against the vandal burgesses of Lichfield, which is found in only one known copy. If other things are equal, the original state is preferable to a new binding—even to the most 'literary' of collectors—not only because a modern binder may have trimmed down the margins unnecessarily (though not as ruthlessly as many in the nineteenth century who cropped the edges of the text), but also because rebinding permits 'sophistication' or the partial reconstruction of an imperfect book with leaves taken from another copy or even another edition. The uncut copy (in which the margins have not been trimmed by a binder's shears) which may also be unopened (with the leaves still joined at the outer folds or 'bolts') can alone be relied on to represent a pristine state.

The old-fashioned ideal of a copy 'just as it came off the press' is a misleading simplification, for subtly different copies of equal or greater interest may have been produced at very nearly the same time. Variations in paper quality, often overlooked, may indicate some factor of interest in the production of a book. In the seventeenth century, and more especially in the eighteenth, it was common to produce fine-paper (often also large-paper) copies of books in such areas as poetry and drama. The *de luxe* version formed perhaps ten per cent of the whole edition, and sometimes preceded the ordinary issue by a few days, selling for a higher price. The text of the fine-paper copies may show readings not found in the ordinary run, and, since the author would have used the superior version for presentation, it is possible that where there are corrections to the text they may be in his own hand. An unusual elaboration appears in a fine-paper copy, now in the University of Kansas library, of a Latin translation of Psalms 1–50 by John Hanway, *Psalmi Davidis quinquaginta priores versibus elegiacis Latine rediti* (1723). This was presented to the Archbishop of Canterbury, William Wake, and has *Ex dono autoris* (the gift of the author) actually printed on the title page.

If size is a clue to the quality of the paper, as it may well be, the desirability of a 'tall' uncut

Psalm I from John Hanway's Psalmi Davidis Quinquaginta Priores Versibus Elegiacis Latini Redditi *(1723).*

copy may not be just aesthetic, as it was for the Elzevir hunters. Yet it may be difficult to establish that a copy is really on fine paper: even a detailed bibliography may not provide the means of distinguishing a separate issue of this kind. Comparison with other copies may give some indications: a different watermark, the omission of the price from the title page or a wider inner margin ('gutter'). The quality of the paper itself is hard to assess, as the process of making paper by hand resulted in differences in appearance and feel, even between sheets from the same mould. In any case, cheaply-produced books were often printed on job lots of paper of varying quality. Frequently, however, the feel of the paper is the only indication of this part of a book's history, and only the collector's experience can provide him with the necessary judgment.

Some booksellers' catalogues should be read with caution, as the term 'large-paper copy' may mean simply 'large copy', where the margins happen to be wide, but there is no evidence that larger sheets of paper were used. Similarly the description, 'fine-paper copy' is sometimes used when there is nothing to prove that all copies were not printed on the same fine paper. Some of the most sumptuous books published in England during the eighteenth century show paper of the same very high quality in all copies—notably editions printed at considerable expense and pre-sold to subscribers, like the magnificent 1757 Virgil, the first book issued from John Baskerville's press at Birmingham. None the less, it is reasonable to suppose that fine-paper copies of books printed before 1800 are much commoner than was once thought, and there is plenty of scope for the discovery of unsuspected items.

The collector of antiquarian books often has to face the problem of deciding whether the lack of some component part is real or only apparent, and, if real, whether it renders the book imperfect or constitutes a legitimate variation from what is accepted as a perfect copy. The question can usually be decided by collating the signatures which enabled the binder to assemble the printed sheets and checking that the order is correct. The principles of collation are explained in the bibliographical manuals. This procedure uncovers many instances of errors in page numbering that are familiar even in the finest productions of the eighteenth and earlier centuries. In Baskerville's 1772 quarto edition of the poems of

Catullus, Tibullus and Propertius, a look at the pagination alone would suggest the absence of pages 201–220, yet the collational sequence is in order and reveals the misnumbering as a mistake by the compositor. However, this method of checking is useful only when the missing component forms part of the original signature-sequence of the book. For instance, when a copy begins with three leaves of which the first is the title-page, and the second and third are signed A3 and A4, there is evidently something missing, probably (in the eighteenth century) a half title but perhaps a blank leaf. First and last leaves— a half title, a blank or a licence leaf (certifying some official permission for the work to be printed) at the beginning, a leaf of advertisements or blank leaf at the end—may be lacking in books which were bound some time after printing, since they often became dirty while the book was in its unbound state and were therefore discarded. Unfortunately, the statement 'lacks final (or preliminary) blank' in a bookseller's catalogue does not always indicate a certainty that the missing leaf was blank.

The problems of leaves added outside the signature-sequence, such as a frontispiece or engraved fly-title before the title-page, engraved plates in the text, or occasional advertisement leaves at the beginning or end, are more difficult. If the book is described fully in a bibliography, or if it is possible to compare the doubtful copy with other examples, it should be possible to decide whether such leaves are missing. Even if they are, however, their absence does not necessarily make the copy imperfect. Many apparent defects may be legitimate variants in the original make-up of the book. Sometimes, for instance, a frontispiece was an optional extra. We know from one of the author's letters that the frontispiece of Defoe's satire *Jure Divino* (folio, 1706) cost a shilling over the normal price of the book. The lists of subscribers in eighteenth-century books published by subscription may be another example. Most copies of Baskerville's 1757 edition of Virgil contain such a list, somewhat longer (by either twenty-one or twenty-four names) in some than in others. It seems that the names of some late subscribers were added after most copies of this part of the book had been printed. But the appearance on booksellers' shelves of copies—not numerous, but too common to be exceptional—without any list at all suggests a further complication. Perhaps, through some confusion in the printing-house, one batch

Laudatur et Alget
Juven. Sat. 1.

graphy of Pope's works and not found in any other copy of the poem. The leaf, headed 'Index to the Ethic Epistles' and outlining Pope's plan for the _Essay_ and its sequel, cleared up a minor mystery, for Joseph Spence had recorded that Pope annexed such an explanatory leaf to a dozen or so copies of the poem for presentation to close friends, afterwards recalling most of them. The discovery of this unique leaf, which is reproduced in the facsimile of this edition published by the Scolar Press of Menston, Yorkshire, in 1969, did not mean that all other known copies had to be regarded as defective, since we know from Spence that Mr Forster's copy represents a separate issue. Even if we had no external evidence, weight of numbers would tend to protect the integrity of the copies without the Index. A less familiar book, the third edition (1726) of

Left: _frontispiece portrait from Daniel Defoe's_ Jure Divino _(1706)._
Below: _title page to Epistle IV of Alexander Pope's_ An Essay on Man _(1706)._

of copies was assembled before the revised list was ready. Variants such as these call into question our idea of the perfect, or in bibliographers' terms, the ideal copy. We may decide that a book is imperfect if its deficiencies are the result of human or mechanical error, or of undiscriminating destruction, but who is to say that a customer brought into being an imperfect copy of Defoe's poem by declining to pay an extra shilling for the frontispiece? A copy with the frontispiece is more desirable for several reasons, notably aesthetic, and the list of subscribers is likely to be of considerable bibliographical and historical interest. These features, though, may not always be what booksellers describe as 'called for', and the collector whose timidity makes him reject all but the ideal may miss much that is of interest, and many bargains.

The concept of the perfect copy is further weakened by the appearance of unique examples of certain books. Just before the last war, Mr Harold Forster bought a fine paper copy of the first collected edition of Pope's _Essay on Man_ (1734), the quarto issue. It was not until twenty-five years later that he discovered on close examination that his copy contained a final leaf which was unrecorded in R. H. Griffith's biblio-

A N
E S S A Y
O N
M A N.
In EPISTLES to a Friend.

EPISTLE IV.

LONDON:
Printed for _J. Wilford_, at the _Three Flower-de-Luces_, behind the _Chapter-house_, St. Paul's. MDCCXXXIV.

Edward Young's *Paraphrase on part of the Book of Job,* which had first appeared in 1719, provides another instance. Three copies of the 1726 edition are known. Only that in the Huntington Library at San Marino, California, has the leaf A1. One side of this leaf bears the words 'A specimen for subscribers', and the other describes a projected subscription edition of Young's works, of which this poem was printed as a specimen, detailing the terms of the subscription. The two copies without this leaf might be thought defective were it not, again, for external evidence, this time in the form of two series of advertisements carried by London newspapers in 1727 and 1729, which suggest that the specimens were sold off as an independent publication two years after the failure of the subscription edition to appear— presumably for lack of subscribers. So an apparent defect may reflect an interesting aspect of a book's history.

Of course, there is a difference in validity between imperfect and complete copies. No collector would normally choose a defective book rather than a complete one, however interesting the reasons for its deficiency. But the more carefully we think about what we mean by imperfect, the better equipped we shall be to decide in individual cases. In *The Elements of Book-collecting* (1927) Iolo Williams advised collectors never to buy an imperfect book, with the almost casually added proviso that they could reasonably hope to obtain a perfect copy in due course. McKerrow, reviewing Williams's book in *Transactions of the Bibliographical Society*, supported him strongly, as most of his contemporaries would have done, 'not only because the advice is in itself sound, but because if followed, it will leave a larger number of imperfect copies of rare books for those students of typography who need "working" copies for bibliographical study and are quite unable to pay collectors' prices.' Since then, the prices commanded by imperfect books have risen in the wake of those fetched by fine copies and, while the principle still applies, fewer collectors would now make it quite such a prime consideration.

The question of incomplete sets is different. A number of possible considerations may justify the acquisition of odd volumes. A complete volume out of an incomplete set often better fulfils the functions of a working copy than an internally defective volume. Eighteenth-century booksellers' made a common practice of collecting sets of the work of an author, binding together series of pamphlets, individually complete and often remainders of earlier publications, with collective title-pages added at the beginning of each volume. This happened more commonly with cheaply-produced editions, and such sets often show signs of hasty reissue for the purpose of clearing old stocks. Most early collected editions of the popular playwrights of the period take this form and, in a number of cases, most copies will be variant since a different combination of earlier editions was used each time. On the other hand, collections of this kind can be handsome productions with new material added. The first collected edition of Samuel Foote's plays consists of eighteen earlier editions of the separate plays put into two volumes by the bookseller William Lowndes with a life of the author; one of the collective half-titles to the whole set states, 'Price 15s in boards'. The separate signature-sequences in each play show that the pamphlets were printed for separate sale as well as for assembly in bound sets. Sometimes, contemporary advertisements (including those bound in at the end of books) make the choice clear. The late eighteenth and early nineteenth centuries saw the appearance of many general collections of English plays published in this way. Bell's *British Theatre* (a number of editions, between 1776 and 1799), Jones's *British Theatre* (1791–5) and *The British Theatre* (25 volumes, 1806–09) edited by Elizabeth Inchbald are among the most familiar. A full bibliographical account would be immensely complicated, but a useful simplified list is given by Carl J. Stratman. A single volume from one of these collections, containing perhaps four or five plays, is a worthwhile collection in its own right.

The other consideration which may redeem an odd volume is the possibility that luck will enable a collector to complete his set from other sources. If this happens, the volumes may well be from the same set (in the same binding, and with the same signs of ownership), if it has been accidentally split at auction or in the dispersal of a library. This general point applies, of course, to modern books as well. Again, a word must be added about apparent incompleteness. Many works which were published volume by volume never attained the total originally intended by the author (or bookseller). A single volume proclaiming itself Vol. I is sometimes also the last, simply commemorating a more ambitious project. Some of the best-known examples are Sir Walter Raleigh's *History of the World* (1614),

George Berkeley's *Treatise Concerning the Principles of Human Knowledge* (Dublin, 1910) and Edward Young's *Conjectures on Original Composition* (1759). None of these extended beyond the first part. The circumstances and details vary, but it is easy for the unwary to mistake books like these for odd volumes. Michael O. Krieg lists (though far from exhaustively) books such as these published in all periods and in all countries.

It might be useful to clarify a few of the terms which have been used here. The words used in specifying formats, such as folio, quarto, octavo and duodecimo, are themselves old and generally retain their original, more precise meanings in relation to early books. However, they are normally used in a different (debased, if we are being pedantic) sense by, for instance, modern publishers. The terms now indicate the size of a book, though not with any accuracy unless qualified as in the description, demy 8vo, which means that the book is one-eighth the size of a sheet of demy paper (now standardised at $17\frac{1}{2}$ins by $22\frac{1}{2}$ins), i.e. $8\frac{3}{4}$ins by $5\frac{5}{8}$ins. Crown 8vo is $7\frac{1}{2}$ins by 5ins, as a crown sheet measures 15ins by 20ins. This way of expressing measurements is possible because we know exactly how big a crown, demy or any other size of sheet is. In the

Above: *engraved title page to Sir Walter Raleigh's* The History of the World *(1614), written during his years of imprisonment in the Tower of London, from a copy belonging to Elizabeth of Bohemia, known as the Winter Queen.*
Left: *from the 1780 edition of Bell's* British Theatre.

days of hand-made paper, these terms had different meanings in each period and with each place of origin. Since, too, margins were usually trimmed indiscriminately before binding, the relation between the size of the sheets on which the book was printed and the dimensions of the finished book is very uncertain. The terms folio, quarto, and so on, indicate not size but how many times each sheet was folded to make up the gatherings of which the book consists—a folio once and a quarto twice (i.e. into quarters). The terms demy and crown are relevant only when the size of the original sheets is ascertainable (which is not all that often). The number of leaves in each gathering, shown by the signatures, does not necessarily indicate the format, or number of folds per sheet, for gathering and sheet need not correspond. Thus a book in gatherings of four leaves does not have to be quarto, but the reader can tell from McKerrow's *Introduction* how relevant this is to his own interests. Certain books were printed at the same time, in the same edition, in more than one format. Sometimes this difference corresponds with differences of paper and other visible signs of fine paper issue, as in some early editions of Pope: both the 1717 edition of his *Works* and the 1734 *Essay on Man* were printed simultaneously in quarto and on two different sizes of paper in folio.

We referred, briefly, to the well-known cancel in the first edition of Johnson's *Journey to the Western Islands of Scotland*. Cancel-hunting is as much a favourite sport with the collector as it is with the professional bibliographer. R. W. Chapman's *Cancels* (Oxford, 1930) is the fullest and most interesting account of the subject, and McKerrow describes the principal forms which cancels take, and the ways of recognising them. He defines a cancel as 'any part of a book which is substituted for what was originally printed.' It may be of any size from a scrap of paper bearing one or two letters, pasted on over those first printed, to several sheets replacing the original ones. The collector is most likely to come across a single leaf replacing the original, and the commonest indication of such a cancel is the stub on which the new leaf has been pasted. The substitution reflects a change of mind on the part of author or printer, or the correction of some error noticed in the course of printing. Cancellation is sometimes retroactive, involving (at least in theory) all copies of a book (especially if the need for a cancel was only recognised after the completion of printing), and sometimes affects only those copies of the leaf which were printed after the decision to make the change. A book which may illustrate both kinds is the first edition of Dryden's *Annus Mirabilis* (1667). In a reference to Sir William Berkeley, vice-admiral of the white squadron at the battle of North Foreland in 1666, the third line of stanza lxvii (on p. 18) originally read 'Berkley alone, not making equal way . . .' It seems that this was considered an undiplomatic reflection on the late admiral, and a leaf was substituted in the majority of copies amending this line to 'Berkley alone, who nearest Danger lay . . .' Forty stanzas further on, on p. 27, Dryden had written of the miraculous invincibility of Prince Rupert's fleet, which

TO
THE METROPOLIS
OF
GREAT BRITAIN,
The most Renowned and late Flourishing
CITY of
LONDON,
In its
REPRESENTATIVES
The Lord Mayor and Court of Aldermen, the
Sherifs and Common Council of it.

AS perhaps I am the first who ever presented a work of this nature to the Metropolis of any Nation, so is it likewise consonant to Justice, that he who was to give the first Example of such a Dedication should begin it
A 2   with

The dedication of Annus Mirabilis: The Year of Wonders, 1666, '*An Historical Poem containing the Progresses and various successes of our Naval War with Holland, under the conduct of His Highness Prince Rupert, & His Grace the Duke of Albemarle and describing the Fire of London' by John Dryden (1667).*

'dead and buried the third Day arose.' Precisely who overruled this blasphemous turn of phrase we do not know, but overruled it was, and in every known copy except one, which is now in the Guildhall Library in London, the leaf with the offending stanza was cancelled. The line now innocuously reads 'And every Ship in swift Proportion grows.' Is it accident, the relative seriousness of the two lapses, or some more practical reason, that caused one to be suppressed more effectively than the other?

It is impossible to guess in how many cases a cancelled passage is really lost for ever, since copies, hitherto unknown of any rare book may turn up at any time to resolve the mystery surrounding cancellation. A fairly well-known example is the unique copy of Robert Greene's *Quip for an Upstart Courtier* (1592) which appeared on the market in 1919 and contained uncancelled, the original, scurrilous attack on the poet Gabriel Harvey, previously only reconstructed from contemporary reports. Similar mysteries, solved by the discovery of an uncancelled copy in the mid 1960s, surrounded the first collected edition of Swift's *Works,* printed in four volumes at Dublin in 1735. Scattered through the remarkable second volume, which contains the poems, there are normally no fewer than nine separate cancels entailing the removal of thirty original leaves and their replacement by twenty-eight new ones. Until recently, we had only the partial explanation given in a letter from Swift to Lord Oxford, written a few months before the *Works* were published. 'I have put the Man [George Faulkner, the printer] under some Difficultyes by ordering certain Things to be struck out after they were printed, which some friends had given him. This hath delayed his work, and as I hear, given him much trouble and difficulty to adjust.' The copy then discovered has all but one of the original leaves still in place, and twenty-seven of the cancel leaves bound in at the end. All the reasons become clear: some stylistic polishing, the omission of lines from certain poems to mitigate some of the more venomous attacks on Swift's contemporaries, and the removal of some whole poems for the same reason—poems which had been included without his permission. This copy is now in the English Faculty Library at Oxford.

Whatever the chances of making such discoveries, cancels are an extremely common feature of old books. R. W. Chapman's suggestion that about a third of eighteenth-century books contained a cancel has not since been refuted so far as I know. In that period, a cancel title-page often proclaimed a new edition while, in reality, concealing the reissue of a previous edition, either because sales of the earlier one needed a boost, or because a new owner wanted to show that the copyright had changed hands. If a title-page looks like a cancel, the chances are that the rest of the book is of an earlier date than the title-page would have us believe. Sometimes, however, in cases where two or more booksellers shared the copyright, different title-pages might be used by each issuing bookseller simultaneously. I have in my own collection a copy of the fourth edition (1652) of Thomas Randolph's *Poems* which has two consecutive title-pages with different imprints. One names two booksellers and the other reads simply 'Printed in the yeare 1652'. The binder has inserted the alternative (first) title-page while neglecting to take out the other. In other cases, cancellation involving substitution was unnecessary, since it was possible to print the different title-pages as part of the same sheet and simply remove the irrelevant one before binding. Books of this kind serve to illustrate the general point that a different title-page is not by any means a reliable sign of a different edition. They ought to be termed different *issues,* though in many contexts—for instance, in A. W. Pollard and G. R. Redgrave's *Short-title Catalogue of Books Printed in England, Scotland & Ireland . . . 1475–1640* and Donald Wing's corresponding *Catalogue* for the period 1641–1700, the standard repertories of their fields—the distinction between separate issue and separate edition is not always drawn.

This account of a few of the hidden features of interest which may lie in an antiquarian book

Title page from A Quip for an Upstart Courtier *by Robert Greene. The capital A is damaged on the original copy.*

A

QVIP FOR AN VP-
ftart Courtier:

Or,

A quaint difpute betvveen Veluet breeches
and Cloth-breeches.

Wherein is plainely fet dovvne the diforders
in all Eftates and Trades.

LONDON
Imprinted by Iohn Wolfe, and are to bee fold at his
fhop at Poules chayne. 1 5 9 2.

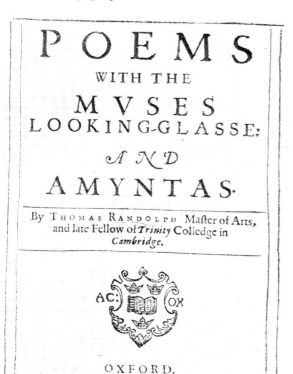

Thomas Randolph, Poems with the Muses Looking Glasse: and Amyntas *(1638); above: Randolph's inscription on a copy dedicated to Richard Weston. The latinized form of Weston's name forms an anagram of 'Vir durus ac honestus'—'a hard and honest man'—if the W is taken as two Vs and V and U treated as interchangeable.*
Below: *title page of the same work.*

includes no attempt to draw the wider picture of what classes of books can be looked for. However, any collector who wishes to taste a thoroughly representative cross-section of the books printed in London in a given period might look at the contemporary catalogues of new publications which were issued during the seventeenth and eighteenth centuries. Catalogues are increasingly accessible in these days of reprints, though the originals are very rare. None of them makes dull browsing for anyone with the least interest in the period. The years 1668–1709 are well covered by the so-called Term Catalogues, edited by Edward Arber (1903–06). In most cases, they state the format and price of each book, occasionally providing other details not given by the books themselves. Their use is limited—though this has some advantages, in helping to clear the ground—by their apparent intention to include books of some importance and ignore a lot of ephemeral and popular literature which is much harder to chart. For the later period there is no one regular guide, but

Title page of a 1764 edition of The British Mazazine.

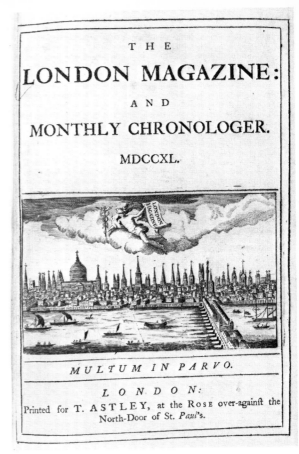

The Monthly Catalogue (1714–17 and 1723–30) and the Register of new publications given in The Monthly Chronicle between 1728 and 1732, both edited by D. F. Foxon (1964), provide a very comprehensive unclassified cross-section of both new works and reprints. The Gentleman's Magazine, from its first appearance in 1731, included more selective monthly lists, as did other new literary periodicals of its generation, such as The London Magazine and The British Magazine. The strange juxtapositions in catalogues like these give some unsettling insights into the bricks and mortar of literary history. The sumptuous first collected edition of John Locke's works, published June 1714 in three folio volumes at £2 10s, appears in The Monthly Catalogue for that month, sandwiched between a popular collection of tales of Troy at two shillings and an anonymous Vindication of the Earl of Nottingham from the Vile Imputations and Malicious Slanders Which Have Been Cast upon Him in Some Late Pamphlets, at one shilling. So the greatest English philosophical monument of

the age rubs shoulders with ladies' drawing-room entertainments and the forgotten pamphlet wars of party politics. It would be a very limited view of eighteenth-century culture which took in only the great landmarks. The book collector is as well equipped as anyone to take the wider view, if only by filling in some unexpected detail which an apparently negligible book can supply. It may seem negligible because of its content or because of its condition. But at a time when the decline—disadvantageous but not paralysing—in the availability of nearly all kinds of old books has been accompanied by a new realisation of the special interest of each individual copy, no collector, whether scholar or amateur, can complain that the possibilities have become unexciting yet.

Right: *vignette from* The Book of the Dead of Nesitanebtashru, *daughter of Pinadjem I, High Priest of Amun, from the Greenfield Papyrus (c1080 BC). Shu, god of the air, raises above his head the body of Nut, goddess of the sky, torn from the embrace of the earth god Geb who lies at his feet. See page 21.*

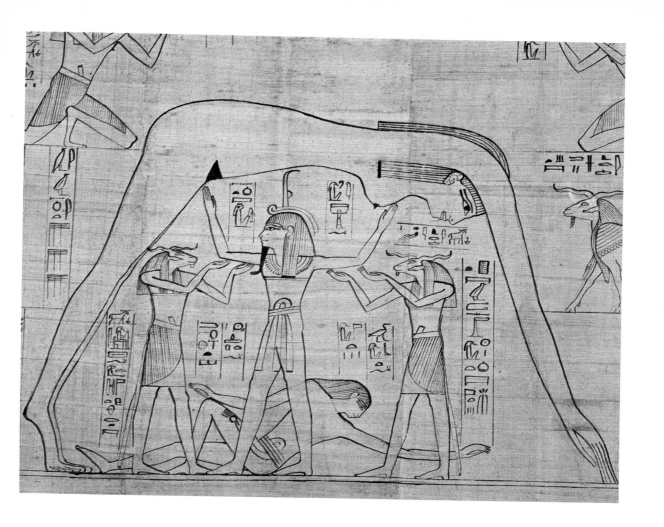

DOCTOR NIKOLA

The Illustrated Book

THIS outline of the techniques and history of book illustration, while mentioning some of the illustrated books which might form part of a collection, will serve primarily as an introduction to the methods of reproduction of illustrations. Unless such books are to be collected purely for their value as an investment, which is often considerable, the only criteria are the collector's own taste and the price and availability of the books themselves. Illustrated books, more than any others, are subject to changes in fashion. This affects the collector, especially when a vogue is part of a more general movement, such as the recent Pre-Raphaelite revival. Then, books of a favoured type are likely to rise very rapidly in price, only to drop as fast when fashions change.

Because the physical limitations of the various processes give them individual characteristics which are usually clearly recognisable, they will be dealt with separately, but some general observations about care and condition may be helpful. Condition is important in all areas of book collecting but particular care is needed in purchasing illustrated books. Since many people understandably feel that good pictures should hang where they can be seen, a great many of those originally found in books are now on walls. Each book should be checked to ensure that all illustrations are present: this is most easily done from the list of illustrations which usually follows the table of contents or chapter headings. If there is no list, checks can be made against the index, a detailed bibliography of the illustrator, or another copy of the book. Alternatively, the actual gatherings of pages may show evidence of the removal of a plate. Apart from the possibility that a plate may have been omitted by the binder or removed by a previous owner, there is the risk that it may have been stolen by one of the people who make a handsome living by abstracting valuable plates from books in shops and libraries. If they have unwittingly sold an imperfect book, most booksellers will take it back and refund the price: some, however, do not, and it can be expensive to find out which they are.

If the book is complete, the next stage is to examine its condition: many modern illustrated books have pictorial or decorated covers, and, obviously, these should be in as good a state as possible. Even the absence of a dust wrapper can render a book technically imperfect, but the collector must adjust his standards according to availability and price. He must also decide the acceptable level of blemishes in the text and plates. Damp-stains and foxing are unfortunately common and may affect the aesthetic and commercial value of a book quite considerably. Books can sometimes be washed and re-sized by a qualified binder, but the operation is expensive and many people consider that even when properly done it detracts from the value of a book, which is no longer in its original state. It is in any case essential to make sure that the reproduction process used for the plates is one that will undergo washing without suffering further deterioration. If in doubt, consult an archivist; if nobody is available to advise, do not have the book washed. Damp and foxing are not the only defects. Plates may have been trimmed too close when the book was bound, and they can be torn, rubbed or scribbled over. Modern colour printed plates, such as those used for the works of Arthur Rackham, are often tipped in— mounted on the page with paste, usually at the top two corners. The other corners may have been folded over through careless handling, and although the crease mark may seem only a minor defect, it may affect the appearance and value of the book. Folding plates are frequently torn or damaged by rough re-folding; plates sometimes also suffer from offset, where they have taken up

Left: a 'Dr Nikola' title by Guy Boothby. See page 148.

ink from the facing page of text. Many books printed before the mid nineteenth century have hand-coloured plates: if the colouring is of a later date than the book, the value may be affected. Original colouring is to be preferred so long as the quality is high, but the most important consideration is whether the colour has been applied with skill, taste and, in botanical or zoological works, accuracy of tone, Steer clear of colouring that runs over the printed areas or is opaque.

Some dealers specialise in 'breaking' illustrated books and removing the plates. Whatever one may think of this practice, which itself often tends to inflate prices, it can provide a useful means of replacing missing plates. An intelligent search in antique and print shops may well uncover replacements, particularly for maps and plates in topographical works which have been removed for framing by a previous owner.

A curiosity which, fortunately, is now seldom found in booksellers' catalogues is the extra-illustrated copy. The term refers to two different articles. The first is legitimate, very desirable, and rare, and is usually one of a few copies of a book which were provided with extra plates or, possibly, original illustrations at the publication stage. What is more often seen is a hybrid resulting from the practice of some misguided nineteenth-century collectors of augmenting their prize copies with illustrations taken from other books. While this produced a number of very interesting volumes, it necessarily caused the destruction of others at the time less fashionable.

Illustration before Printing

This is not intended as a source of information for potential collectors of illustrated manuscripts. Anyone contemplating such a field will need quantities of money and of reliable specialist advice. However, it will be useful to outline the origins of illustration, which is, after all, much older than printing. Egyptian papyrus rolls were illustrated, and it is arguable that the early Chinese books were pictorial, as the characters themselves are ideographic. However, the first books to be consistently illustrated in a modern sense came from Byzantium and were illuminated in a style which combined Islamic elements with a naturalism inherited from the early Christian period. The illumination of manuscripts became widespread during the Middle

Ages and developed in three fairly distinct forms, although these are sometimes found combined where several artists have collaborated on the same work. The principal, and probably the oldest form is the miniature, which interrupted the text and was not always directly relevant to it. Moreover, the artist's interpretation of the text often varied from the author's intention. From the miniature sprang the mainstream of modern illustration and, possibly, the concept of painting as a separate entity. The marginal illustration, rarer and usually less elaborate, was more useful in creating an impression of continuity and was the equivalent and precursor of the modern comic strip. The third category, historiated initials, enjoyed a revival in the Victorian era, but took on a decorative rather than an illustrative function.

Chapter headings, unrelated to the text, by Aubrey Beardsley for Volume I of The Birth, Life and Acts of King Arthur *by Sir Thomas Malory (J. M. Dent & Co., 1893).*

Woodcuts and Wood engraving

Woodcuts were used to produce playing cards long before the first printed books appeared, and survived in broadsides and cheap works until the early nineteenth century. Woodcuts are different from wood engravings, and the two processes produce markedly different results. While the woodcut process is cheap, its physical limitations mean that the resulting illustrations are mostly crude and lifeless. There are obvious exceptions: Aldus Manutius' *Hypnerotomachia Poliphili* (1499), with its excellent typography, woodcutting and printing, is one of the most beautiful books ever produced, and there were many other books con-

Doctor Hawke felt her pulse,
and shaking his head,
Says, I fear I can't save her,
because she's quite dead.

She'll do very well yet,
then said Doctor Fox,
If she takes but one pill
From out of this box.

Doctor Hawk's a clever fellow,
Pincht her wrist enough to kill
her.

Ah! Doctor Fox,
You are very cunning,
For if she is dead,
You'll never get one in.

4

There were four jovial huntsmen,
As I once heard Tom say;
And they would go a hunting,
Upon a summer's day.

All the day they hunted,
And nothing could they find,
But a ship a sailing,
A sailing with the wind.

5

One said it was a ship,
Another did say nay;
The third thought it a house,
With chimney blown away.

All the night they hunted,
And nothing could they find,
But the moon a gliding,
A gliding with the wind.

6   JACK AND THE BEAN-STALK.

Jack arrives at the Giant's House.

JACK AND THE BEAN-STALK.   7

The Giant with his Wonderful Hen.

know you are acquainted with your father's history, till you see me again.

"Go along the direct road, you will soon see the house where our cruel enemy lives. While you do as I order you, I will protect and guard you; but remember, if you disobey my commands, a dreadful punishment awaits you."

When the fairy had concluded, she disappeared, leaving Jack to pursue his journey. He walked on till after sunset, when, to his great joy, he espied a large mansion. This agreeable sight revived his drooping spirits; he redoubled his speed, and soon reached it. A plain looking woman was at the door—he accosted her, begging she would give him a morsel of bread and a night's lodging.

She expressed the greatest surprise at seeing him; and said it was quite uncommon to see a human being near their house, for it was well known that her husband was a cruel and very powerful giant, and one that would eat human flesh, if he could possibly get it.

This account greatly terrified Jack, but still trusting to the fairy's protection, he hoped to elude the giant, and therefore he again entreated the woman to take him in for one night only, and hide him where she thought proper. The good woman at last suffered herself to be persuaded, for she was of a compassionate and generous disposition, and at last took him into the house.

First they entered a fine large hall, magnificently fur-

nished; they then passed through several spacious rooms, all in the same style of grandeur, but they appeared to be quite forsaken and desolate.

A long gallery was next; it was very dark, just large enough to show that, instead of a wall on one side, there was a grating of iron, which parted off a dismal dungeon, from whence issued the groans of several poor victims whom the cruel giant reserved in confinement for his own voracious appetite.

Poor Jack was half dead with fear, and would have given the world to have been with his mother again; for he now began to fear that he should never see her more, and was almost inclined to give himself up for lost; he even mistrusted the good woman, and thought she had let him into the house for no other purpose than to lock him among the unfortunate people in the dungeon: still, he recollected the fairy, and a gleam of hope forced itself into his heart.

At the farther end of the gallery there was a spacious kitchen, and a very excellent fire was burning in the grate. The good woman bid Jack sit down, and gave him plenty to eat and drink. Jack, seeing nothing here to make him uncomfortable, soon forgot his fear, and was just beginning to enjoy himself, when he was disturbed by a knocking at the gate, which was so loud, as to cause the whole building to shake.—Just as he was considering what he

Early nineteenth-century chap-books: top left: 'Dr Hawke felt her pulse' from The Life and Death of Jenny Wren 'for the use of Young Ladies and Gentlemen, being a very small book at a very small charge to teach them to read before they grow large.

Printed and sold by T. Batchelor, d. Alley, Moorfields'. Top right: London Jingles and Country Tales for Young People. Above: Jack and the Beanstalk. *J. Catnash, Printer, 2, 3, Monmouth Court, Seven Dials.*

taining woodcuts of a high standard, particularly those printed in sixteenth-century France. Generally, however, woodcuts lack subtlety and do not lend themselves to the expression of detail or tone. It was simple, if laborious, to produce a block: the artist or draughtsman drew his design on a piece of wood, usually pear, which had been cut with the grain; the block-cutter trimmed away all the wood surrounding the lines of the drawing, which then stood clear of the background and could be inked and printed at the same time as the type. Occasionally the process was reversed, so that the drawing itself was carved in the wood: when printed, the result took the form of white line against a solid black. This type of woodcut, closer to wood engraving, was little used and often crudely executed.

Early examples of woodcut illustrations are now difficult to find, and even the worst tend to be expensive. Yet, despite their limitations, it should not be thought that there is no satisfaction or scope in collecting woodcuts. Examples from the fifteenth, sixteenth and seventeenth centuries are virtually unobtainable in any quantity: by the end of the sixteenth century the illustration of fine books was the province of the copper engraver, and the woodcut was relegated to cheap popular works. These are the chapbooks of the eighteenth and early nineteenth centuries, and are still to be found, though never cheaply and seldom in fine condition. To find them requires much correspondence and patient searching in catalogues. Although even damaged or incomplete copies are likely to be expensive, there is still scope for assembling an interesting collection of these quaint and amusing little books. Many are crude, worn and badly printed, but occasionally a simple woodcut appears which has a freshness and direct strength often lacking in more refined illustrations.

Wood engravings are often classified with woodcuts: it is sad that the clear and useful distinction between the two techniques is so often ignored. The making of a woodcut, which entails the removal of all but the basic lines of the design, admits of little or no tone, and few fine details. It is cut along the grain of relatively soft wood. Wood engraving is an altogether more expressive medium, capable of reproducing extraordinarily fine detail. Box wood is normally used, cut across the grain so that the engraving is carried out on a hard surface, free from the problems of grain variations. The majority of

THE PHEASANT.

(*Phasianus Colchicus*, Linn.—*Faisan vulgaire*, Temm.)

Illustration on page 339 of A History of British Birds: '*Volume I containing the history and description of Land Birds*' *by Thomas Bewick (1847 edition).*

woodcuts have small areas of printing surface, and large areas of white space. Wood engraving at its most sophisticated makes use of many thousands of carefully engraved lines and cross-hatchings to give a wide range of tone, as well as almost complete control over perspective. It is perhaps the most expressive of all illustrative techniques, and while it may lack the elegance of the engraving on metal, or the realism of photomechanical processes, it achieves a power and apparent texture which are outside the range of these techniques.

Modern collectable wood engraving began with the work of Thomas Bewick. During the seventeenth century copper engraving had almost completely ousted the use of wood, and the artistic traditions of wood illustration had been forgotten. During the first three-quarters of the eighteenth century such wood blocks as were used were almost without exception of indifferent quality, but in 1779 there appeared the first of the series of books with illustrations engraved in wood by Bewick. His accomplishments both as a craftsman and as an artist and draughtsman were to effect an entirely new wave of enthusiasm for the medium. His work has a lasting freshness through his perceptive view of

The opening of Covent Garden Theatre (now the Royal Opera House) from The Illustrated London News *(April 1847)*

subject and medium, as well as a never-failing charm springing from his humour and vigorous naturalism. His two greatest works, the *General History of Quadrupeds* (1790) and the *History of British Birds*, produced in two volumes, *Land Birds* (1797) and *Water Birds* (1804), are justly celebrated. It is still possible to form a good Bewick collection, although the current revival of interest in his works certainly means that in five years time it will no longer be feasible to make such a collection complete. As his books ran into many editions, the blocks became worn, and printers were not always careful to prepare them correctly for the press. The wide variation in the quality of the impressions from one copy to another will affect the price. Good early editions of the *Quadrupeds* and the *Birds* are fairly uncommon but may be found for up to £100 or $200, while many of the lesser works can be found for less than half that figure.

Throughout the nineteenth century, wood engraving flourished and continued along the lines established by Bewick. The impetus carried on well into this century, although the number of good wood engravings produced now is regretably small. Examples from the period after Bewick divide neatly into three categories which can be used as a basis for collecting. The first is formed by pictorial records. The publishing boom of the early nineteenth century created an enormous demand for illustration. The technique most commonly used in the eighteenth century had been copper plate engraving—slow, complicated and expensive. The later demand was for cheap books, available quickly in large quantities. Wood engraving made this possible, and a host of popular illustrated books and periodicals began to appear, many of them containing pictures which, while they were originally intended simply to convey information, often display considerable charm and a high standard of craftsmanship. Some are of local or topical interest and can form an excellent basis for a collection. Odd volumes of nineteenth-century periodicals such as the *Illustrated London News* can be picked up quite cheaply, and the huge variety of such magazines, many of them full of wood-engraved illustrations, provides tremendous scope for assembling complete sets, representative examples or selected subjects. However, the reason for the abundance of these magazines is the extensive destruction of bound volumes during the last twenty years. The large amount of insignificant material contained may seem amply to justify the breaking of issues to form a collection of illustrations and interesting articles. One can make fascinating collections of wood engravings on anything from the Boer War or the famine and the land troubles in Ireland, to advertisements for patent medicines. Many of the news journals of the period sent artists to make on-the-spot sketches of important events, so that the opportunities for assembling albums of illustrative material on nineteenth-century history are very exciting. This type of illustration also occurs in manuals of instruction. None the less it is most inadvisable to consider breaking these books: there are usually enough of them to form an inexpensive collection, and, if the subject chosen is well defined, the collector can build a valuable and significant body of work.

Apart from pictorial themes, the other possibilities lie in the development of colour printing from wood and in the mainstream of monochrome wood engraving. Individual collectors may of course wish to define narrower limits within these divisions or to cut across them and concentrate on the work of particular illustrators.

Early experimental colour prints from wood engravings, though often charming, were seldom entirely successful. Newton's work in optics had suggested that realistic reproduction of natural colour could be achieved by combinations of three basic colours. Separate wood blocks engraved for each primary colour were inked and printed successively in exact register. Examples from various stages in the development of the process are not difficult to obtain, nor are they expensive. In some cases the successive layers of coloured ink have built up curious glossy areas. One of the most successful colour printers was Edmund Evans, who worked with artists such as Walter Crane, Kate Greenaway and Randolph Caldecott, and produced results that could hardly be excelled today. Evans embarked on his process in the 1870s, and by 1880 was using as many as nine separate printings for an illustrated book. Modern processes are normally restricted to four colours: red, yellow, blue and black, and to use even six colours is unusual and very expensive.

Wood engravings printed in colour can still be found, but the fairly high demand for the work of the better-known illustrators has raised

Engraving from The New and Complete Newgate Calendar, or Malefactor's Universal Register *'by William Jackson Esquire of Inner Temple, Barrister at Law; assisted by other gentlemen, 1818. A new edition with great additions, illustrated with elegant copper plates'.*

the price of good examples. To make a full collection of, say, Kate Greenaway would require much labour and expense. So much of nineteenth-century colour printing is likely to have been absorbed into collections by the end of the 1970s that anything remaining on the market will be very costly. The same demand will affect other types of wood engraving, although probably less dramatically. For some reason colour is felt to be extremely desirable, but it is surely wrong to overlook the effective results achieved in black and white by nineteenth-century engravers. Unlike Bewick's work, most of the monochrome wood engravings of the nineteenth and early twentieth centuries is little sought after, and a great many opportunities remain in this field.

The early printed books reflected to a large extent the high standards of art and design in the manuscript tradition from which they developed. Some of the great fifteenth-century examples remain unequalled specimens of the printing art. Yet, while the types used by the early masters captured many of the qualities of the most refined of the manuscript hands, the woodcut illustrations were less successful compared with the achievements of the manuscript painters. The process of engraving on metal therefore developed rapidly and, together with the closely related technique of etching, required the application of new methods of printing.

The engraver worked on a flat plate, usually of copper, with a needle-like graver. The design was drawn on paper, traced and transferred to the surface of the metal. The tone and strength of the final impression was determined by the depth and width of the engraved lines. Much finer detail could be achieved on metal than on wood, and there was also the advantage of being able to correct errors by beating the metal to raise it, then smoothing and re-engraving it. While it did not allow the printer to reach the illustrative excellence of the manuscript, the copper plate provided a satisfactory alternative. The plates had to be printed separately from the type, since the ink was transferred to the paper not from a raised surface, as from type or a woodcut, but from an engraved recess. In this process of intaglio printing, the ink was rubbed well into the engraved lines and the surplus wiped off the flat surface. Paper was then applied to the plate under considerable pressure, and was usually previously moistened to make it more pliable. The incomplete absorption of ink that often resulted produced a pleasing relief effect.

A characteristic result is produced by the similar technique of dry-point engraving. In line engravings the graver or burin is pushed along the metal away from the body, raising a burr along the line which is then removed. The dry-point engraver draws the tool towards himself, raising a finer and more regular burr which is left on the plate. This method, much favoured by Rembrandt, produces a delicate plate capable of making very few impressions. For this reason it has seldom been used for book illustration. Etching, although more often used than dry-point, is again not common. In this process the artist transfers his design to an acid resistant var-

Etching and aquatint from Graphic Illustrations of Hogarth, *'from Pictures, Drawings and Scarce Prints in the possession of Samuel Ireland, Author of this work' (2 volumes, 1794–99). London, R. Fauldner, New Bond Street, and J. Egerton, Whitehall.*

nish coating on a metal plate and the lines to be etched are scratched through the varnish. The plate is immersed in sulphuric acid, and the depth, and thus the final tonal effect, is determined by the length of time the acid is allowed to act on the metal. Afterwards the varnish is removed and prints taken in the same way as from an engraving.

The eighteenth century saw a rise in the popularity of several other intaglio processes. Some English artists used stippling, where the engraved lines are replaced by fine dots, whose density controls the variation in tone much as do the dots in modern half-tone reproductions. However, the two most popular processes were mezzotint and aquatint. In mezzotint engraving a copper or steel plate is worked with a rocking-tool, a semicircular steel instrument with a roughened edge which is moved back and forward across the entire surface to produce many thousands of minute dents in the metal. The roughened surface will hold ink and prints completely black. The engraver then scrapes away metal to the required depth to produce lighter tones and highlights. It is possible to achieve a tonal range in mezzotint which surpasses that of etching or line engraving, but the process has also been used badly to produce dull, flat prints. Aquatint engravings closely resemble mezzotints and are often confused with them. The technique was first practiced by J. B. Leprince in 1787 and is characterised by a coating of fine particles of resin on the plate, which is heated to make them adhere. The design is scratched through this coating and acid then applied to etch out not only the lines but also the minute spaces between the resin grains. The printed results are often very similar to wash drawings.

Finished mezzotint and aquatint plates are delicate and suitable for printing runs varying from 300 to 600. Books with illustrations produced by these techniques are difficult to find and generally expensive, particularly when colour has been used. Good examples begin at about £75, $150, and may fetch ten times that amount. With all these intaglio processes, books containing early impressions made when the plates are clear and fresh will cost considerably more than later versions where they have become flattened through repeated pressure and constant wiping. Another factor to be contended with is the state of the impression, since in many cases modifications were made after a few copies had been struck off. The engraver or artist may have wished to add further detail, strengthen the design, correct errors or remove some of the subject. Variations in the state of well-known engravings are fairly thoroughly recorded, and careful study of such documentation can often help to locate particular bargains. An amusing example of state variation occurs in the celebrated late eighteenth-century book of Irish views, Malton's *Picturesque Views of Dublin*, which contained very fine line engravings of the city's architecture. The early state of the illustration of the Irish Houses of Parliament showed a farmer coaxing some pigs past the beautiful Georgian building, but as a result of Dubliners' sensitivity about this pig-in-the-parlour image, later states of the print lack this pastoral touch. Complete copies of Malton are now very rare, as most of the plates have long since been hung on drawing-room walls: on the infrequent occasions when they are sold, early editions command at least double the normal price.

Photogravure

Photogravure is the only intaglio process in common use today, and was first developed as a sophistication of the mezzotint method in the late nineteenth century. The subject is printed photographically on a copper plate or cylinder through a screen of crossed lines, and the plate etched so that it is covered with a fine mesh of minute pits whose depths vary according to the density of the image. The finished plate is inked, the surface ink scraped off, and the impression made. The prints can be recognised by the crossed line effect.

Lithography

In 1798 the Bavarian, Aloys Senefelder, stumbled on one of the most direct means of illustration while experimenting with the local Kelheim stone to find a relief method of printing his own work. His discovery created a revolution in printing in the nineteenth century, and, through its later development, a greater revolution in modern publishing. The process depends on the fact that printing ink and water will not mix. The lithographer draws his design on a smooth flat stone with a wax crayon. Water is then poured over it, and flows off the wax-covered areas while remaining on the porous surface of the stone itself. When ink is rolled on, it in turn is repelled by the wet surface, but is retained by the waxed areas for transfer to the paper. This process, first in monochrome and later in colour or chromolithography was widely used from the middle of the nineteenth century. Most illustrated books today are printed by offset photolithography: the stone has been replaced by a zinc plate surface with photo-sensitive emulsion. The image is exposed through a fine dot screen on to the plate, which is chemically developed. Unexposed areas of the emulsion are dissolved, whereas sections affected by light are hardened and form a layer, broken into tiny dots by the screen, which fulfils the same function as the wax on the stone. The further sophistication of transferring the image first to a rubber roller, or blanket, and then to the paper, gives rise to the term offset lithography. This relatively inexpensive method of printing has the advantage of great flexibility in book design: type and illustrations can be laid out in ways which would be difficult or impossible in other processes. It has also made it possible to produce facsimile reprints of important out-of-print books at a fairly low cost.

Collotype

Like lithography, collotype depends on the inability of water and printing ink to mix, but, unlike other photographic printing processes, it does not entail the use of a screen to break up tonal areas. Of all modern methods it gives the

A Daumier Lithograph from a series entitled Les Chemins de Fer *(c1845).*

> *'Conducteur! Conducteur! Arretez au nom du ciel. J'ai la colique!'*
>
> *'Impossible . . . L'Administration le défendi. Mais donc deux heures un quart nous ferrons à Orleans!'*

finest results, but it is also the most expensive and the least used. The photographic image is projected on a heavy glass plate coated with emulsion, and again the areas which receive the most light, the darkest in the finished print, are rendered hardest. The plate is placed in a special press where it is flooded with a mixture of water and gelatine. The emulsion retains moisture in proportion to its hardness, so that the amount of ink carried may extend across the full tonal range. However, a plate will not produce more than two thousand impressions. When used in colour, the process may require as many as a dozen separate plates and printings. Books illustrated with collotypes are rare and invariably expensive: Muirhead and Gertrude Bone's *Old Spain* was published in 1936 at 100 guineas, a colossal price at the time, which it is only now beginning to reach on the collector's market.

Half-tone engraving

Modern printing normally makes use of either offset lithography or letterpress, the traditional system of metal type applied direct to the paper. Letterpress illustrations now usually take the form of half-tone engravings, where the image is transferred photographically to the block or plate through a dot screen. Acid etching leaves the dot pattern in relief on the metal surface, with the density of the dots increasing in the darker areas. The dotted effect is clearly visible in newspapers, where the rough texture of the paper demands a coarse screen. While it is more expensive to print in colour from letterpress blocks than from offset lithographic plates, the results may show a strength sometimes lacking in the

less direct method. Good letterpress blocks do however require a considerable amount of hand work by the engraver to supplement the etching process. A variant of the basic letterpress process block is the photo-line engraving, where the dot structure is replaced by a pattern of fine lines to give a result similar to that of a wood engraving.

For the collector of illustrated books the question of availability is important. Woodcuts from the nineteenth century are interesting and collectable on a small scale. Wood engravings from the nineteenth century to the present day are very attractive and well worth acquiring; the work of some engravers such as Eric Gill is hard to find but in general the books of the last hundred years which are illustrated with wood engravings have a relatively small number of devotees, so that there is plenty of room for collecting even within a limited budget. Many superbly illustrated books by Claire Leighton, Gwen Raverat and Robert

Above: *from the 1938 edition of* Days in Old Spain, *by Gertrude Bone with illustrations by Muirhead Bine.*

Below: *half-tone illustration from the second edition (1895) of the Cycling volume in* The Badminton Library of Sports and Pastimes, *edited by His Grace the Duke of Beaufort. This volume was written by the Rt. Hon. the Earl of Albemarle and G. Lacy Hillier. First printed in 1887 by Longmans, Green & Co.*

Above: *steel-engraved plate by Gustav Doré for* The Rime of the Ancient Mariner *by S. T. Coleridge (Hamilton Adams & Co., and the Doré Gallery, 1876). Above right: Sheet music from the early 1890s. Below right: title page by Charles Robinson for* The Sensitive Plant *by Percy Bysshe Shelley (William Heinemann, London and J. P. Lippincott, Philadelphia).*

Gibbings, for example, can be found at under £10 or $20.

An eighteenth-century copper plate book or a nineteenth-century book of aquatint views is now an expensive item, with well-known works costing thousands of pounds. The only scope for collecting on a reasonable budget is probably in the field of books of nineteenth-century steel engravings. These were produced in large quantities, and some are mere curiosities while others are interesting and attractive. Already those of more topical appeal, such as books of local views, have risen steeply in price. Illustrated literary works or those with classical or religious themes are still easily available more cheaply. However, one prime area which remains virtually untouched is that of wood, or more usually, steel engraved portraits published in volumes with titles like *Illustrious Personages* or *Eminent Men*. These should be collected before they are destroyed or vanish, and could be acquired either generally or in selected categories. As many booksellers

attach little importance to these books, the buyer has the advantage of low prices but will have to be thorough in his searching as they seldom appear in catalogues.

Early lithographic books have also become expensive, particularly as many of them contain the coloured topographical plates so much sought after. The only opportunities here for collecting at modest prices lie in the area of illustrated covers of Victorian sheet music. These attractive productions, many of them brightly coloured lithographs, served the same eye-catching purpose as the modern record sleeve. Strictly this is not book collecting at all, and the stock of prints is dwindling as they are particularly well suited to framing. Nevertheless it is still possible to find a large, dull looking volume of collected Victorian music sheets, some of them bound in their original covers.

The works of the well known illustrators, Greenaway, Caldecott, Crane, Beardsley, Rackham, Dulac, the Robinsons and others are now very fashionable and much collected. It should not be difficult to find booksellers with a good stock of their books, but the prices will be high.

Walter Crane: left: *endpiece to Book III, Canto XII* of The Faerie Queen *by Edmund Spenser, edited by Thomas J. Wise (George Allen, 1895).* Below *and* bottom: *illustrations to Volume III, Book II, Canto II and Volume I, Book I, Canto IX of* The Faerie Queen.

To restrict a collection to one or two artists would be extravagant and impractical, and it would be more advisable to take a particular theme, for instance fairy stories or the tales of the brothers Grimm. Representative examples of the work of the greater and the lesser illustrators could be assembled in this way with a smaller initial outlay.

Two other prime areas for collecting which are based largely on the photo-line engraving process are provided by the pen draughtsmen and the cartoonists. The late nineteenth and early twentieth centuries saw the development of a fashion for pen drawings which are seldom coloured and lack the vividness of masters such as Rackham but display subtlety and considerable attention to detail. Apart from their aesthetic appeal their great attraction is their low price. The draughtsmen have been sadly neglected because they are more in the tradition of illustration than the producers of the now fashionable and highly priced picture books. Rather than creating a collection of pictures with an accompanying text they worked within the discipline of the written material and their plates are integrated with the type. This field is very much open to collectors at the moment, but will probably not be in a few years time.

Cartoons fall into a similar category. Hundreds of books of cartoons are published every year on a wide range of subjects. They provide a unique and often admirably satirical view of a particular period or event, and many are skilful and attractive as well as amusing. Some of the early twentieth-century cartoonists, however, are now much sought after: it is very hard to find good examples of the amazing drawings of Heath Robinson or the German cartoonists of the Weimar era. Cartoons appear all the time, and a comprehensive collection of books dealing with the Cold War, Vietnam or Watergate will be of great interest ten years from now.

The illustrated book provides a varied and attractive field for the collector, with many specific opportunities, some of which have been indicated here. Yet, whether he selects on the basis of the process used, on the illustrator, the subject or the era, his only sensible course, as always, is to set his budget and rely on his own taste.

Two pages from The Sirens Three, *a poem written and illustrated by Walter Crane (Macmillan & Co., 1886).*

OH, LISTEN TO A TALE OF "WO"

'Oh, Listen to a tale of "Wo"' by Phil May from
The Phil May Album *collected by Augustus M.
Moore (2nd and cheaper edition, Methuen & Co.,
London 1904).*

Natural History

THE scope of natural history books is necessarily limited to the study of natural objects, such as plants and animals or their remains, and the properties or activities associated with them. Sometimes a title that includes the term 'natural history' heads nothing more than a collection of information on a specified subject. *The Natural History of Nonsense* is obviously going to say a lot about nonsense, but is unlikely to contain much information about natural objects. Here, 'natural history books' are those with the study of natural objects as their primary purpose. Many diverse subjects may scrape into that definition: bee-keeping, gardening, geology, conchology, botany, microscopy and others. Books dealing with the exact sciences, such as mathematics, chemistry and physics are excluded. Nor is there room here for medical books (except those which are primarily herbals), or works on astronomy or meteorology.

Our authors will include giants, whose writings helped to change the course of science, or even of world history, but the names of most of them are almost forgotten. The works of Mrs Loudon, J. G. Wood, Shirley Hibberd and Anne Pratt are little known in the world of learning but they, and many like them, may mean more to potential collectors of natural history books than those of Linnaeus, Audubon, Redouté and Charles Darwin. It is better to build up a collection of attractively produced and relatively cheap books by numerous minor figures than to pursue a rapidly dwindling number of expensive and not invariably attractive books by a handful of major writers.

Ultimately, all natural history books have been inspired or influenced by four men whose own works span well over two thousand years of history: Aristotle, Dioscorides, Linnaeus and Darwin. The writings of Aristotle, dating from the fourth century B.C., were accepted largely without challenge for two thousand years. Aristotle's wide knowledge of zoology is clear from the *History of Animals,* one of the books most reliably ascribed to him. He appears, however, to have paid little attention to botany. *De Materia Medica* of Dioscorides, dating from the first century A.D., must therefore be considered of great importance. Although concerned only with healing herbs, it became the prime source of botanical knowledge until, like the work of Aristotle, it was gradually superseded by more sophisticated productions during and after the Renaissance.

Despite rapid progress in the scientific study of animals and plants in the late seventeenth century, naturalists still suffered from the lack of a system. Many attempts were made at a comprehensive and rational classification of living things, none of them successful. In the seventeenth century, the Englishman, John Ray, almost achieved a workable classification of plants and, to a lesser extent, of animals. However, it was not until the following century that the Swedish naturalist, Linnaeus, perfected a system, which was universally accepted and revolutionised the study of botany and zoology. By introducing a uniform system of identification, using a latinised generic and specific name for each animal and plant, he made possible the discussion of living things in terms which remain intelligible to any naturalist, whatever language he speaks. The *Systema Naturae* and other Linnaean classics profoundly influenced later writers on natural history. Essentially, however, Linnaeus introduced no new philosophy of nature. The belief in man as a separate entity from the brute creation had been central to Western thought for many centuries. Equally, he and his followers failed to challenge the age-old belief in the immutability of species. For all their lavish illustrations and much improved typography and presentation, subsequent books differed very little in philosophical content from those written before the time of Linnaeus.

Charles Darwin altered all that. *On the*

CAROLI LINNÆI

EQUITIS DE STELLA POLARI,

ARCHIATRI REGII, MED. & BOTAN. PROFESS. UPSAL.;
ACAD. UPSAL. HOLMENS. PETROPOL. BEROL. IMPER.
LOND. MONSPEL. TOLOS. FLORENT. SOC.

SYSTEMA NATURÆ

PER

REGNA TRIA NATURÆ,

SECUNDUM

CLASSES, ORDINES,
GENERA, SPECIES,

CUM

CHARACTERIBUS, DIFFERENTIIS,
SYNONYMIS; LOCIS.

TOMUS I.

EDITIO DECIMA, REFORMATA.

Cum Privilegio S:æ R:æ M:tis Sveciæ.

HOLMIÆ,
IMPENSIS DIRECT. LAURENTII SALVII,
1758.

THE ORIGIN OF SPECIES

BY MEANS OF NATURAL SELECTION,

OR THE

PRESERVATION OF FAVOURED RACES IN THE STRUGGLE
FOR LIFE.

BY CHARLES DARWIN, M.A., F.R.S., &c.

SIXTH EDITION, WITH ADDITIONS AND CORRECTIONS.

(ELEVENTH THOUSAND)

LONDON:
JOHN MURRAY, ALBEMARLE STREET.
1872.

The right of Translation is reserved.

Origin of Species, the most important and influential biological book ever written, showed that species underwent modification. The implication that man was an animal equally susceptible to evolutionary processes was later developed in his *Descent of Man.* In these and numerous other books, Darwin demolished the cosy idea of man as the creature made in God's image, replacing it with a view of man as a competitive and highly organised animal. Ever since Darwin's works gained wide acceptance, the great majority of books in the field of biology have been written under their influence.

In a direct sense, the importance of an idea leads to the desirability of a book. Although the tenth (and most important) edition of the *Systema Naturae* is unillustrated, cheaply produced and quite unreadable, it contains the full expression of an important idea and is now commercially desirable as the conveyor of that idea. The value now placed on any early Linnaean item depends simply on the publication of one important statement by its author.

The first edition of Darwin's *Origin* is also unillustrated, cheaply produced and difficult to read. It, too, represents the culmination of a significant idea and is valuable on this account. Nearer our own time is Desmond Morris's *The Naked Ape,* a brilliant exposition, developed ultimately out of Darwin's work. Though entertaining to read, this is also unillustrated and cheaply produced. Only the idea has any value. Indeed, it secured immense sales for the book even before publication and will almost certainly make the first copies issued from the press desirable collectors' items.

Having established the relevance of ideas to book collecting, it is easy to find themes to suit most temperaments and most pockets. The traditional collector, who acquires books for their own sake, may specialize in work on gardening or bees partly because he's interested in the subject but mostly because he's interested in the books, particularly rare examples in fine condition. He is just as likely to increase his col-

Right: *plate 15 from* Alpine Plants *(1st series, 1872) by* D. Wooster.

GENTIANA ANDREWSII.

Papilio Ulysses

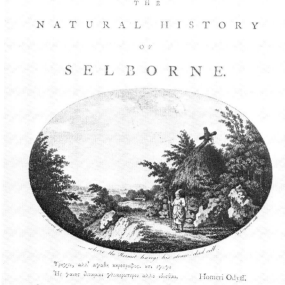

Above: *engraved title page to Gilbert White's* Natural History of Selborne *(first edition 1789).* Right: *plate XXVII from P. H. Gosse's* Naturalist's Rambles on the Devonshire Coast *(1853).*

lection with books on other subjects if they meet his usually exacting standards of quality and rarity. Most collectors do not operate in this way; in any case they cannot afford to. They are usually attracted to books whose subjects already interest them.

By far the most familiar type of collector now is the one whose acquisitions are motivated by current fashion. He is not being sheep-like; he is being human. Changing social conditions are powerful dictators of trends and always have been. Today, for instance, in the Western world, the strong desire exists for a return to a more natural life style. Now keenly aware of an imperilled heritage of nature and a rapidly changing or vanishing rural scene, we are witnessing the encroachment of artificial and largely imported urban ways of life. To many, this new life style is alien but inevitable. Some of us escape from it at weekends by taking a car ride into the country. Many of us do the same thing vicariously by watching television. But nothing can recap-

Left: *plate 21 from* Epitome of the Natural History of the Insects of India *by Edward Donovan (1800).*

ture the peace and quiet of earlier days better than books written by those who lived in those days. How else can we explain the perennial popularity of Gilbert White's *Natural History of Selborne* or Henry David Thoreau's *Walden, or Life in the Woods?* A visit to Selborne or to Walden may simply accentuate the fact of today's changing world, but the books in which those places are immortalised are unchanging and evocative. If you are interested in the animals and plants of the seashore, a visit to Babbacombe in South Devon or Tenby in South Wales may be to your liking. But to rediscover the natural riches of these places as they were in mid-Victorian times you will have to refer to the captivating *Naturalist's Rambles on the Devonshire Coast* and *Tenby: a Seaside Holiday* by Philip Henry Gosse. If you have the collecting instinct you will probably find that one copy of White's (or Thoreau's) masterpiece is not enough. You will want to own copies of the many different editions. Finally you will be satisfied only with a first edition. If you are fascinated by Gosse, you will be compelled to look for first editions because, in the case of the works mentioned and several others, there are no others.

There are, too, collectors who begin by wanting certain books on specialist topics to help them in their work. They usually find themselves building up a collection which extends well beyond their primary needs. Sooner or later, a geologist working in a fairly restricted field, say metalliferous mining, will begin to broaden his interest with the acquisition of a volume by an early writer on geology. His purchase of a late edition of Hugh Miller's *Old Red Sandstone,* for example, may lead him to want more of Miller's books, then the earlier editions of them and, finally, to build up a collection of classical geology authors, such as Lyell, Murchison, Mantell, and Sedgwick. He is discovering the roots of his own knowledge. He tries to approach as nearly as possible the giants whom he may fondly believe to be his spiritual ancestors.

In the search for books, there is sometimes no alternative but to scavenge in secondhand bookshops and to form a satisfactory relationship with booksellers. In the field of gardening, for instance, Gertrude Jekyll is a household word. During the early twentieth century, she was the arbiter of good design, colour scheme and quiet efficiency in the garden. Her well-written books, abounding in sound common sense and practical advice, are as useful now as they were when they were first published. Many garden lovers prefer her books to those of modern writers on her chosen subjects. Some of her titles such as *Home and Garden, Wall and Water Gardens, Wood and Garden, Colour in the Flower Garden* and *Lilies for English Gardens,* were once very commonly seen in secondhand bookshops. That is not surprising, as many were reprinted several times. They are now becoming increasingly scarce, and the demand much exceeds the supply. Strangely enough, they have not recently been reprinted, despite the demand, and those who want Jekyll titles must therefore beg, borrow or, occasionally, steal them. Inevitably, the scarcity of Miss Jekyll's books has made them collectable for their own sake and, even if they are reprinted, there will still be the same demand for the original editions as products of the Jekyll era. The attraction of the original edition, even of a book published during the twentieth century, is well illustrated by another gardening book, or rather a trilogy: *My Garden in Spring, Summer, Autumn*

'Of the Reyner, or Rainger' from History of Four-Footed Beasts *by Edward Topsel (1648).*

by E. A. Bowles. First published in 1914–15, the three volumes are a sheer delight to read, and attractively illustrated with coloured and monochrome plates. In 1973, copies of this edition retailed at around £65 for the set. The price was in no way affected by the existence of a modern reprint which could be obtained at the same time for £10.50 the set. The omission of coloured plates from the reprint only partially explains the much greater value placed on the original edition. The original has character and a history and, even in less than fine condition, will be preferred by the true collector to a sparkling new reprint.

The age of a book, contrary to popular opinion, does not necessarily make it valuable. Books published in the sixteenth and seventeenth centuries are not in short supply and there are still bargains to be had by lovers of old books. Old natural history books are not easily found, however, and are usually very expensive, particularly if they are illustrated. Seventeenth-century and later editions of the *Natural History* of the Roman writer, Pliny, may sometimes be obtained at reasonable prices. They are nearly always in Latin and unillustrated. Such books appeal to very few collectors and most copies end up in major institutions. Of far greater appeal are the works of a handful of sixteenth-century scholars who, between them, satisfied the demand for encyclopaedic works on natural history and science in Europe for almost two centuries. Aldrovandi, Belon, Gesner and Mattioli were contemporaries but each worked in isolation. Whereas Mattioli wrote on plants, the others concentrated on animals. The lasting appeal of their works can be attributed to the illustrations, the more absurd the better. The widespread belief of the period in monstrous animals was perpetuated in books such as Aldrovandi's *Serpentum et Draconium Historiae* and Gesner's *Historiae Animalium*. Monsters have not lost their appeal, and early books illustrating them are in great demand. The illustrations of fantastic creatures in Edward Topsel's *History of Four-footed Beasts* (1658), perhaps the monster-collector's favourite book, show the stuff natural history was made of in the seventeenth century. From the point of view of production and scientific content, these books are light years away from those of the eighteenth and nineteenth centuries, but they are still great favourites with collectors.

Thomas Moffet's *Insectorum sive Minimorum Animalium Theatrum* (1634), one of the earliest scientific studies of insects, is still fairly regularly seen for sale, often with a photocopied title page. By contrast, the first scientific exposition of shells, *Historia Conchyliorum* (1685–92) by Martin Lister, is much rarer. It is worth buying even in an incomplete state; no two copies are exactly the same. If any of the sectional title-pages are printed in red and black, the copy is worth considerably more than one printed only in black. John Ray wrote so many natural history books, most of which went into several editions, that he may appear the commonest natural history author of the late seventeenth and early eighteenth centuries. Indifferent copies of his *Synopsis Methodica Stirpium Britannicarum* (1690) and a second edition (1696) are frequently offered for sale at reasonable prices. Perfect copies are worth much more, however. Francis Willughby's monumental illustrated folios on birds and fishes, the *Ornithologiae* (1676) and *De Historia Piscium* (1686), were both edited by Ray. Both are now beyond the means of most collectors. Edward Tyson's *Anatomy of a Pygmie* (1699), a thin folio volume, is now worth at least £10 per

page, for the very good reason that the book is a landmark in the history of science, despite its unpromising title. As with so many important books, its appearance does not seem commensurate with its high price. The appearance of a book may mislead the inexperienced or unwary collector in the fields of natural history and science more than in any other. For the collector of prose and poetry, condition is paramount. The value of a scientific work is often unaffected by its condition, provided that it is more or less complete.

The first half of the eighteenth century is an

Plates from Historia Conchyliorum *by Martin Lister (1770 edition).*

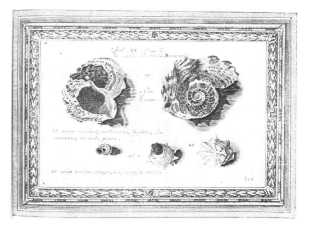

extension of the late seventeenth, in a natural history context. It was not dominated by the works of Linnaeus although many Linnaean books and dissertations were published before the 1750s. Early works by this great naturalist are all worth seeking in any edition. With the numerous dissertations, it is advisable to collect originals rather than later reissues, although complete or near-complete sets of the *Amoenitates academicae,* in which the dissertations were gathered together, are certainly worth having. Searching out such material is a specialised task, since the most likely sources of unrecognised pamphlets are bound volumes of miscellaneous tracts. As Linnaeus wrote much on medical matters, it is sometimes possible to unearth small items from collections of loose or bound pamphlets, primarily medical in character.

Among the most popular of all natural history books are those which come into the category of herbals, books in which wild and cultivated herbs are discussed principally in relation to their usefulness to man. Ever since Dioscorides wrote on the healing properties of herbs, mankind has been deeply interested in them and their uses in medicine and the culinary arts, and in recent years this interest has increased. All modern herbals are based to some extent on earlier ones, and they are in many respects identical. It cannot be claimed that the study of herbs is essentially associated with the British Isles, but some of the most familiar herbals have been published there. The names of Culpeper, Gerard and Hill are almost household words and, at one time or another, few households in the Western world have been without an edition of one of their works. From the fifteenth century herbals have been published in all shapes and sizes. They were often illustrated, either with woodcuts or, later, with hand-coloured figures that varied in quality from the most crude to the most beautiful in the history of botanical art. Among early herbals, Mattioli's *Commentarii in Sex Libros Pedacii Dioscoridis* (1544) cannot be considered rare as it went into more than forty editions and many thousands of copies. The better known *Herball* (1597) of John Gerard, though expensive these days, is also not rare. The later edition by Thomas Johnson (1633) is much more scholarly and much larger; it is also more common but no less desirable. Nicholas Culpeper's *Complete Herbal* is undoubtedly the best known of all and has been constantly in print ever since its first publi-

cation in 1652. Possibly, no one knows how many different versions of Culpeper have appeared (although many of them bear little resemblance to the first version), and it must be recognised as one of the most successful natural history books of all time. The collection of herbals can be very rewarding and very frustrating. Because they were meant to be put to everyday use, many of them are worn, grubby and defective. Often, it is difficult to discover how many plates should be present in a particular copy. Often too, the most conspicuous lacuna is the title page. The number of copies of Gerard's *Herball* which lack several pages (the title page is very often supplied in facsimile) probably exceeds those which are complete. Even so, the defective copies now in circulation bring high prices. Early herbals in good condition rightly sell for high prices, but some collectors are so mesmerised by this particular branch of natural history literature that they are willing to pay ridiculous sums for pocket editions published no earlier than the late nineteenth century. Infatuation is sometimes

The first edition of Gerard's Herball *(1597).*

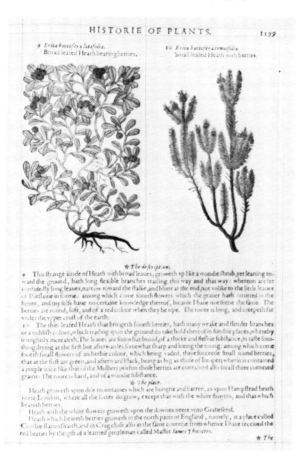

allowed to outweigh discretion. As herb lore and herbal recipes are now very much in vogue, prices are certain to increase sharply, and money spent on an early example in fine condition will be well invested.

The systematic writings published by Linnaeus at the height of his career achieved a revolution in botany and zoology. Linnaeus did not merely devise a useful method of naming and classifying plants. He made natural history interesting and exciting by showing the limitations of Greek, Latin and Hebrew texts, and the classical authors, as sources in the study of natural objects. His work and, indeed, his entire personality enabled others to look at nature without superstition or prejudice and unhampered by doctrinaire judgements. Most of his books are modest in appearance. Intended to be working tools for the practising botanist or zoologist, they paved the way for the production of many sumptuous natural history books by others. For many years, botanical books, in particular, were often based solidly on a Linnaean foundation. The universally accepted system of naming plants began with the publication of his *Species Plantarum* (1753), and that of naming animals with the publication of the tenth edition of *Systema Naturae* (1758). Consequently, these two books are highly esteemed and extremely costly. Other editions of these two works, though less valuable, are keenly collected by major institutions and a few private collectors.

Although the second half of the eighteenth century was dominated in a scientific sense by Linnaeus, the natural history books produced during that time were not all Linnaean in character; nor did they employ his system of nomenclature. Relatively few books were written to popularise limited aspects of natural history but several encyclopaedias were compiled. Two of the better known are Buffon's *Natural History* and Goldsmith's *History of Animated Nature*. Both were widely translated and went into many editions. Goldsmith's book was kept in print until late in the nineteenth century. The fact that Buffon ignored the Linnaean system renders his multi-volume work far less important scientifically than it might have been. Had he not used his own largely meaningless system of nomenclature, his book would now be one of the most expensive in the field of natural history literature. The edition most likely to be found is that of Barr which is not worth very much. The Sonnini edition of 1798–1807 in 129 volumes is unlikely to come into the hands of a collector, except at auction. Barr's Buffon occurs in sets with different numbers of volumes. When first published in 1792–93, it comprised fifteen volumes. The 1797–1808 reissue should have sixteen volumes; an extra volume on birds was published for the first time in 1808. Sets comprising less than fifteen volumes occur in the trade with disconcerting frequency and should be ignored. Late editions of Goldsmith's work, illustrated with hand-coloured plates, used to be available very cheaply. They now command a relatively high price because the plates are suitable for mounting and framing.

A few words on the important subject of illustrations may not be out of place here. For most of us, the illustrations form the principal attraction of a natural history book. In an age accustomed to a bombardment of picture language, it might be expected that pictorial art should be more popular than printed words. Unfortunately, the pictorial element in a book is now often considered to be so important that it is ripped out to be mounted and framed for sale, while the text is discarded. The rights and wrongs of this practice are not our concern here. In any case, it would need more than an indignant protest to stop the traffic in 'breakers'—the affectionate trade expression for books destined to be torn apart—which evidently exists to satisfy popular demand. A good natural history book with its full complement of coloured plates is going to become a thing of the past. Already, the dismembering of such books has brought about a rapid reappraisal of the commercial value of items previously held in low esteem. This is in line with current trends in the world of antiques and fine art and is not an isolated phenomenon. It has long been beyond the capabilities of most collectors to buy any of the great bird books by Gould, Lear and Audubon, for example, and the great flower books by Redouté, Hooker or Roscoe. The time is also approaching when the more prosaic works of minor Victorians like Anne Pratt and Gosse will have become the playthings of affluent collectors. The law of supply and demand is operating with such ruthless efficiency in the world of the illustrated natural history book that there is already a shortage of books which were, very recently, grudgingly given space on a bookseller's shelves. Clearly, any natural history book containing hand-coloured plates is potentially rare and valuable as a book or a breaker. Books illustrated

with photographs are potentially valuable too, especially if they were published before 1870.

The nineteenth century is the Golden Age of natural history, and of books on the subject. There is so much fascinating material to choose from that selection is difficult. The Industrial Revolution inevitably had a great effect on the printing trade. The development of the steam-powered printing press, improvements in the supply and quality of paper, and the widespread use of lithography and stereotype inevitably provided better books in greater quantities. Optional extras, such as colour printing, nature printing and photographic reproductions were all available long before the close of the century. These and other processes were suited to the portrayal of colourful natural objects; indeed, nature printing was invented for the purpose. It was also an age of great travellers, writers, scientists and artists.

Despite the Napoleonic wars, many natural history books were published during the first quarter of the nineteenth century, particularly in France. These were the great days of French natural history and many renowned naturalists, including Cuvier and Lamarck, were alive then. They were also the days of immensely talented illustrators such as Redouté, the most famous of all flower painters. Among the best publications on natural history were the illustrated accounts of exploratory voyages undertaken by the French. Such publications are now rarely seen outside auction rooms and high-class book-sellers' establishments.

In England, the *Botanical Magazine* of William Curtis, begun in 1787, was constantly supplemented (and additions are still being published today). The most sumptuous of all illustrated botanical books, the *Temple of Flora* by R. J. Thornton, was published between 1799 and 1807. Rightly, this exquisite book, which bank-rupted its author, is now so highly esteemed that any of its twenty-eight plates can retail at around £100. Most collectors never even see a copy. For a few pounds, they may buy a copy of the same author's tiny book entitled *Easy Introduction* to the Science of Botany, through the Medium of Familiar Conversations between a Father and his Son (1823), in which a few of the Temple of Flora plates are reproduced, duodecimo size.

The production, at relatively low cost, of popular substitutes for the expensive illustrated books may be said to begin at this time. Thornton's Easy Introduction is one of the less familiar examples. At the same time, many charming little 'guides' and 'companions' were published, which combined a conversational, elementary style with simple but pleasing illustrations. Books with titles like The Botanical Keepsake, The Floral Garden and The Elements of Conchology are now well worth adding to a collection and may still be picked up for reasonable prices. Their usually small format makes them unsuitable as breakers.

In the zoological field, the works of Edward Donovan are typical of the illustrated books of the British school. Each of his titles usually comprises more than one volume, and there are nearly always many hand-coloured illustrations. All Donovan's works are collected, particularly his Natural History of British Insects (1792–1813), Natural History of British Birds (1792–97), Natural History of the British Shells (1799–1803) and his Epitome of the Natural History of the Insects of India (1800–1804).

Donovan's Catalogue of the Leverian Museum (1806), merely an auction sale catalogue of items formerly in the collection of Sir Ashton Lever, is far rarer than any of his illustrated works. Indeed, such catalogues are nearly always rare, because most of them were disposed of after the sale. They are always worth picking up as items of interest, and occasionally of value, despite their often tatty appearance, the more annotated, the better. A few catalogues are noteworthy and have always been sought after. J. Lightfoot's Catalogue of the Portland Museum (1786) is one of the most famous and most extensive. Well known because it advertises the sale of the Portland (or Barberini) Vase, it is also important to naturalists as an early source of scientific names for shells and other natural objects. William Bullock's Catalogue . . . of the Roman gallery . . . and the London Museum of Natural History (1810) is another extremely rare sale catalogue. Its value would be easy to underestimate. Bullock's Companion to the London Museum, which went into several editions before 1820, is not a sale catalogue but a description of his collection; it is not rare as yet. Two of the more important

sale catalogues issued during the early nineteenth century are especially interesting. Both advertise the contents of important shell collections. That of Mrs Bligh (wife of the navigator, William Bligh) was illustrated by William Swainson and published in 1822. That of the Earl of Tankerville was illustrated with coloured plates by G. B. Sowerby (the first of that name) and published in 1825. Very few of the natural history sale catalogues produced later in the nineteenth century are as important and as valuable as these.

Some of the best work by the celebrated wood engraver Thomas Bewick was completed in the same period. Bewick's incomparable woodcuts of animals and rural scenes began to appear in the late eighteenth century, but most of those available today date from the early nineteenth. Bewick collecting is a specialised subject, requiring much patient study, good judgment and, as always, a lot of luck. It is still comparatively easy to buy good copies of Bewick's own works such as the General History of Quadrupeds and History of British Birds. The addicted Bewick collector does not stop there, however. Bewick illustrated many books by other authors, and it is among these that bargains and rarities are still to be found. It is not generally known, for instance, that some of his woodcuts are to be found in books as diverse as Dovaston's Poems and James Anderson's Recreations in Agriculture. When inspecting Bewick's woodcuts, you should bear in mind that clean, sharp block impressions are important in determining the value of an item. The description of a volume illustrated by Bewick as the 'large paper issue', or the 'first issue in this form', or the 'best issue' does not necessarily make it an essential acquisition. To judge the desirability of a Bewick item, it is necessary to know, for instance, that the first volume of the first edition of British Birds (1797) should have an 'indelicate' woodcut at page 42 which does not occur in many subsequent editions. There are so many variant issues that the Bewick hunter is constantly adding to his collection. But this is the perennial attraction, the essence of specialist book collecting.

Since book publishing in North America was not highly organised during the first half of the nineteenth century, many writers preferred to place their manuscripts and drawings with publishers abroad, principally those in London. The magnificent Birds of America, for instance, would probably never have appeared before the American public had Audubon not come to

THE HOLSTEIN OR DUTCH BREED

has been introduced with great fuccefs, and is now the prevailing ftock in all the counties on the eaftern coaft of this kingdom.—In good paftures, cattle of this kind grow to a great fize*; and the Cows yield a greater abundance of milk than thofe of almoft any other kind.

* An Ox was fed by Mr Edward Hall, of Whitley, in Northumberland; and killed in March, 1789. when feven years old; it weighed, without offal, 187 ft. 5 lb.—And a Cow, bred and fed

Above: *plate 56 from* American Conchology, *written, printed and published by Thomas Say (1830–32).*

London in the first place. Some naturalists, notably Thomas Say, preferred to print and publish some of their books themselves. Say, sometimes considered to be the father of American natural history, helped found the settlement of New Harmony in Indiana and published most of his books there. The paper was of poor quality and the typography crude, but the hand-coloured plates were often of high quality, considering the difficulties of working in a little settlement, far from any cultural centre. Lucky is the collector who can lay his hands on a copy of *American Entomology* (1824–28) or *American Conchology* (1830–32) with the evocative New Harmony imprint. Works like these, in the original parts, with the wrappers intact as issued, comprise some of the rarest Americana ever published.

Collectors of Americana have long been aware of the work of that eccentric genius, Constantine Samuel Schmaltz Rafinesque. Con-

vinced that everything in nature could be named and described, he spent most of his life travelling, collecting natural objects, writing endlessly, and bringing out the oddest series of publications in the annals of natural history. Anyone who names and describes twelve species of thunder and lightning is, perhaps more of an eccentric than a genius, and all the world loves an eccentric. All his writing is collectable, although in book form, such as *Annals of Nature* (1820) and *Circular Address on Botany and Zoology* (1816), it is extremely rare and costly. Collectors seeking the work of Rafinesque, or of Say, would do well to look in the periodicals to which they contributed, *Silliman's American journal of science* and the *Journal of the Academy of Natural Sciences of Philadelphia,* for example. Early numbers of such journals are scarce, but they are usually inexpensive if not part of a long run.

For the collector of natural history books, the most varied and most appealing material is that published during Victorian times. Books of the period now form the backbone of most collectors' libraries, especially those specialising in natural history. It was in Britain, under Victoria's long reign, that the production of natural history books flourished to an extent unmatched anywhere up to that time. That was the era of Gould, Gosse, Kingsley, Darwin, Lyell, Pratt, J. G. Wood, Shirley Hibberd, the Sowerbys, Lear, Reeve and Frank Buckland. A bewildering array of books was produced in all shapes and sizes, illustrated or unillustrated, and ranging in price from a few pence to hundreds of pounds. Many of the books are still in circulation and many of them are not very expensive, at least for the time being.

One result of the Industrial Revolution was an increased regard for the wonders of nature. From about 1850, there appeared a spate of books devoted to the study of plants and animals of the country and the sea shore. Writers like Charles Kingsley and the novelist, George Eliot, dabbled in rock pools and marvelled at new varieties of ferns growing in Wardian cases in their drawing rooms. The study of nature became respectable, instead of simply odd, and an insatiable demand arose for books on all aspects of natural history. Naturalist authors, such as Gosse, George Henry Lewes (who lived with George Eliot) and the

Plate 9 from Glaucus *by Charles Kingsley (fourth edition, 1859).*

Rev. J. G. Wood satisfied the demand for cheap illustrated literature. The formula adopted by such writers was a fairly consistent mixture of accurate (and sometimes not so accurate) scientific observation, wonderment and piety. Usually some snatches of sentimental poetry were thrown in at frequent intervals.

Another type of book catered for those who sought a deeper understanding of a particular group of animals or plants. Books of this kind, written in matter of fact scientific language, usually provided descriptions and illustrations of a good proportion of the species in a group. The Ray Society was formed expressly to publish them and continues to do so today. Gosse could supply this kind of demand as well as write the more superficial popular books and so, to a certain extent, could Anne Pratt. Another able performer in both these fields was M. C. Cooke, who published books on a number of aspects of natural history, chiefly fungi. The collector may not be able to spend hundreds of pounds on Cooke's eight-volume *Illustrations of British Fungi* (1881–91), but he may still buy for a few pounds the same author's *Rust, Smut, Mildew and Mould* (1898), or his *Handbook of British Fungi* (1871).

Astronomical prices are now being asked for John Gould's great folio works on birds, but acceptable substitutes for some of them may be acquired in miniature, for a very small outlay. Jardine's *Naturalist's Library,* a long series of

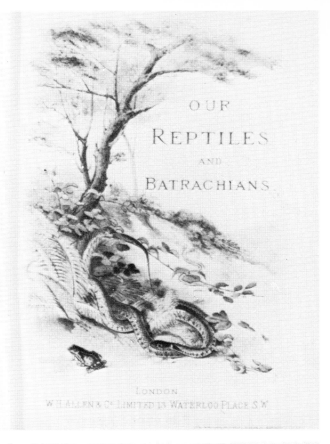

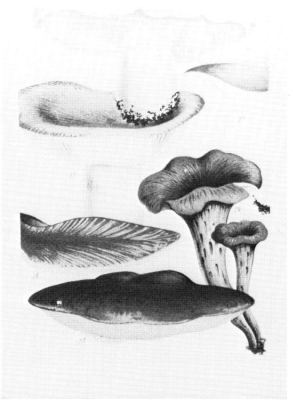

Top: *title page and frontispiece of* Our Reptiles and Batrachians *by M. C. Cooke (1893).* Left: *plate 11 from Cooke's* British Edible Fungi *(1891).* Above: *plate 1 from* Humming Birds, *Volume I of* Ornithology *in Jardine's Naturalist's Library.*

attractively produced volumes, includes several on birds, well illustrated with hand-coloured plates, mostly based on Gould's *The Natural History of Humming Birds* (1834) is the most desirable item of the series and is usually more expensive than the others.

All the works of P. H. Gosse are now eagerly collected. The hand-coloured plates are the main attraction. For many years his *Actinologia Britannica, a History of the British Sea-anemones and Corals* (1858–60) was easily and cheaply available. Rightly, its merits are now being appreciated and it is likely to increase in price. It is now difficult to understand why this book, with its beautiful colour-printed plates by W. Dickes, was for so long treated with disdain by collectors. The name of Gosse has been kept alive by the exquisite illustrations of marine life which embellish most of his books. Only his *Naturalist's Sojourn in Jamaica* (1851), *Tenby* (1856), *Land and Sea* (1865) and one or two other books may be considered readable. On the other hand, he wrote several obscure pamphlets and tracts of a religious nature, such as *The High Numbers of the Pentateuch: Are They Trustworthy?* (1871) and *The Humanity of the Son of God* (1886). Naturally, they are not to be expected on the same shelves as his other books. They are more likely to be stocked by a bookseller who deals in theological works. Here is a lesson for the collector: look in unlikely places for the titles you want. A large part of Gosse's considerable output was in the form of articles contributed to journals and, often, the articles include plain or coloured drawings. It is well worth attempting to bring together a collection of such articles.

With few exceptions, the works of the Rev. J. G. Wood are not illustrated in colour. However, the line engravings by first-class illustrators, such as Wolf and Whymper, are always of high quality, and the text is usually extremely readable. There are so many titles to collect that a shelf may be filled very easily. Possibly, many of us have been attracted to the subject of natural history in our youth by one or more of his books, and retain affectionate memories of titles such as *Homes without Hands, Insects at Home, Insects Abroad, Common Objects of the Sea Shore, Common Objects of the Microscope,* and *Common Shells of the Sea Shore.* Few of us could have foreseen that these books, once available at giveaway prices, would become the treasured possessions of future collectors, each retailing for pounds rather than pence.

Fashions change for a number of reasons, and the interest of one collector in a particular author may be enough to attract the attention of a wider public. The descendant of an author,

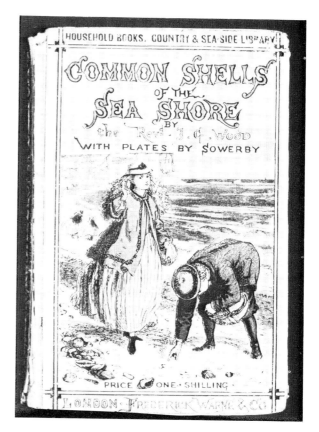

attempting to assemble his ancestor's complete writings, will alert booksellers to the sales potential of the works and the possibility of asking higher prices for them. There is evidence that this may be one of the reasons for the increasing scarcity and expense of the works of Anne Pratt. Her *Flowering Plants of Great Britain,* published about 1861, has been available cheaply until very recently. The three-volume set was priced at £32 in a bookseller's catalogue in 1974. Of course, the inclusion of 238 coloured plates printed by the Baxter process contributes to the notably high price. Fortunately, she wrote, as did J. G. Wood, many smaller books which still sell for prices within the reach of modest collectors.

Since they usually lack coloured plates, geological books have been ignored until comparatively recently. They are avidly collected, now, because of the greatly increased interest in the history of geology. With the exception of hand-coloured maps which accompany many of them, they have little aesthetic appeal. Not until the nineteenth century did geology come into its own as a science; its short history is easily comprehended. The economic importance of geology in the modern world does not need to be stressed here: most important geological insti-

Grasses, Sedges and Ferns of Great Britain, *by Ann Pratt (1866).*

tutions maintain libraries, often well endowed, which absorb geological literature of all kinds. Undoubtedly, nineteenth-century geological books are going to grow more expensive in the near future. Even now, however, it is comparatively easy to obtain early editions of some geological classics at bargain prices. It may seem that early editions of the works of an outstanding pioneer, such as Charles Lyell, are common enough to justify low prices. The situation could change in a year or less. *Principles of Geology, Elements of Geology* and *Antiquity of Man,* to name three of his better known titles, were very popular in their day, and many copies were published. Their popularity continues, however, and the demand for them is now greater than it was in the lifetime of their author. It is safe to predict that the only copies readily available in a few years' time will be twentieth-century reprints.

R. I. Murchison's monumental *Silurian System* (1839) is already approaching the £500 mark and will soon be reasonably priced at that figure. At the present time, the collector tends to reject any copy lacking the large folding map which should accompany the two text volumes. Such fastidiousness is already unrealistic. All the works of that pioneer of dinosaur hunting, Gideon Mantell, are now becoming scarce. Even *Thoughts on a Pebble,* his least significant contribution to geological literature, will become hard to find simply because he has an honoured place in the history of geology.

Before discussing the pivotal figure of nineteenth-century science, Charles Darwin, we can look at a few lesser figures and their work, and at some publishing concerns connected with the production of illustrations. Several different processes were developed for the reproduction of illustrations, some more successfully than others. Lithographic reproduction was the most popular and effective method of obtaining good quality pictures. Most of the great illustrated books contained plates produced by this process. Steel and wood engraving also remained very popular; colouring was usually applied by hand.

An early form of colour printing was perfected by George Baxter, whose prints were published separately or in books. They usually bear the caption 'Printed in Oil Colours by G. Baxter' and are nearly always finely detailed and beautifully drawn. Books containing Baxter prints are being dismantled at an alarming rate, now that the collection of his work has become so popular. Those that remain frequently have badly foxed plates. Often, the only Baxter print in a book is the frontispiece, nevertheless this is usually the best feature of the book. A typical example is found in *Shells and Their Inmates,* published by the Religious Tract Society in 1841. The frontispiece forms the principal redeeming feature of this book; the other is the attractive pictorial cover. Incidentally, the Religious Tract Society and the S.P.C.K. (Society for Promoting Christian Knowledge) brought out many attractively illustrated books on natural history, usually pocket sized and anonymous. A series of volumes published by these religious organisations can still be amassed fairly cheaply, in spite of entailing much tedious hunting.

Henry Bradbury learned the art of nature printing in Vienna and introduced the process to Britain in the 1850s. Plants and other natural objects were pressed into soft metal to produce impressions from which intaglio printing plates could be made. The ink impressions taken from the plates were exact representations of the ob-

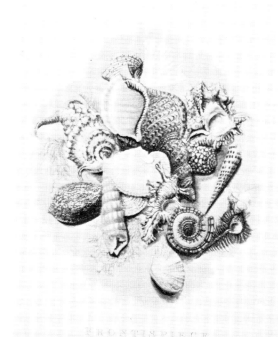

SHELLS

AND THEIR INMATES.

Art's finest pencil could but rudely mock
The rich grey mosses broidered on a rock,
—And those gay watery grots he would explore,
Small excavations on a rocky shore,
That seem like fairy baths, or minute wells,
Richly embossed with choicest weed and shells,
—As if her trinkets Nature chose to hide,
Where nought invaded but the flowing tide.

JANE TAYLOR.

LONDON:
THE RELIGIOUS TRACT SOCIETY;
Instituted 1799.
SOLD AT THE DEPOSITORY, 56, PATERNOSTER ROW,
AND 65, ST. PAUL'S CHURCHYARD; AND
BY THE BOOKSELLERS.

1841.

jects. As nature-printed plates are now eagerly collected, books illustrated with them are very expensive. They were largely ignored by collectors during the first half of the twentieth century, possibly because, glued in rather than sewn, they have an annoying tendency to fall out of the books. *The Nature Printed British Seaweeds* (1860) by W. G. Johnstone and A. Croall is one of the best known English examples of this process. Other outstanding examples are *Ferns of Great Britain and Ireland* (1855–56) by T. Moore and J. Lindley, and Moore's *The Nature Printed British Ferns:* octavo edition (1859). Such books are being collected because of an interest in the printing process and for the attractiveness of the plates. This is not good news for those naturalists who need them in their work, but it does ensure that nature-printed plates in books which are of no practical use will be rescued from oblivion. It is better for them to hang on a wall than be lost altogether.

A Victorian book may make dull reading and may or may not be attractively illustrated. Many of them, however, have attractive external features which make them collectable. The original cloth bindings, often decorated with designs picked out in gold or blind tooled, are now being collected for their own sake by buyers who appreciate the appearance of books more than the content. It is very satisfying to collect titles from a series brought out by one publisher. There are many series to choose from; usually they were produced in large numbers at modest prices. The firm of Groombridge & Sons published many books which are as attractive inside as they are outside. The illustrations are colour printed, the pages gilt-edged, and the covers decorated with agreeable pictures or designs. In the 1870s, Groombridge published several books by the Rev. W. Houghton and other equally obscure writers. Nothing can be more visually pleasing to collectors of attractive book covers than a shelf containing Houghton's *Country Walks of a Naturalist, Seaside Walks of a Naturalist, Walks of a Naturalist with his Children,* and *Sketches of British Insects.* H. J. Slack's *Marvels of Pond Life* and Sara Wood's *Dwellers in Our Gardens* are equally delightful to look at. The publishing firm of Reeve, Benham & Reeve also produced several attractive series of modestly priced books. John van Voorst, a leading London publisher of natural history books, was also fond of pictorial covers; a gloriously rustic example adorns the front of J. E. Harting's *Rambles in Search of Shells* (1875). The Victorians did not do things by halves.

The nineteenth century abounded in illustrators. More often than not, a drawing prepared by an artist was engraved, etched or lithographed by someone else, and coloured by yet another hand. It was rare to find a book illustrated from first to last by one person, or in one establishment, as in the operation of the Sowerby family. It would be difficult to imagine a library of nineteenth-century books on natural history which contained no Sowerby illustrations. The whole Sowerby family worked together, most of them in the same building, and each had an allotted place and task. Between them, they illustrated books on nearly every aspect of natural history for over a century. Always, they maintained high standards. James, James de Carle, George Brettingham and his son and grandson of the same name, John Edward and Henry drew, engraved, lithographed and coloured thousands of illustrations for others. Some members of the family wrote books as wall, although it is difficult to see how they found time to acquire the necessary knowledge. Among the most famous of the books they illustrated are J. E. Smith's *English Botany* (1790–1814 and later editions), with more than 2,500 coloured plates by James Sowerby, *Thesaurus Conchyliorum* (1842–87), with thousands of figures of shells drawn natural size by George Brettingham Sowerby (first, second and third) who also wrote the text, and R. I. Murchison's *Silurian System* (1839), with plain plates by James de Carle Sowerby. These are beyond the purchasing power of most collectors, although numerous slighter works with Sowerby illustrations, such as J. G. Wood's *Common Objects of the Sea Shore, Popular British Conchology* (1854) by G. B. Sowerby (the second), and Anne Pratt's *The Ferns of Breat Britain* (1861) are well within their reach. The work of many other illustrators of natural history books is worth collecting together. There is obviously a rich field for discovery here.

Darwin was already a distinguished man of science when he published his *Origin* in 1859, and he continued to publish carefully reasoned, rather turgid books on animals and plants until his death in 1882. Consequently, there are enough Darwin titles to keep a collector busy for a long time. His books are common because some of them went into many editions, but it was not until 1965, when Freeman published *The Works of Charles Darwin,* that collectors could begin to make sense of them. As is so often the case when a bibliographical hand list is published, the collecting of Darwin's works became a fashion, with some a passion. Some collectors now feel

Plate 28 from Volume I of J. E. Smith's English Botany *illustrated by James Sowerby (first edition).*

that it is not enough to collect every English edition—though that is a formidable enough proposition, considering that at least a hundred different issues of the *Origin* alone were published in England between 1859 and 1965—but they must also have all the editions in foreign translations too. This is too much of a good thing for most collectors. An acceptable compromise for them is to restrict themselves to English editions published up to the time of Darwin's death, or to those issues from the first to the last definitive. These, with few exceptions, were all published by John Murray and, with the single exception of the first edition of *The Fertilisation of Orchids* (1862) which was issued in plum cloth, all were issued in green cloth. As some of the variant issues are distinguishable only by small differences in the lettering and ornamentation on the spine, the collector considers the original bindings vital rather than optional extras.

One or two pointers to assist the potential Darwin collector may not be amiss here. The first edition of the *Origin* should be in good condition and in original cloth to justify the high price which will inevitably be asked. All editions and issues up to, and including, 1876 are important; some are as scarce as the first. That of 1872 (11th thousand) is widely considered to be the final version of the text as Darwin left it, but that of 1876 contains one or two minor differences and is the definitive text. Subsequent issues were from stereotypes of the 1876 issue. There should be a folding diagram in each issue. The first issue of the first edition of *The Descent of Man* (1871) may be distinguished from the second issue, despite the identical appearance of their title pages, inserted advertisements and bindings. The first issue has eight Errata on the verso of the title leaf to Vol. II; in the second issue there are no Errata, but nine other works by Darwin are listed. The first issue also has a tipped-in leaf (pp. ix-x) in the same volume referring to a 'serious and unfortunate error'. To distinguish between issues of Vol. I, look at page 297. It is a first issue if the first word on the page is 'transmitted', a second issue if the word is 'When'. A copy of the first issue usually costs considerably more than a copy of the second. *The Variation of Animals and Plants Under Domestication* (1868) also has two issues of the first edition; the earlier is more desirable. They may be distinguished by their Errata. In the first issue, there are four Errata on page vi of Vol. I and seven on page viii of Vol. II. In the second issue, these are corrected, but there is a new one on page vi of Vol. II.

Other prominent evolutionists contemporary with Darwin were his friend and champion, T. H. Huxley, and A. R. Wallace, joint proposer, with Darwin, of the theory of evolution through the action of natural selection. Both of them published many books which were popular in their day and are worth collecting (and reading) now. First editions of Huxley's books are in demand, although his superb writing and well-reasoned arguments deserve recognition in any edition. Most sought after are his *Evidence as to Man's Place in Nature* (1863), *Lay Sermons* (1870), *Critiques and Addresses* (1873) and *American Addresses* (1877).

Wallace's more varied (and more variable) output presents the collector with some puzzles.

Masterpieces such as *The Malay Archipelago* (1869), *Geographical Distribution of Animals* (1876), *Island Life* (1880) and *Darwinism* (1889) are compulsory purchases for the collector of evolutionary material. His later preoccupation with spiritualism and social problems resulted in a number of distinctly inferior books. The Wallace collector, like the Darwin collector, has many titles to choose from but, before he plunges too deeply into Wallaceana, he should realise that his author, unlike Darwin, had to produce a lot of hack literary work to earn a living. Darwin's complete works represent the life blood of a man totally committed to science. Wallace's, unfortunately, do not.

It is already clear that many natural history books published during the twentieth century are now, or soon will be, collected as eagerly as any published previously. Because we are more aware of them and understand them better, and because many of them are of high quality, they are, in general, more coveted than early productions. Collectors are less concerned, today, about whether books are antiquarian, or of a past generation. They are most interested, naturally, in what is available. Collectors of bird books are more than content if they can obtain any books illustrated by Archibald Thorburn. Entomological enthusiasts are only too pleased to have a copy of F. W. Frohawk's *Natural History of British Butterflies* (1914), a beautifully illustrated folio in two volumes which would not have been written or published without the financial backing of Lord Rothschild. In some ways, after all, nineteenth-century ideas and methods lingered on into the twentieth century. In the 1920s, for instance, it was still possible, though only just, to produce hand-coloured illustrations of natural objects. In 1925, the Rev. E. G. Alderson published his *Studies in Ampullaria,* a monograph on a group of large freshwater snails; fifteen of the 150 copies issued were hand-coloured by the author.

But the twentieth century is the era of photography, and modern book production would be nowhere without it. It may well be that future generations will look upon present day book production with the respect and admiration with which we regard Victorian books. It is just possible that our standards of production cannot be sustained for much longer. If this is so, certainly many of the books being published now will become the collector's treasures of tomorrow.

Philosophy and Religion

IT is still possible for anyone to form an interesting, worthwhile and valuable collection of books and pamphlets from the vast range of theological and philosophical works. There have probably been more books and pamphlets published of a theological and philosophical nature than in any other subject. Where have they all gone? Up to the second world war many bookshops had a substantial section of these books and their owners had a reasonable knowledge of the books themselves. Many booksellers now exclude theology from their shelves and where the books do survive it is often in the history or miscellaneous section.

One of the reasons for the reluctance of booksellers to buy theology is that the libraries of parsons, priests or ministers, the main source of supply, are so much alike in the books which they contain. Unfortunately this constantly recurring mass of theology books is of a popular sort; 'soft theology', for which there is virtually no demand even at the cheapest prices. Few libraries, of parsons, contain the works of some of the more significant English philosophical theologians of the last thirty years for example, Ian Ramsey, T. F. Torrance, Ninian Smart, E. I. Mascall, Austin Farrar, Leslie Dewart or John MacQuarrie, fewer still those of the highly influential theologians from the continent.

Perhaps one of the causes for the dire straits the Churches feel themselves to be in is this division between the minister in the parish and the theological scholar. It was in no way surprising that John Robinson's *Honest to God* should have caused such a great theological upheaval in England some years ago. Most of the important ideas had been discussed and written about for quite a long period especially on the European continent and were skilfully brought together in Robinson's book. Instead of a gradual sifting and assimilation of the various ideas there was an undesirable polarisation between reaction and enthusiasm.

There are still large quantities of theology books about but you may have to travel far to find them. Do not be put off by thinking the books will be so expensive that it is not worth starting to collect them. Start right away, money should be no obstacle to starting your collection. I know students who, on modest grants supplemented by vacation work, build themselves outstandingly good working libraries in a specialised field, and in certain cases end up their time at University with much better holdings in their area than their University library. However, almost irrespective of how much money you can afford or are prepared to spend, it is essential to define your area of interest, and initially make it as narrow as possible. Once you start collecting you will discover more books than you ever imagined published in your particular field; if you try and expand on too broad a front you will not be able to build your collection in sufficient depth to be of real interest and value.

It would be incorrect to assume that works of the seventeenth and eighteenth century are so expensive that it is not worth while thinking of collecting in this period, there is still a surprisingly large number of such books and within the whole field it is possible to collect, for example, first or early editions of classic works of British philosophy and philosophical theology. One of the particular attractions of many of these works is their 4to format, there is a singular delight in handling one of these volumes bound in contemporary full calf, printed on excellent quality paper, it opens well and invites you to read on. A folio volume is a splendid thing but you need strong arms and a stout table, a 12mo volume is a cringing mean thing by comparison, although it comes into its own for tracts and controversial items, the 8vo format has proved itself over time but it is utilitarian and lacks the generosity of the 4to.

As good a work as any to start such a collection would be William Wollaston's (1660–

[1]

A

DISCOURSE

On the

MIRACLES of our SAVIOUR, &c.

F ever there was an useful Controversy started, or revived in this Age of the Church, it is *this* about the *Messiahship* of the Holy Jesus, which the *Discourse of the Grounds*, &c. has of late rais'd. I believe this Controversy will end in the absolute Demonstration of Jesus's *Messiahship* from Prophecy, which is the only way to prove him to be the *Messiah*, that great Prophet expected by the *Jews*, and promised under the Old Testament. And tho' this way of Proof from Prophecy seems to labour under many Difficulties at present, and tho' some *Writers* against the *Grounds*, being distressed with those Difficulties, are for seeking Refuge in the Miracles of our
B
Saviour

Above: *frontispiece of the fifth edition of William Wollaston's* The Religion of Nature Delineated. Right: *the first page of* A Discourse on the Miracles of Our Saviour, &c. *'by Thomas Woolston, sometime Fellow of Sidney Sussex College in Cambridge, Printed for the Author, sold by him near Moregate and by the Booksellers of London and Westminster'.*

1724) *The Religion of Nature Delineated*, first edition published anonymously in 1724, though a few copies were printed for private circulation in 1722. 10,000 4to copies sold between the first edition and the sixth in 1738. For this reason it is still possible to buy copies of the work at reasonable prices. I have recently seen good copies for sale between £6 and £14. This was one of the important Deist works, many of which were published anonymously, some also posthumously.

William Wollaston should not be confused with Thomas Woolston (1669–1733) another Deist whose *A Discourse on the Miracles of Our Saviour* was published in six parts between 1727 and 1729. This work also had an enormous circulation, Voltaire estimating it at 30,000. Part of the success was due to its racy and irreverent style. Woolston was taken to court in 1729 and convicted of publishing a blasphemous libel; he was sent to prison for a year and fined £100.

He refused to pay the fine and died in prison four years later.

Christianity as old as the Creation; or, the Gospel a Republication of the Religion of Nature, first edition 4to 1730 written by Matthew Tindal (1657–1733) but published anonymously, is perhaps the classic Deist text: early editions are still to be found at a reasonable price, although the first is now quite scarce.

One of the most acute thinkers of the seventeenth century was William Chillingworth (1602–1644), and his major work *The Religion of Protestants, a safe way to Salvation*, first edition folio 1638, is an important and desirable work. The first edition is now quite rare and expensive in good condition, however, there were ten reprints in folio till 1742, and this, the tenth and last, is considered the best critical edition of the folios. The sixth edition of 1704 should be avoided because of printing errors. The best late reprint of his works is a three-volume set published in 1838 which can cost about the same as one of the later of the folio editions.

Samuel Clarke (1675–1729) published his Boyle lectures in 1705–06 under the titles *A discourse concerning the Being and Attributes of God* first edition, 8vo 1705 and *A discourse Concerning the Unchangeable Obligations of Natural Religion and Truth* first edition, 8vo 1706. These works are becoming scarcer but are still to be found at a reasonable price; the two 'Discourses' were later published in one volume under the joint titles. Clarke wrote other important works but he should not be confused with another Samuel Clarke (1599–1682) an historian, best known for his *A General Martyrologie* 1673 published earlier under the title *A Collection of the Lives of Ten Eminent Divines,* first edition, 4to 1662. As well as having the same names, a further problem for a quick identification arises because on some title pages Clarke the historian is mentioned as Minister of St Bennet (Fink), and the philosopher Clarke is described as rector of St Bennet's (Paul's Wharf).

Robert Barclay (1648–90) in his *Apology for the True Christian Religion, as the same is set forth and preached by the People called in Scorn 'Quakers',* first English edition 4to 1678 wrote one of the great apologetic works in the English language. This edition is now scarce but there are still many early 8vo versions to be found. The work was originally printed in Amsterdam in 1676 in Latin under the title *Theologiae Verae Christianae Apologia,* and in this form is even rarer than the first English edition.

Another work more truly philosophical, and in fact one of the greatest and most famous philosophical works in the language, is *The Analogy of Religion, Natural and Revealed, to the Constitution and Course of Nature* by Joseph Butler (1692–1752). The first edition was published in 1736 in 4to. At the time it was considered as providing a comprehensive refutation of the basic Deist tenets, and has subsequently influenced many of the important British philosophers. The first edition of the work, while not common, can still be bought by the vigilant collector at a surprisingly low figure. I have seen good copies for sale within the last year at £12, £14, and £27. The second edition came out in two 8vo volumes.

Portrait of Bishop Butler from the 1860 edition of The Analogy of Religion.

These and many other similar works appear ridiculously cheap in view of their age, their influence, their comparative scarcity, and their fine bindings. What work or object of similar age, quality and distinction within the fields of pictures, glass, furniture, can be bought for anything remotely as low a price? To make such a comparison is full of difficulties; a picture is unique whereas a book is only one of a number of the same, but one book is perhaps the great creative achievement of a lifetime from a brilliant mind and obtainable in its original form as published.

For the ambitious collector the 1678 first edition of *The True Intellectual System of the Universe wherein all the Reason and Philosophy of Atheism is confuted, and its Impossibility Demonstrated* by Ralph Cudworth (1617–1688), the greatest of the Cambridge Platonists, is a scarce and desirable book to have. Massive as the folio volume is, and although it is Cudworth's major work, it was never completed. His *Treatise concerning Eternal and Immutable Morality* was not published until 1731. The earlier work should have a full engraved title page before the plain type title page, quite frequently it is missing. Many important seventeenth century works

A

VIEW

OF THE

EVIDENCES OF CHRISTIANITY.

IN THREE PARTS.

Part I. Of the direct Historical Evidence of Christianity, and wherein it is distinguished from the Evidence alledged for other Miracles.

Part II. Of the Auxiliary Evidences of Christianity.

Part III. A brief Consideration of some popular Objections.

BY WILLIAM PALEY, M. A.

ARCHDEACON OF CARLISLE.

THE FIFTH EDITION.

IN TWO VOLUMES.—VOL. I.

LONDON:

PRINTED FOR R. FAULDER, NEW BOND STREET.

M.DCC.XCVI.

Above: *Title page illustration from* The True Intellectual system of the Universe *'wherein all the Reason and Philosophy of Atheism is confuted, and its Impossibilities Demonstrated' by Ralph Cudworth*

have, or should have, these two title pages. There was a good four volume edition of Cudworth's works published in 1829.

Another of the Cambridge Platonists, Henry More (1614–87), is scarce in first edition and considerably more expensive than some of the works mentioned earlier. First editions of Locke, Berkeley, Hobbes, tend to be even more expensive. However, their works in slightly later editions are still moderately common and inexpensive.

It is curious that the first editions of William Paley (1743–1805) do not appear more often. His major works are *The Principles of Moral and Political Philosophy,* first edition 1785, *Horae Paulinae,* 1790, possibly his most original work, *View of the Evidences of Christianity,* 1794, and

Natural Theology, 1802. Perhaps the reason that first editions of his works are not all that common is because they became such standard texts that they suffered unusual wear and tear. His works abound in various nineteenth century editions and handsome calf sets can still be bought quite cheaply. It is sad to say that during the past five or six years many interesting books bound in calf have vanished from the bookshops and into the hands of interior decorators and designers.

Dugald Stewart (1753–1828), the greatest of the Scottish School of this period, published his *Elements of the Philosophy of the Human Mind,* under one general title but each of the three volumes was published one at a time in 1792, 1814, 1827. Each volume in first edition was in 4to and all are now becoming quite difficult to find. The third volume was never reprinted except in the collected works edited by Sir William Hamilton in eleven volumes 1854–60. If the opportunity arises it is well worth while

ELEMENTS

OF THE

PHILOSOPHY

OF THE

HUMAN MIND.

By DUGALD STEWART, F. R. S. Edin.

PROFESSOR OF MORAL PHILOSOPHY IN THE UNIVERSITY OF EDINBURGH.

LONDON:

PRINTED FOR A. STRAHAN, AND T. CADELL IN THE STRAND;
AND W. CREECH, EDINBURGH.

M DCC XCII.

TRAITÉ
DES ETUDES
MONASTIQUES,

DIVISÉ EN TROIS PARTIES;

AVEC UNE LISTE DES PRINCIPALES
Difficultez qui fe rencontrent en chaque fiécle dans la
lecture des Originaux, & un Catalogue de livres choifis
pour compofer une Bibliotéque ecclefiaftique.

Par Dom JEAN MABILLON *Religieux Benedictin de la
Congregation de S. Maur.*

A PARIS,

Chez CHARLES ROBUSTEL, rue S. Jacques,
au Palmier.

M. DC. XCI.

Avec Privilege du Roy, & Permiffion des Superieurs.

---

getting the volumes of the first editions singly, as each is something of a prize.

This selection of writers and important works in philosophy and philosophical theology omits many distinguished names, but there is not sufficient space, nor would too long a list be helpful. What I have endeavoured to do is to point out some important works which are still to be bought at reasonable prices, and which would form the basis of a most interesting small library.

Those who are interested in Patristics and have a weakness for old folios will know the work of the Benedictine scholars of St Maur. These Maurist versions of the Fathers are still relatively common and in many cases are the best critical editions. Perhaps the greatest of all the Maurists was Jean Mabillon (1632–1707): his works are not common in England or America, but when they do appear can be bought quite inexpensively as they are not always recognised. One of his most famous works was written in defence of the scholarly life and work of monks, *Traité des Etudes Monastique* first edition, 4to. Other important works were his *De re Diplomatica,* 1681 and *Liturgica Gallicana,* 1685. Most of his scholarly patristic and historical work was taken up with his edition of St Bernard, his *Acta Sanctorum* and *Analecta.*

The Abbé Migne (1800–75) was not a scholar of the calibre of Mabillon but in an assessment of his life's work he must surely be reckoned one of the most remarkable figures in the whole history of publishing. His aim was to publish all the documents of what constituted Catholic 'tradition'. All the volumes were to be inexpensive so that the clergy could buy them, and all were to be of uniform size. The general title of the whole work was *Bibliotheque Universelle du Clergé ou Cours complet sur chaque branche de la science Ecclesiastique.* The original material for this great enterprise lay in libraries and archives throughout Europe in manuscript and book form. He had no official backing, either ecclesiastical or lay. The final results were due to his own great ingenuity and unflagging resolve. Eventually he had his own presses, type-foundry, bookshops and bindery: not satisfied with that, he had an adjoining factory making ecclesiastical furnishings, organs, altars and such.

The most famous and useful legacies of his work are the Latin and Greek Patrologies. The Latin Patrology was published between 1844 and 1855, and covers the work of 2,614 writers down to 1216 in 220 volumes plus four index volumes. The Greek Patrology was published between 1857 and 1866 in 161 volumes. For all his works the proofs were checked six times. He paid a special bonus for all misprints spotted in the proofs of the Greek Patrology. Despite this vigilance numerous misprints have been discovered, but all patristic scholars and early historians acknowledge the great and lasting debt owed to Migne for this great work.

Many people think this is the sole work associated with Migne; not so; published simultaneously with the Patrologies were 68 volumes of the works of French pulpit orators, about 150 volumes of the works of certain Catholic authors, such as St Teresa and St John of the Cross, the works of St Thomas Aquinas in 26 volumes, and nearly 170 volumes of encyclopaedias. But even this is not the whole picture, for simultaneously with the joint efforts already described, there was a continuous demand for reprints; in 1864, for example, there were 400 volumes waiting to be reprinted.

Migne never reached his target of 2,000 volumes for the *Bibliotheque Universelle*: fire destroyed all his premises in 1868 and put an end to his great vision. Not all his volumes are of equal value, the encyclopaedias being the least, but I know of several patristic students and scholars who are building up their own sets of the *Patrologiae Cursus Completus*.

For a collector with an entirely different and slightly unusual approach, there are very interesting possibilities in assembling the various editions of single titles. A collection of all different editions of *The Imitation of Christ* would take some years to get anywhere near complete as there would be several hundred if not thousands of volumes. The *Imitation* is one of those few spiritual works which have crossed almost all denominational barriers, although occasionally it has been edited with certain passages removed or altered to suit some partisan viewpoint. These variations could be traced. In such a collection would be simple pocket editions, folio editions, illustrated editions of every variety, finely bound editions, private press editions, in fact the collection would contain a number of histories or surveys in miniature; typography, binding and illustration.

Bunyan's *Pilgrims Progress* is another book that would result in an interesting collection, and there are many more. However, it is worth checking to find out that the particular book you would like to collect has sufficient variations and reprints to make it a worthwhile task.

It is also possible to concentrate on a single subject rather than a single author, and form, for instance, a collection of different Lives of Jesus. Even if this were restricted to Lives in English

John Bunyan's Dream, the frontispiece to the first edition of Pilgrim's Progress.

it would include F. D. Strauss' *Life of Jesus* translated by George Eliot in 1843. Not only was it the first attempt at a 'Life of Jesus', but such was its methodology and so negative the results that it is seen as one of the theological milestones of the century. Since then there has been a continuous stream of new lives of Jesus reflecting every denominational, theological, and purely personal viewpoint. Surely someone will make a study of them and attempt to assess their influence, their similarities and contradictions. Many of the lives had remarkable sales. F. W. Farrar's *Life of Christ, 1874*, went through eleven editions in its first year. There have also been lives cast in the form of novels. Such a collection, which at a guess I would estimate at about 200 lives could be collected at quite a small cost.

Another area of interesting study, which would certainly make a most unusual, and in its way amusing, and attractive collection, would be the field of books which make analogies between religion and sport: cricket, mountaineering or what ever appealed to the author. There was a minor vogue for this type of book between 1880 and 1914. As good an example as any is Thomas Waugh's *The Cricket field of the Christian Life*. In the preface he describes two types of person, those who are spiritually inclined and those who take no interest in the Church or Christ's saving purpose. For both types he hopes:

> In presenting the Christian life to them under the figure of a game of Cricket, to help the former class into closer fellowship with the Lord and into a deeper sympathy with his saving purpose, and do something to win many of the latter class to accept him as Saviour and Captain . . . they understand the game so well, and the game suggests and illustrates so many points and phases of Christian life that they may read the book with an interest that in the end means the winning and saving of their fine young lives . . .

What the effect this type of book has, it is impossible to say, but I cannot see it producing the results so optimistically expected. Books and sermons of an improving tone are rarely bought by the people they were written for. However, books of this type are worth preserving as an example of one of the many methods employed to make men turn again and listen.

Holman Hunt's engraving 'a Carpenter's Shop near Nazareth', frontispiece to The Life of Christ *by Frederick W. Farrar, (two volumes, Petter & Galpin, London, Paris and New York, 1874).* Top right: *frontispiece illustration to* The Cricket Field of The Christian Life *by the Rev. Thomas Waugh (published for the author by W. J. Tyne & Co. Ltd., The Edgeley Press, Stockport).*

Entirely different are the very distinctive works printed and published by the Mechitarist Society from the island of St Lazaro in Venice. This Society is virtually unknown in England or America, but their works can still be found; they used a particularly attractive type face which once recognised is easily identifiable. The Mechitarists were an Armenian order who developed publishing as a speciality of particular value in their missionary work. Not all their books are printed in Armenian nor are they all of a theological or religious nature. Byron studied oriental languages at the Monastery and was partly responsible for the publication of an Armenian–English grammar by Dr Aucher. Their Armenian Bible of 1733 was particularly distinguished. Among their other works were an edition of *Robinson Crusoe* in 1817 and Young's *Night Thoughts* in 1819. Perhaps the work which occurs most frequently is an Armenian prayer book printed in 24 languages in 1813; the work was reprinted and expanded and by the 1860s it was in 33 languages and over 500 pages long.

Of nineteenth century English publishers the books of William Pickering are most attractive and there have been collectors at work for many years trying to reassemble the whole corpus. However, there are still many about and the new collector has an excellent chance to acquire choice works. The publishers Bell and Daldy have never been collected in the same way as Pickering, although their work was of the highest quality. Bell and Daldy probably offer better opportunities for the collector than Pickering.

There is a private press run by the Nuns of Stanbrook Abbey, Worcester, England, which issues works from time to time, usually of quite exceptional quality. They should be even better known than they are. To anyone interested in books from private presses, and especially one which prints works of a religious nature they are well worth investigating and not expensive for the quality of work they produce.

I have strayed from the highways of philosophical classics to the byeways of forgotten books and private presses, but in between there are many books and many paths and even more collectors trying to preserve what they can find. One of these paths leads to the ever increasing interest in the phenomena of religious experience and mysticism and the psychology of religion. For centuries, of course, there has been great interest in this subject and much has been written, but as a subject with its own separate discipline it is really in the twentieth century that a systematic study has been developed. The founder of this discipline was William James, the great American psychologist and philosopher, famous for his contributions in three fields. His *Principles of Psychology* first edition, two volumes, 1890, is one of the few classic works in its field and much sought after in first edition. He was also the most distinguished of the Pragmatist philosophers, but perhaps his work of more lasting interest are his Edinburgh Gifford Lectures 1901–02 published as *The Varieties of Religious Experience*, 1902. This is the major pioneer work in its field. Perhaps all the credit should not be given to James, for there is a little known work by Edwin Diller Starbuck, *The Psychology of Religion,* first edition 1899, which James in his preface to the work describes as having 'broken ground in a new place.' It is now quite a hard book to find, but one which should have an honourable place in any collection.

As the subject is a relatively new one there is still the chance for the student and collector to build up a really excellent small library of, say, 500 books, which would include the major mystical writers as well as the twentieth-century academic works on the subject. Works of interest and importance which are becoming hard to find would include the following, and more besides. *The Psychology of Religious Mysticism* first edition 1925, by James H. Leuba, one of the pioneers in the field, as was E. S. Ames in his *The Psychology of Religious Experience*, 1910. Other important early works also by Americans are W. E. Hocking's *The Meaning of God in Human Experience*,

THE PHILOSOPHY OF MYSTICISM

BY

EDWARD INGRAM WATKIN

AUTHOR OF
"SOME THOUGHTS ON CATHOLIC APOLOGETICS"

LONDON
GRANT RICHARDS LTD.
ST MARTIN'S STREET
MDCCCCXX

1912, and E. A. Bennett's *A Philosophical Study of Mysticism*. In 1920 E. I. Watkin published *The Philosophy of Mysticism,* a work which should be reprinted, this time with an index. Chapter fifteen contains a very interesting discussion on the mystical element in the writing of Richard Jefferies (1848–87). Jefferies' very remarkable spiritual autobiography *The Story of My Heart,* first edition, 1883, in spite of its ghastly title, is becoming accepted as one of the very few great works expressive of nature mysticism.

Of more recent works, some to look out for are Marghanita Laski's *Ecstasy,* 1961, John E. Smith's *Experience and God,* 1968, and Sir Alister Hardy's Gifford lectures *The Living Stream* and *The Divine Flame*. A new dimension was added to the discussion by the publication of Aldous Huxley's *Doors of Perception* in 1954. This brought in the question of the relationship between drug experiences and religious experience. R. C. Zaehner's *Mysticism Sacred and Profane,* 1957, was the first serious answer to the work and its implication; since then many books have dealt with this subject.

I should not like to leave this area without mentioning a few interesting but isolated works of the nineteenth century: Charles Buck's *A*

The first boke of Mo-ses, called Genesis.

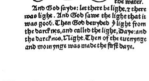

Left: *first page of the Coverdale Bible (1535) showing the six days of creation.* Above: *title page to the New Testament of Matthew's Bible (1537).*

Treatise on Religious Experience, second edition 1807, S. C. Wilks' *Essay of the Signs of Conversion and Unconversion in Ministers of the Church,* second edition 1817, and finally *The Religious Feeling,* by Newman Smyth, New York 1877.

The serious collectors of Bibles have always been a fairly small group and I am sure always will be. There are still many interesting Bibles to be found in shops. Where does the beginner start? The different editions are so numerous, well over 2,000 in English alone, and there are so many minor variants in sixteenth and seventeenth century editions that the inexperienced collector can find himself landed in a bibliographical quagmire. It would be quite impossible in the space of a few lines to do more than point out some of the most famous editions, almost exclusively those in English, and suggest one or two points.

The pioneer was William Tyndale, who published the first edition in English of the New Testament in 1526 and revised it in 1534 and 1535. He also translated parts of the Old Testa-ment and in 1530 the Pentateuch. The first edition of the complete Bible in English was also published in 1535, translated by Miles Coverdale. It is Coverdale's translation of the Psalter which was incorporated into *The Book of Common Prayer.* A new folio edition (1537) of Coverdale's Bible was the first Bible to be printed in England.

In 1537 Matthew's Bible was published with the Kings 'gracious Lycence' and is thus the first Authorized Version. It is called Matthew's Bible, but Thomas Matthew is reckoned to have been a pseudonym for John Rogers. None of the editions to that date was considered wholly satisfactory, so, with the support of Henry VIII, and under the immediate patronage of Thomas Cromwell, Coverdale produced a new edition in 1539. This is the first of the 'great Bibles' so called because of the size: it is sometimes also referred to as 'Cromwell's Bible', and later editions are known as 'Cranmer Bibles'. In Queen Mary's reign the great flood of Bible printing was halted and existing Bibles were ordered to be burnt. Geneva became the home of many refugees and it was from there that a new translation of the New Testament was published in 1557. This version attributed to William Whittingham 'forms the first critical edition of the *New Testament* in English'; it has the now usual notes and tables and was also the first English testament to use verse divisions and to be printed in Roman type. The 'Geneva Version' of the Bible was published in Queen Elizabeth I's reign in 1560; this and subsequent editions are often referred to as Breeches Bibles' from the wording of Genesis III, 7. There are quite a number of nicknames attached to various editions of the Bible but none of them are much use in helping to identify the edition.

In Queen Elizabeth I's reign the 'Great Bibles' were reprinted and set up again in Churches. Archbishop Parker wished to see a new authorised edition prepared by the Bishops, the work was carried out, and what is known as the 'Bishops' Bible' was published in 1568. This edition is considered aesthetically one of the finest ever printed in England.

Below: *the 'Breeches Bible' (1560).* Right: *title page of the Bishops' Bible.*

Apart from some later reprints of the 'Bishops'', 'Geneva' and 'Great' Bibles the others mentioned are unobtainable or excessively scarce. The Roman Catholic translation of the New Testament printed at Rheims in 1582 is now very scarce. It is the first English Roman Catholic translation of any part of the Bible. This translation by Gregory Martin was used in the great 'Authorized Version' of 1611. The second edition of this work was published in 1600 and printed in Antwerp. The Roman Catholic translation of the Old Testament did not appear until 1610, its delay due to 'our poore estate in banishment' (preface). The edition was in two volumes, the first being dated 1609 and the second 1610. Work on the Authorized Version of 1611 began in 1604 at the request of King James: its publication forms a landmark in English history. Now it is very scarce and expensive and many copies sold are defective but nevertheless much prized. Since 1611 there have

been innumerable other versions of the Bible, among them unusual editions which can often be found quite inexpensively. Most of these are modest looking productions, but the title page may suggest that a further examination would prove interesting. For example in 1798 there appeared a *Translation of the New Testament from the Original Greek,* with the unusual line 'humbly attempted by Nathaniel Scarlett, assisted by men of piety and literature: with notes'. Scarlett was a bookseller in the Strand. The translation attempts to give the language a contemporary idiomatic sound. The text was divided up by Scarlett into sections and the narrative broken up and divided between speakers.

Another translation of the New Testament was made in 1719 by Cornelius Nary, a parish priest in Dublin. He is quite explicit in his preface about the manifold deficiencies, as he sees them, of the Rheims-Douay translation. It was too large, too expensive, the language too antique and the words in 'a number of cases so obsolete, the orthography so bad, and the translation so very literal, that in a number of places it is unintelligible and all over so grating.' Unfortunately Nary's edition met with even less success than Scarlett's. For the collector, however, these odd isolated editions of the Bible or parts of it are a special delight alongside the main stream of the history of the printed Bible.

The first Bible printed in Scotland was produced at Edinburgh in 1579; in Ireland there are reasons for believing there was printing before 1714 but the earliest extant copy is of that year. The first Bible was printed at Cambridge in 1591 and at Oxford in 1675. An important date in the history of Bible publication is 1804, the year in which the British and Foreign Bible Society was founded. The quantity and variety of its editions in all languages has been quite prodigious: of English Bibles and New Testaments alone, over 900,000 copies were sold in the first eleven years of the Society's existence.

The first American Bible is John Eliot's famous Indian Bible printed at Cambridge, Massachusetts in 1663. The first Bible in a European language was a German one printed in Philadelphia in 1743. It was in Philadelphia also that the first English Bible was printed in 1782 by Robert Aitken in two 8vo volumes. The reason for this late printing of a Bible in English was that the Crown restricted the printing of Bibles in England and the colonies to a few named British printers. There had in fact been various schemes put forward in America but they had failed mostly through lack of funds. However, after the War of Independence none of these difficulties remained and there was a fairly rapid expansion. Anyone with a Bible printed in America in the early years may well have a very rare and valuable book, and even Bibles of a much later date should be looked at closely as among them may be the first Bible to be printed in a particular State.

The collector will find it very hard and frustrating to find continental antiquarian books in bookshops in England and America. At no period has there been any great import of foreign language works. Books in Latin are perhaps the most common, then those in French and German; other European languages seem to be represented by a very modest selection. There are specialist dealers for most languages, but the prices naturally tend to be high. Despite the scarcity of books, the collector who is prepared to scour the bookshops will often come across remarkable and sometimes spectacular bargains, for the chance that a bookseller has more than a working knowledge of one or perhaps two foreign languages is not high. You might come across the first edition in Danish of Søren Kierkegaard's first important work *Either—or* published in Copenhagen in two volumes in 1843 as *Enten-Eller. et livs—Fragment udgivet af Victor Eremita.* I have seen Ludwig Holberg's *Epistler,* in five volumes, Copenhagen 1748–54, being offered at a give away price when to the specialist they would be rare and expensive.

Early editions of the Reformers are mostly recognised and are now becoming scarce and expensive even in the less sophisticated areas of the antiquarian book trade. However, the writings of some of the important Catholic Counter-Reformation writers, even those as famous as Cardinal Bellarmine, can often be found at a much cheaper price. For anyone wishing to study some of the less distinguished theologians and Biblical commentators of seventeenth and eighteenth centuries, there are still large quantities of the works in old folios to be bought cheaply in some of the large bookshops.

If important antiquarian continental works are difficult to find, there are still sufficient copies of translations of key works from the nineteenth century onwards. Many of these works have been highly influential. George Eliot translated two works, both of which were destructive of the traditional Christian standpoint. Her translation of D. F. Strauss' *The Life of Jesus,* published in 1843, was one of the milestones of nineteenth-century thought. The first German edition, published in 1835–36, created such a storm that it virtually finished Strauss' career as an academic. Yielding to some of the criticisms the second and third editions were modified but he regretted having made these alterations: the fourth edition, which is the one translated by George Eliot, is virtually the same as the first. In 1864 Strauss wrote his *New Life of Jesus* which is a quite separate and distinct work from the earlier *Life of Jesus.* 'The New Life' was translated into English in 1865. If D. F. Strauss opened a whole new era of New Testament studies and religious thought then in the field of Old Testament studies Julius Wellhausen's work translated into English in 1885 as *Prologomena to the History of Israel* was similarly important.

The other work translated by George Eliot was Ludwig Feuerbach's *Essence of Christianity,* first English edition 1854. Its major influence on Karl Marx and many of the important thinkers of the nineteenth and twentieth centuries is generally accepted. It is surprising how long Friedrich Schleirmacher's speeches on religion had to wait before being translated in 1893 by Caird. However, their influence on the romantic movement in the early years of the nineteenth century and later on the works of A. Ritschl, A. Harnack and E. Troeltsch and others have affected the whole understanding of the idea and function of religion and the particular stress laid on 'feeling' in religion.

The dominant Liberal Protestant view developed in the late nineteenth and early twentieth centuries is best captured in A. Harnack's *What is Christianity?* translated by T. Baily Saunders in 1901. It presents what many people thought and think is a much too cosy a view of Christianity. The book was remarkably unteutonic, being short, unambiguously clear and readable, and has been reprinted many times. A very much more radical book presenting a less comfortable interpretation of the Bible and the teaching of Jesus was written by A. F. Loisy and translated into English in 1903 as *The Gospel and the Church.* It is equally readable but maintains that the Liberal Protestant interpretation of the New Testament was almost totally incorrect and that the stress should be put on Judgement: Loisy claims the eschatological element is paramount. Views similar to these were expressed at great length and in even more radical form in Albert Schweitzer's great work translated in 1910 as *The Quest of the Historical Jesus.* Other works which have had a permanent and lasting influence in their fields are Rudolf Otto's *The Idea of the Holy,* first English edition 1923, and H. Kraemer *The Christian message in a non-Christian World,* 1938, although this work is not strictly a translation. There are many other works which have made significant and enduring contributions to the religious life and thought of the Anglo-Saxon countries; a collection of all these works would be a magnificent collection indeed.

A number of the translated works mentioned above were written during a period when in England and America there was a great philosophical revival. It is the period of D. Josiah Royce, William James, John Dewey, George Santayanna, and C. S. Peirce, all of them among the most distinguished American philosophers. In England T. H. Green, Edward Caird, F. H. Bradley, William Wallace, John McTaggart, G. E. Moore and Bertrand Russell are only a few of the many outstanding philosophers of the period. Their works are always sought after,

THE QUEST OF THE HISTORICAL JESUS

A CRITICAL STUDY OF ITS PROGRESS

FROM REIMARUS TO WREDE

BY

ALBERT SCHWEITZER

PRIVATDOZENT IN NEW TESTAMENT STUDIES IN THE UNIVERSITY OF STRASSBURG

TRANSLATED BY

W. MONTGOMERY, B.A., B.D.

WITH A PREFACE BY

F. C. BURKITT, M.A., D.D.

NORRISIAN PROFESSOR OF DIVINITY IN THE UNIVERSITY OF CAMBRIDGE

LONDON

ADAM AND CHARLES BLACK

1910

especially in first edition, but none more so than Russell. In complete contrast to the proliferation of Russell's books and pamphlets stand the three volumes of the *Works of T. H. Green* published posthumously between 1885 and 1888 and edited with a memoir by R. L. Nettleship. These are scarce and always in demand, as is the two-volume *Statement and Inference*, 1926, which contains the unpublished works of John Cook Wilson (1849–1905).

The Idealist philosophy dominant in the early years of the century eventually failed to sustain itself and virtually disappeared under the rising tide of linguistic philosophy. There are signs that there is a reassessment of some of these Idealist philosophers John McTaggart Ellis McTaggart must surely be recognised as one of the truly great British philosophers. His works are always in demand. His major work is *The Nature of Existence,* two volumes, 1921. There is another work, published in 1906, *Some Dogmas of Religion,* which has under the table of contents a brief outline of the argument of the whole work chapter by chapter. The following outline

argument is of the concluding chapter and is very striking as it gives a glimpse of the seriousness of purpose and the excitement of philosophical inquiry at its best.

Sect	CONCLUSION
241.	The result of our inquiries has been almost entirely negative. This is to be expected.
242.	No religion is justifiable unless it is based on metaphysics. This involves that religion is justified for few people.
243.	But this would not prevent the good in which religion believes being true.
244.	And some results of the loss of religion would not be undesirable.
245.	And the extent to which it would be lost may be exaggerated.
246.	Still, the result is tragical.
247.	But that does not disprove it.

For the collector interested in the philosophy of religion and philosophical theology a collection of the Gifford lectures would contain most of the important work in that area from the late 1880s up to the present. The Gifford lectures are delivered at the Scottish Universities under a foundation left by Lord Gifford. The lectures for the most part have been of great distinction and often form the major work of a particular philosopher or theologian. It would not be possible to mention them all but they include *The World and the Individual* by Josiah Royce, two volumes, 1900, and William James' *Varieties of Religious Experience* both of which have been mentioned earlier. In 1918 *The Philosophy of Plotinus* by W. R. Inge appeared, and in 1920 *Space, Time and Deity,* two volumes by that now much neglected but important philosopher Samuel Alexander. In 1929 was published A. N. Whitehead's seminal work *Process and Reality.* The list goes on and on and many of the major continental thinkers have delivered important series of lectures, Karl Barth in 1938, Gabriel Marcel in 1949–50, Rudolf Bultmann in 1955.

Clearly there are other important books which are always being sought by collectors such as *The Natural and the Supernatural,* 1931, by John Oman, and F. R. Tennants' two-volume *Philosophical Theology,* 1928, which was at one time a standard work. Two important but unjustifiably neglected works, and ones which are difficult to find are G. T. Ladd's *The Philosophy of Religion* two volumes, 1906, (Ladd was professor of philosophy at Yale), and *Studies in the Philosophy of Religion* by A. A. Bowman, two volumes, 1938, edited with a memorial introduction by Norman Kemp Smith.

Returning to the nineteenth century we enter areas so rich in material for the collector and student. Innumerable controversies raged, most of them now long forgotten. So many research projects now relate to these events that in ten years any interesting nineteenth-century material may be extremely hard to find. We have seen over the past fifteen years a quite remarkable development of studies into the Tractarian and Oxford Movement and J. H. Newman in particular; this interest has been world wide, and there are constant requests for all of Newman's works, requests which are becoming more and more difficult to fulfill. Sets of *Tracts for the Times,* 1833–41, are also elusive, and unfortunately some sets lack the last volume containing Newman's famous Tract 90, no doubt kept by the owner as being the most famous. It is well worth while building the set one volume at a time rather than waiting to find a full set. W. G. Ward's *The Ideal of a Christian Church,* 1844, is very hard to find, as are most of his works. On the other hand, works by E. B. Pusey are still to be found. Early works by minor figures such as T. W. Allies are scarce. A few years ago biographies and autobiographies of nineteenth century ecclesiastics were plentiful in most bookshops, but now these are rapidly disappearing, and it is unusual to see more than a copy a year of J. Fowler's life of that curious and interesting figure *Richard Waldo Sibthorp* (1880), or of the *Autobiography of Isaac Williams* edited by Sir George Prevost in 1892, or later again the *Life and letters of Ambrose Phillipps de Lisle* by E. S. Purcell, two volumes 1900. The best opportunities in collecting biographies are for those outside the main stream of nineteenth-century theology, the local preacher, the Quaker, Unitarian and other denominational lives. In them there is to be found the most revealing picture of the Church of the period and how it responded at a local level to some of the great theological debates as well as to changing social conditions.

From the sixteenth century, to the last quarter of the nineteenth the pamphlet and tract gauged the temperature and feelings of the times, and in many instances they reflect the development from week to week of particular debates. This is nowhere more evident than in the nineteenth century. One of the real opportunities for the collector lies in this area. There are still many pamphlets about and they are sold very cheaply. With patience very interesting collections can be made. In the last year I have had through my hands over forty of the pamphlets relating to the very important but now half forgotten Gorham controversy which was at its height about 1850. There were more pamphlets of a polemical nature between Anglicans and Roman Catholics than of any other single type. There was a constant and increasing flow of material throughout the whole century, much of it vitriolic. Reading and handling these pamphlets one can only be amazed that such fury and panic could be roused over what appear incredibly minor matters; on the other hand they convey a most distinct impression of vitality, of men passionately concerned for their religious beliefs. How extremely dull the twentieth century will appear in comparison.

The Churches, as well as being torn by theological debates, also had to come to terms with external movements of every description, in particular the great expansion of industrialization. This caused constant examination of the true function of the church. One of the responses was the 'Christian Socialist' movement whose main figures were F. D. Maurice, J. M. Ludlow and Charles Kingsley. Their more practical efforts, made in the late 1840s and early 1850s included the publication of a short lived penny magazine called *Politics for the People*. Another journal was started in 1850 under Ludlow's editorship called *The Christian Socialist* and both these publications are very scarce collector's items. However it is still possible to find early copies of Kingsley's novel *Alton Locke* which is one of the best sources for understanding what the 'Christian Socialist' hoped for and was fighting against. The movement developed along different avenues after 1855 with the development of the Working Men's College. This particular venture failed, but, despite the establishment's opposition to it, its influence was lasting.

A major cause of disquiet was the publication of the evolutionary theories of Charles Darwin. There are still many interesting books and pamphlets to be found relating to this debate. The small pamphlet illustrated is an example of a minister attempting a practical application of the argument from design in an attempt to disprove and ridicule evolutionary theory. In 1830, many

THE

TESTIMONY OF A DEWDROP TO ITS CREATOR.

WHAT IT CAN TELL US; AND WHAT IT CANNOT TELL.

WITH

SOME OBSERVATIONS ON THE PHILOSOPHIES AKIN TO ATHEISM OF THE PRESENT DAY.

BY

H. NOEL, M.A.

LONDON:
JAMES NISBET & CO., 21 BERNERS STREET.
MDCCCLXXXIII.

Above: *title page of a pamphlet attempting to refute Darwin's theory of evolution.*

years before the Darwinian theories caused such a storm in theological circles, the 'Bridgewater Treatises' had been published. Lord Bridgewater left the very substantial sum of £10,000 to be spent on a theological work which should illustrate the 'Power, Wisdom, and Goodness of God, as manifested in the Creation.' In his will Lord Bridgewater added that 1,000 copies of the work should be printed. He also suggested a few ideas for discussion as instances of the creative power of God: 'the variety and formation of God's creatures in the animal vegetable and mineral Kingdoms; the effect of digestion, and thereby of conversions; the construction of the hand of man . . .'

The trustees took the suggestions literally and the end results are some of the more weird sounding titles to be found in the whole field of natural theology, for instance Sir Charles Bell's *The Hand: its mechanism and vital endowments, as evincing Design.* Medically this is still a classic text; as a theological work it is just curious. The

last of the 'Bridgewater treatises' is the most strange-sounding of all and not just in its relation to natural theology: it was written by William Prout and titled *On Chemistry, Meteorology, and the Function of Digestion.* The Bridgewater Treatises, despite their anomalous position in regard to theology are nevertheless much sought after. In the last few years certain of the scientific treatises have fetched high prices in first editions.

The Ritualist controversies of the 1850s and 1860s now seem some of the more absurd episodes in the history of the century but at the time there were no issues more bitterly fought over or more divisive. Traditional Anglican churches had played down any forms of complex ritual and ornate decoration either in the church or around the altar in particular. The Roman Catholic churches, altars and ceremonies were just the opposite. It is probably for this reason alone that there was such a strong reaction when attempts were made to enliven by ornamentation and dress the churches and ministers of the Church of England. Nothing captures the aspirations of the ritualists better than the illustrated frontispiece of F. G. Lee's edition, 1865, of the *Directorium*

Frontispiece to the Directorium Anglicanum.

THE · HOLY · EUCHARIST·

Anglicanum. Here is a feast of every permissable piece of ecclesiastical finery and ornamentation. But as well as illustrating the Ritualist ideal, it also reflects the fussy attention to details for which the movement was justifiably criticised. Pusey and the Ritualists were interested in ornament and ritual not for its own sake but as a means of rekindling religious life. Many of them were foremost in the fields of missionary work in the most deprived areas.

From the whole great wealth of material to be found relating to this controversy, I will select one or two passages from a now long forgotten little book published in Bristol in 1888 called *The Church Goer*. It is a record of life in some West Country churches from the 1850s to 1880s. The writer records how a friend likes an 'ugly church' because he knows the 'ritualists have not been there playing their pranks'. In another church the writer describes the consternation and fury when the parson introduced an intoned 'Amen' at the end of the prayers. As the service progressed the half dozen 'Ritualists' remained standing and intoned 'Amen'. The writer expressed his personal predicament and his compromise:

> 'If I stand up they will call me "high", if I sit down, "low" and high and low are literal terms judging from the postures of the parties; yet I consider myself neither one nor the other but a rare mean between both. Such is my vanity! Mine was the difficulty of a moderate man, a situation which a person who tries to be sensible will sometimes find himself in. There was no via media here, but a crooked position between erect and sitting—an attitude of almost suspended animation, which, if not ridiculous, is certainly uncomfortable. Yet it was all the physical demonstration left to me; and, by way of compromise, I bent myself as nearly as possible to an angle of 45°. I was thus driven to a mathematical illustration of my own peculiar and intermediate school of theology.'

The seventeenth and eighteenth centuries, like the nineteenth century, still provide a wealth of pamphlets and tracts for the collector. During this time the pamphlet was the universal medium for most controversial matters, it was the age of the pamphlet shops which ultimately were superseded by the newspaper. Many of the pamphlets were printed sermons. The word sermon now

has rather a poor dull image, but in the seventeenth and eighteenth centuries they had a much greater influence, the 'Fast Sermons' preached between 1642 and 1649 being perhaps the most crucial of all. H. Trevor Roper says of these that on certain occasions they prepared 'The way for dramatic episodes. They would foretell the death first of Strafford, then Laud; declare the Civil War; initiate the inconoclastic programme; and finally, they would announce the most dramatic, most revolutionary gesture of all; the execution of the King himself'.

It is still possible to buy sermons of this period quite cheaply. Among the most interesting are the funeral sermons, many of them forming valuable, even unique, sources of historical material. Some also are highly polished literary works, or are visually attractive with intentionally quaint titles such as the 1659 *Divine Arithmatic, or The Right Art of Numbering Our Days*. The seventeenth century was the golden age of the sermon, the period of Donne, Taylor, Baxter, and Barrow. John Evelyn and Samuel Pepys were indefatigable church goers and listened to a great variety of preachers and they recorded impression in their Diaries. The popularity of the sermon extended well into the

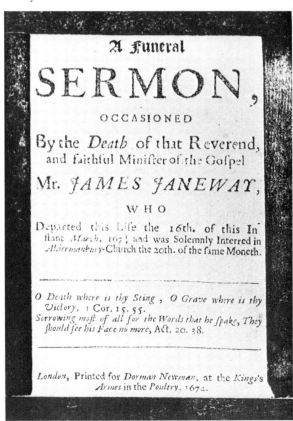

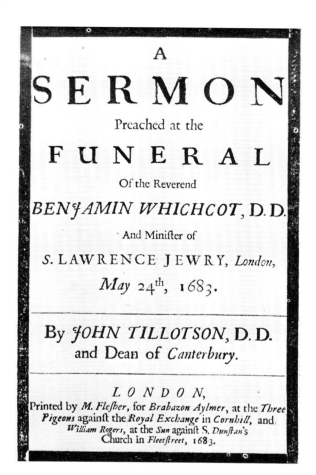

A
SERMON
Preached at the
FUNERAL
Of the Reverend
BENJAMIN WHICHCOT, D.D.

· And Minister of ·

S. LAWRENCE JEWRY, *London*,
May 24th, 1683.

By JOHN TILLOTSON, D.D.
and Dean of *Canterbury.*

LONDON,

Printed by *M. Flesher*, for *Brabazon Aylmer*, at the *Three Pigeons* against the *Royal Exchange* in *Cornhill*, and *William Rogers*, at the *Sun* against S. *Dunstan's* Church in *Fleetstreet*, 1683.

Title pages from two seventeenth-century sermons preached at funerals.

eighteenth century. For many years this was the backbone of the book trade. Lawrence Sterne reckoned in the 1760s that two volumes of sermons would earn him twice as much as he earned from good sales of *Tristram Shandy.*

Generally the works most sought after are those by the Puritans from the middle of the sixteenth to the mid seventeenth century. There is still quite a wide selection of books on the market but the important works are now becoming very expensive. It is difficult to envisage a worthwhile collection of sixteenth-century books being developed without very considerable expenditure. But from the middle of the seventeenth century onwards the field is still wide open for the collector in the general run of antiquarian books, although as in all periods there are plenty of very rare and expensive books.

In publishing and bookselling there are always accidents of fate or design which make certain books rare or worthy of particular note to the collector, and these accidents happen as much

now as in earlier centuries, for example a number of books unfortunately get thrown away because they are thought to be odd volumes of a set. Volume one of C. N. Shutte's life of Bishop Phillpots and volume one of J. G. Frazer's *The Worship of Nature,* are examples of 'volume one all published' the works never being completed. Phillpots served an injunction on Shutte preventing the completion of the work. Frazer hoped to finish his work, but never managed to. Likewise Bertrand Russell's *Principles of Mathematics,* volume one, 1903; volume two never appeared, although in 1910–13 there appeared his and A. N. Whitehead's *Principia Mathematica.* In contrast to these there is another sort of work that looks complete but is not. An example of this is one of the most famous and controversial works published in England in the nineteenth century; Richard Hurrell Froude's *Remains* edited by J. B. Morley. Two volumes were published in 1838 and two more in 1839. The title page of volume one describes the work as being in 'two volumes'. The full set is very scarce and expensive, although it was volume one that caused the controversy and is well worth having on its own.

There is a further group of books which once published are withdrawn or bought in. This happened with Ronald Knox's new edition of the *Manual of Prayers.* The work was published in 1942 with the full authorisation of the entire Roman Catholic Hierarchy. In six months the work was withdrawn; as far as one can see as a result of some slightly devious ecclesiastical politics. It is now quite scarce.

It would be possible to write a book on various unusual or curious books but space does not allow it within this chapter, which must be concluded with a short list of useful bibliographical works starting with W. T. Lowndes *Bibliographers Manual of English Literature* revised by H. G. Bohn in six volumes, a standard and very useful work as is James Darling's *Cyclopedia Bibliographica A Manual of Theological and General Literature,* two volumes 1859. Perhaps the best of the general works is S. A. Allibone's *Dictionary of English Literature and British and American Authors,* three volumes. The essential reference for the Bible collector is Darlow and Moule's *Historical Catalogue of the Printed Editions of the Holy Scripture,* in four volumes published in 1903. In 1968 the volumes dealing with English Bibles was revised and expanded by A. S. Herbert. For American imprints *The English Bible in*

America edited by Margaret T. Mills, revised edition 1962, should be consulted. A useful guide to the full sets of works such as the *Parker Society* and *Camden Society* publications will be found in *Texts and Calanders, an Analytical Guide to Serial Publications,* by E. L. C. Mullins, 1958. Useful for patristic studies are the volumes of Johannes Quasten's *Patrology,* where he lists all the critical editions, their translations, and monographs on them. Valuable books for information on Roman Catholic writers and their works, are Joseph Gillow's *A Literary and Biographical History and Bibliographical Dictionary of the English Catholics from the Breech with Rome, in 1534, to the Present Time,* five volumes 1885, and John Kirk's *Biographies of English Catholics 1700–1800,* published in 1909.

The standard books for listing early works are A. W. Pollard and G. R. Redgrave *A Short-Title Catalogue of Books printed in England, Scotland and Ireland, and of English Books Printed Abroad, 1475–1640,* and the *Short-Title Catalogue of Books Printed in England, Scotland, Ireland, Wales and British America and other English Books Printed in other Countries 1641–1700,* compiled by Donald Wing in three volumes.

For details about the early printers a book to consult is *A Dictionary of Printers and Booksellers in England, Scotland, and Ireland and of Foreign printers of English Books 1557–1640,* edited by R. B. McKerrow, reprinted in 1968. For identifying the obscure and unknown the standard work is Halkett and Laing, *Dictionary of Anonymous and Pseudonymous English Literature* in twelve volumes. A work of a very different nature to those mentioned is C. H. Spurgeon's *Commenting and Commentaries* reprinted 1969. The book contains his pithy assessments of over 4,000 commentaries and expositions on the Bible. The book seems to be standard for all those enthusiastic students and collectors of books of an evangelical tendency.

Two seventeenth-century anti-catholic pamphlets.

Travel and Topography

MOST bookshops have a section labelled 'Travel and Topography', but, to the experienced collector or dealer, the two terms have markedly different connotations. 'Travel' implies the discovery of new territories—the 'voyages' of the great explorers. The most expensive books in this category were the direct outcome of major journeys sponsored either by governments or privately—full-scale affairs complete with an artist to provide visual evidence of the expedition's achievements to its backers. Rare and beautiful works like Lord Kingsborough's *Antiquities of Mexico* (1830), Captain James Cook's *An Account of a Voyage Round the World* (1773), Mark Catesby's *The Natural History of Carolina, Florida and the Bahama Islands* (two volumes, 1731 and 1743) and Daniels' *Oriental Travels*, for instance, provide ample evidence of the scope and dynamism of Britain's pre-industrial trading empire.

'Topography' is the delineation of a particular locality—whether it be parish or continent—and often has, for the academic collector, a close association with genealogy. Indeed, the American bookseller, Goodspeed's of Boston, which owes much of its reputation to a distinguished connection with the scholars of Harvard, has made a speciality of these two related disciplines. In its conventional application, however, 'topography' is an elastic term, encompassing the valuable works of sixteenth and seventeenth century surveyors and gazetteers, numerous substantial town and county histories from the eighteenth and nineteenth centuries, slim volumes of local history recorded by conscientious nineteenth century clergymen, the proceedings of local history societies, local descriptions furnished by travellers all over the world, and, ultimately, all literature and ephemera linked to a specific area.

Because there is a wealth of material in the field, and because even the most casual book-buyer can be expected to evince an interest in his own district, travel and topography are the

'*A Maori Indian, March 1770 New Zealand*', an illustration from An Account of the Voyages undertaken by order of his present Majesty for making Discoveries in the Southern Hemisphere, '*successively performed by Commodore Byron, Capt. Carteret and Capt. Cook in the Dolphin, the Swallow and the Endeavour, printed for W. Strahan; and T. Cadell in the Strand, 1773*'.

mainstay of the second-hand book trade throughout the world. There is, therefore, a degree of expertise in the trade which makes bargains difficult to find, while, generally speaking, it is not worth buying books in poor condition, as they represent a risky trade-in proposition. In some areas of book collecting a theme, once established, will begin to turn up relatively obscure works, but the market for travel and topography books, which are, in any case, rather obviously classifiable, has been so much exploited that some

Above: 'The Ribbon Snake and Winter's Bark', from Volume II of The Natural History of Carolina, Florida and the Bahama Islands; 'containing figures of Birds, Beasts, Fishes, Serpents, Insects, and Plants: particularly the Forest-trees, shrubs & other plants, not hitherto described or very incorrectly figured by Authors' by Mark Catesby (two volumes, 1731 and 1743). Right: title page of Paesi Novamente Retrovati.

ingenuity is required if a rich new vein is to be discovered. It might be rewarding to adopt the approach of Dr Andrew Osborne, who, over the last 15 years, has collected some 3,000 books written by Australians living in America. His collection, now in the possession of McMaster University Library in Ontario, vividly illustrates many hitherto unsuspected connections between two countries at remarkably similar stages of development, and includes the stories of those transportees who were able to jump ship in Sydney Harbour and swim to an American vessel, of the fugitive who rose to be a Confederate general and of the Melbourne gold-miners who joined the California Rush of 1849. One of Australia's most famous convict novels, John Mitchell's Gaol Journal, incidentally, first appeared in the New York Herald in 1861. Dr Osborne's collection is an excellent example of the way in which a new theme can unite a large number of neglected books into a coherent and

instructive whole. Many of the volumes were acquired very cheaply, but took on a new value when placed in their proper context.

Travel books containing the first systematic accounts of newly explored regions inevitably command the best prices. These prime texts begin with the first printed version of Marco Polo's journals, published in Nuremberg in 1477. The first collection of voyages was the *Paesi Novamente Retrovati*, compiled by Francanzano da Montalbaddo and published in 1507. This work, which contains accounts of all three of Columbus's voyages, the Pinzon brothers' expedition and the third voyage of Amerigo Vespucci, is the first detailed record of the New Worlds of the West, the far South and the East.

The *Decades* of the Spaniard Pietro Martire Anghierra, published over nine years from 1511, continued and consolidated the authoritative catalogue of exploration. The author was a member of the Council of the Indies, the official directorate of Spanish exploration, and was personally acquainted with Columbus and Vespucci. Parts of it were translated into English in 1555 by Richard Eden as *The Decades of the Newe World, or West India,* which was instrumental in

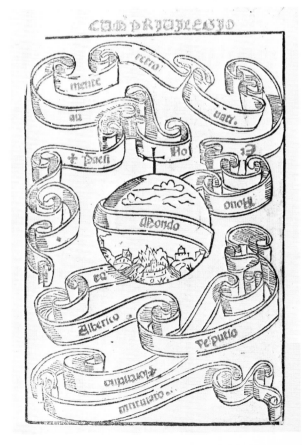

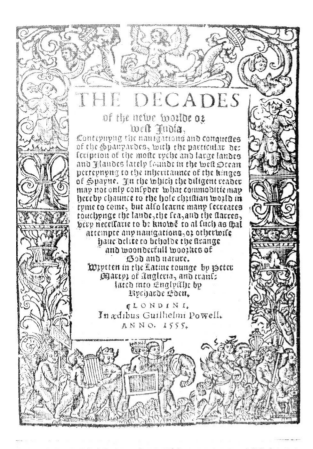

firing England's own territorial ambitions. In 1577 the posthumous publication of *The History of Travayle in the West and East Indies and other Countreys . . . with a Discourse on the Northwest Passage . . . Augmented and finished by Richard Willes* offered an abridged translation of further sections of Martyr's *Decades* with a number of new narratives. The first account of Magellan's rounding of Cape Horn, *Le Voyage et Navigation faict par les Espaignols des Isles de Mollucques,* appeared in 1525 in Paris. As the pace of exploration quickened, the foundation texts were superseded by a series of monumental compilations:

Left: engraved frontispiece to The Decades of the Newe World or West India *by Richard Eden (1555). Below: from* The History of Travayle in the West and East Indies and other countreys lying either way, towards the fruitful and rich Moluccas 'as Moscovia, Persia, Arabia, Syria, AEgypte, Ethiopia, Guinea, China in Cathayo and Giapan: With a discourse of the Northwest Passage. Gathered in part, and done into Englyshe by Richard Eden. Newly set in order, augmented, and finished by Richard Willes. Imprinted at London by Richard Iugge' *(1577).*

---

rounde about the worlde.   456   *What they sayled dayly.*

they sayled dayly betweene l.lx.to.lxx.leagues . So that in fine, if God of his mercy had not gyuen them good weather, it was necessary that in this so great a sea, they should all haue dyed for hunger . Which neuerthelesse they eſcaped ſo hardly, that it may be doubted whether euer the lyke viage may be attempted with ſo good ſucceſſe . They conſidered in this Nauigation that the pole *Antartike,* hath no notable ſtarre, after the ſorte of the pole *Artike.* But they ſawe many ſtarres geathered togeather, which are lyke two cloudes, one ſeparate a little from an other, & ſome-what darke in the myddeſt. Betweene theſe, are two ſtarres, not very byg, nor much ſhynyng, which moue a little: and theſe two are the pole *Antartike.* The needell of their compaſſe varied ſom-what, and turned euer towarde the pole *Artike,* neuertheleſſe, had no ſuche force, as when it is in theſe partes of the pole *Artike:* Inſomuch that it was neceſſarie to helpe the needle with the lode ſtone (commonly called the Adamant) before they coulde ſayle therewith, bycauſe it moued not, as it doeth when it is in theſe our partes . When they were in the myddeſt of the gulfe, they ſawe a croſſe of fyue cleare ſtarres, directly towarde the Weſte, and of equall diſtance the one from the other.

The ſtarres about the South pole.

The needle of the compaſſe.

The lode ſtone.

Kkk.iiii.   The

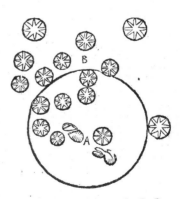

The viages of the Spanyardes
The order of the ſtarres about the pole An-tartike, ſome haue figured in this maner.

A. The pole Antartike.   B. The Croſſe.

The Equinoc-tiall line.   In theſe dayes they ſayled betweene the Weſt and South, ſo farre that they approched to the Equinoctiall lyne, and were in longitude from the place from whence they firſt departed, a hundred and twentie degrees . In this courſe they ſayled by two Ilandes of exceedyng heyght, whereof the one named Ci-panghu, is twentie degrees from the pole *Antartike:* and the o-ther named Sumdit, fyftiene degrees. When they were paſſe the Equinoctiall line, they ſayled betweene the Weſt & Southweſt, at the quarter of the Weſt, towarde the Southweſt more then a C leagues, changing their ſayles to the quarter of the Southweſt, vntyll they came to the thirtiene degrees aboue the Equinoctiall towarde the pole *Artyke,* intending as much as were poſſible, to approche

The Ilands of Cipanghu and Sumdit.

---

the viage of the Spaynar ... a ... the world from Asia ...
... and america ...

Jo: Jenman

506

THE THIRD AND LAST PART OF THE
principall Nauigations and Discoueries of the English nation
made to the West, Northwest, and Southwest parts of the world, with
the Letters, Priuileges, Discourses, Obscurations, and other
necessarie thinges concerning the same.

The voyage of Madoc the sonne of Owen Gwyneth Prince of Northwales,
to the West Indies, in the yeere 1170: taken out of the hi-
storie of Wales, lately published by M. Dauid
Powel Doctor of Diuinitie.

Page 506 of the third part of The Principall Navigations Voiages and Discoveries of the English Nation *'made by sea or over Land, to the most remote and further distant Quarters of the Earth at any time within the compass of these 1500 yeares' by Richard Hakluyt (1589).*

Della Navigationi et Viaggi by Giovanni Battista Ramusio, first published in Venice in three parts (1550, 1556 and 1559), related the discoveries of Cortez and Cartier's first voyage to Canada, and was reprinted many times; Richard Hakluyt's *Principall Navigations, Voiages and Discoveries of the English Nation* (1589) was expanded into three volumes and published as *Principall Navigations, Voiages Traffiques, and Discoveries* in 1598, 1599 and 1600. Dr Samuel Purchas's massive five-volume updating of Hakluyt appeared between 1624 and 1626 as *Hakluytus Posthumus or Purchas His Pilgrimes. Contayning a History of the World in Sea Voyages, and land-Travells by Englishmen and others.*

These seminal works command prices commensurate with their rarity and historical importance, but any collector would be well-advised to search for nineteenth and twentieth century reprints or facsimiles—more likely to be selections than complete texts—to give his library some flavour of the epic period of exploration The Hakluyt Society in England and the Cortes Society in America have published a number of scholarly and accurate re-editions.

Travel literature of the eighteenth century reached its peak with the meticulous and finely-illustrated accounts of the circumnavigators George, Lord Anson and Captain James Cook. Anson's voyage, made from 1740 to 1744, is recorded in *A Voyage Round the World* (1748, London). Cook's accounts of his first, second and third voyages were published in nine volumes (including an atlas) in 1773, 1777 and 1784. Although eighteenth century illustrated travel books will probably be beyond the resources of the new collector, there are many unillustrated books of the same period still available at reasonable prices. The books to look out for are abridged reprints of the great sixteenth and seventeenth century voyages, and, especially, English translations of continental works. Further opportunities lie in privately published journals and diaries—often produced as a memorial to some globe-trotting ancestor—many of which did not appear until the nineteenth or the twentieth century.

By the end of the eighteenth century, travellers and cartographers were beginning to strike deep into unexplored interiors. The first reliable book on Africa was written by the Scottish surgeon-explorer Mungo Park (1771–1806) as *Travels in the Interior Districts of Africa* (1799). Captain Meriwether Lewis and Lieutenants William Clark led the first east-west overland crossing of North America in 1804–1806, a pirated account of their expedition being published by Longman in London (1809). The first official version, now a £900 book, was *History of the Expedition under the command of Captains Lewis and Clark to the sources of the Missouri, thence across the Rocky Mountains, and down the river Columbia to the Pacific Ocean, Performed during the years 1804–5–6. Prepared for the press by Paul Allen,* two volumes (Philadelphia, 1814). The Australian counterpart of this book, *Two Expeditions into the Interior of South Australia* by Charles Sturt (1795–1869) came out in 1833. Sturt's book now fetches about £100—the same price as *First Footsteps in East Africa* (1856) by Sir Richard Burton (1821–1890). Burton, whose other most important book, *Abeokuta and the Cameroon Mountains,* two volumes (1863), may

Above: 'H. H. Ahmed Bin Abibakr, Amir of Harar', an illustration, originally in colour, by Edward Douglas, lithographed by M. & N. Hanhart, for First Footsteps in East Africa, or An Exploration of Harar by Richard F. Burton (Longman, Brown, Green & Longmans, London 1856). Above right: from How I Found Livingstone; 'Travels, Adventures and Discoveries in Central Africa; including Four Months Residence with Dr Livingstone' by Henry M. Stanley (Sampson Low, Martson, Low & Searle, London 1872). Below: a plate from chapter 25 of David Livingstone's Missionary Travels and Researches in South Africa (John Murray, London 1857).

still be found relatively cheaply, was the first non–Muslim to visit Mecca, a hazardous enter-

prise he recounts in Personal Narrative of a Pilgrimage to El-Medinah and Meccah, three volumes (1869). Another classic of African travel literature, A Journal of the Discovery of the Source of the Nile by John H. Speke (1827–1864) had been published six years earlier. In 1857 David Livingstone (1813–1873) published his Missionary Travels in South Africa, a book which was so popular at the time of its publication—there were more than 3000 copies in circulation at Mudie's Library in 1863—that it may still be obtained at a reasonable price. Otherwise, trailblazing literature is getting more expensive—My Travels to Africa (1886) by H. M. Stanley (1841–1904) has risen from £5 to £10 in the last decade, while his How I Found Livingstone (1872) is also pretty scarce.

BOAT CAPSIZED BY AN HIPPOPOTAMUS ROBBED OF HER YOUNG.

Frontispiece photograph of Admiral Robert E. Peary from The North Pole.

A travel book is always likely to fetch a higher price in the country it describes than elsewhere. Thus, *Antiquities of Mexico* has been sold, in Mexico City, for even more than the £8,000 it has reached at Sotheby's, while Ward's *Mexico*, an £80 book in England, sells for £110 there. Books on areas more recently opened up have generated a great deal of travel literature still obtainable at relatively modest cost, but prices are now beginning to rise, as in the case, for instance, of Frank Kingdon-Ward, a distinguished botanist who travelled extensively in China and Tibet. His first, and scarcest, work, *Land of the Blue Poppy* (1913) fetches up to £30 and his small, black undistinguished volume on Tibet, *The Riddle of the Tsangpo Gorges* (1926) £20. Kingdon-Ward's *From China to Hkamti Long* (1924) and *Plant Hunting on the Edge of the World* (1930) should still be available in first edition for £15 and £12 respectively.

In the nineteenth century, there was a tremendous increase in the number of books produced, with a corresponding surge of curiosity about strange lands over the sea. The expanding boundaries of the British Empire created communities of expatriate British all over the world—in Canada, South America, the Pacific, Australasia, the Far East, India and Africa, and the vast literature created in the constant bustle of Imperial business provides limitless opportunities for collecting. From the valiant efforts of the missionary societies to enlighten the heathen flowed an endless stream of educative material designed to instil English and Christianity into the subject races. Innumerable personal memoirs, journals and anecdotes were penned by the men and women who followed the flag, on every subject from table manners at Simla to the opium trade in China. In England, adventure stories for boys, by writers like G. A. Henty and R. M. Ballantyne, told stirring yarns of action and excitement in faraway places, while intrepid naturalist travellers extended the realms of scientific knowledge.

Among the most widely read nineteenth century books on India are *Major James Rennell and the Rise of Modern Geography* (1895) by C. R. Markham and *Forty One Years in India* (1897) by Field Marshal Sir Frederick Sleigh Roberts, both of which should still be fairly easy to find. The works of English scholars in India during the nineteenth century are much collected. Ferguson for instance, was at work on the definitive book on Himalayan architecture while Sleeman was

Of the explorers' chronicles to have appeared since the nineteenth century heyday of European colonisation, *The North Pole* (New York, 1910) by Admiral Robert E. Peary USN (1856–1920), *Scott's Last Expedition,* two volumes (1922), edited by Leonard Huxley and *The Ascent of Everest* (1953) by Sir John Hunt are obvious milestones, while the world's first single-handed circumnavigator, the American Captain Joshua Slocum (1844–1909) published his account as *Sailing Alone Round the World* in New York in 1900. A European curiosity, published in 1904, *Unexplored Spain* by Abel Chapman now sells for around £30. Today, with remote areas of the world—New Guinea and the Amazon basin, for example—still imperfectly known, the annals of exploration are by no means complete, and the vigilant collector may still expect to secure first accounts as they are published.

APPENDIX P.

BHILSA GANGS IN 1829.

Numbers.	List of the Men of Feringeea's Gang at Bhilsa, beginning of 1830.	Remarks by Captain W. H. Sleeman, General Superintendent.
1	Feringeea, son of Purusram,...	Approver.
2	Kurhoree, adopted of ditto, ...	Ditto.
3	Radhee, adopted of ditto, ...	Hung at Jubulpore 1830.
4	Hureea, adopted of Feringeea,	At large.
5	Gunesh, adopted of ditto, ...	Died in Jubulpore Jail.
6	Rumma, adopted of Purusram,	Approver.
7	Somere Sing, Rajpoot, ...	Died in Jubulpore Jail 1831.
8	Bhowannee Pershad,...............	Hung at Jubulpore 1830.
9	Murdun Kolee, ...	Ditto ditto ditto.
10	Beharee, son of Boodhoo, Brahmin, ...	Ditto ditto ditto.
11	Odeya, son of ditto, ditto, ...	Ditto ditto ditto.
12	Jhurha, son of Dureear, ditto,...	Ditto ditto ditto.
13	Pultooa, son of Dunna, Rajpoot,	Ditto ditto ditto.
14	Gunesh, son of Bhugwan, Brahmin, ...	Approver.
15	Kunhey, son of Laljoo, Mussulman, ...	Ditto.
16	Budhooa, son of Khamdee, ditto,	Died in Saugor Jail.
17	Purunna, son of Innent, Mussulman, ...	Hung at Saugor 1832.
18	Dulele, son of Saadut, ...	Died in Jubulpore Jail.
19	Bhujuna, son Punchum, Mussulman, ...	In Jubulpore Jail.
20	Purunna, son of Laljoo, Mussulman, ...	Died in Jubulpore Jail.
21	Mungul, son of Budhoo, Brahmin, ...	Approver.

Above: *a page from* Ramaseeana *or 'A Vocabulary of peculiar Language used by the Thugs, with an Introduction and Appendix description of the System pursued by that Fraternity and of the Measures which have been adopted by the Supreme Government of India for its Suppression' by W. H. Sleeman (G. H. Huttmann, Military Orphan Press, Calcutta 1836).*

writing his treatise on *The Vocabulary of the Thugees*. The intensification of British domination in India after the Indian Mutiny came at a time when the most beautiful colour plate books were being produced in England. Williamson's *Oriental Field Sports* was probably the most popular of the many books which sought to do justice to the colour and variety of the sub-continent. The large edition of the book now sells for £400 and the small £150. Such books, with others like *The Siege of Rangoon* by Marryat and Moore and Daniels' *Voyage to India* remain the jewels of any Indian collection. Huge numbers of books were produced during the nineteenth century on the subject of British military involvement in India, especially the small wars on the Afghan frontier and the Indian Mutiny,

but these are now rapidly disappearing from the bookshops. It is well worth searching through regimental archives and histories for mid-century Indian material, since in five years' time it is likely to be scarce. British periodicals, like the *Edinburgh Review* and the *Quarterly Review*, devoted considerable space to Indian affairs, and these can be found in single volumes at reasonable prices. (Odd, bound volumes of periodicals can often be a bargain: they are worth less than they would be as part of a complete set or run, but they may well contain material relating to the theme of your collection.) Although nobody has so far made a complete collection of the Anglo-Indian novel from Kipling to John Masters, the literature of the Raj since the end of the nineteenth century is fairly common. On the other hand, the earliest fruits of English scholarship in India are rising significantly in price—Sir William Jones's has gone from £40 to £250 over the last ten years.

As far as China and Japan are concerned, it is the Americans who, thanks to Captain Perry, have been responsible for the most prolific and significant literature, while the English have been inclined to write about these areas in a somewhat desultory and anecdotal fashion, as in Lady Brassey's *Voyage on the Sunbeam* (1878), a very

WANDERINGS

IN

SOUTH AMERICA,

THE

NORTH-WEST OF THE UNITED STATES,

And the Antilles,

IN THE YEARS 1812, 1816, 1820, AND 1824.

WITH ORIGINAL INSTRUCTIONS FOR THE PERFECT PRESERVATION OF BIRDS, &c.
FOR CABINETS OF NATURAL HISTORY.

BY CHARLES WATERTON, ESQ.

LONDON:
PRINTED FOR J. MAWMAN, LUDGATE-STREET.

1825.

popular book in the nineteenth century. In Central and South America, the British were extensive travellers during the nineteenth century. Waterton's *Wanderings in South America* (1821) is a classic of the age. The author, an expert taxidermist and an authority on retaining the colour in a toucan's beak, had a famous museum of monsters including a monkey stuffed to resemble a contemporary member of parliament.

Many of the great naturalists—Linnaeus, John Ray (1627–1705) and Francis Willughby (1635–1672), for example—have travelled widely, but the most sought-after author in the field of natural history remains Charles Darwin (1809–1882), whose first book, usually abbreviated to *Journal of Researches* or *The Voyage of the Beagle* was published in 1839. First editions of Darwin are currently fetching anything from £20 to £1000, so that it may be necessary to search out subsequent editions and reprints. The most important twentieth century writer in the travel/natural history category was Reginald Farrer who wrote what are probably the best books ever produced on botanical exploration in *Eaves of the World,* two volumes (1917) and its sequel *The Rainbow Bridge* (1921). Both are

A plate from Volume II of On the Eaves of the World *by Reginald Farrer (Edward Arnold, London 1917)'*

An illustration from African Game Trails: An Account of the African Wanderings of an American Hunter-Naturalist *with illustrations from photographs by Vernon Roosevelt and other members of the expedition (John Murray, London 1910).*

about the Himalayas, and good first editions fetch £25 and £15 respectively. Farrer plunged to his death, a rhododendron clasped in his hand, on an expedition to Upper Burma, a story told by his colleague and friend E. H. M. Cox in *Farrer's Last Journey* (1926), which is now rather scarce, a good copy selling for around £15.

American collectors, especially, should look out for the work of Ernest (Chinese) Wilson, whose *China, Mother of Gardens* and *A Naturalist in Western China* (1913) and other books fetch premium prices. Big game hunting is also a subject much in demand by book collectors. The United States president Theodore Roosevelt published an account of his experiences on African safaris in *African Game Trails* (1910), which now costs about £20. A keen self-publicist, Roosevelt was in the habit of signing a great number of books, so an autographed copy should not be considered a rarity. Almost all the books of Frederick Courteney Selous are valuable, his *African Nature Notes and Reminiscences,* for instance, currently fetching £20.

A vast body of travel literature was produced in the Victorian era by those dauntless ladies, who, despite the submissive role society had assigned their sex, set off for the wildest and remotest parts of the globe, enduring physical hardship, ridicule and, often, ill-health. Their work was not, at the time, taken seriously by the male establishment. The first proposal to admit ladies to the Royal Geographical Society was rejected out of hand in 1847, and later attempts met with the same fate. The Society did, in fact, give a medal to Lady Franklin in 1860, but this was in recognition of her providing the finance for a series of expeditions—she herself was no traveller. In 1892, however, the Society invited Isabella Bird to address them on her travels in Tibet. She snubbed them, choosing instead to address a society which admitted women. By November of that year the Royal Geographical Society had 15 women members, although legal action was subsequently taken to debar them, and it was not until 1913 that the business was finally settled. Isabella Bird was perhaps the most remarkable of the Victorian lady travellers. In 1872, at the age of 41, she set off for Australia on an 18-month tour to recover her health. After a few months, she became bored and sailed to the Sandwich Islands to begin an unparalleled travelling career. Usually alone, and in the most rigorous conditions, she remained on the move until her death in 1904. Her earlier books, *Six Months in the Sandwich Islands* (1875), *A Lady's Life in the Rocky Mountains* (1879), *Unbeaten Tracks in Japan* (1880) and *The Golden Chersonese* (1883) were largely put together from letters to her sister, sparkling and conversational. The last three of her seven books, written after the deaths of her husband and sister, are more sombre in tone, although *Journeys in Persia and Kurdistan* (1891), *Korea and her Neighbours* (1898) and *The Yangstze Valley and Beyond* (1899) all bear testi-

Illustration for the title page of A Lady's Life in the Rocky Mountains *by Isabella L. Bird (sometimes catalogued as Mrs J. F. Bishop).*

A photograph from Icebound Heights of the Mustagh: '*An Account of the two seasons of pioneer exploration and high climbing in the Baltistan Himalaya' by Fanny Bullock Workman and William Hunter Workman M.A. M.D. (Archibald Constable & Co., London 1908).*

mony to her indomitable spirit which, despite rheumatism, heart and lung trouble, kept her constantly engaged on hazardous exploration until her death in 1904. *Life of Isabella Bird* by Anna Stoddart was published in 1906.

The Victorian age produced a host of other women travellers, their exploits, perhaps, overshadowed by Isabella Bird's, but remarkable ladies nevertheless. Marianne North, the botanical illustrator whose work can be seen in the gallery named after her at Kew Gardens, travelled in North and South America, visited Japan, Singapore, Sarawak, Java and Ceylon, and, at the suggestion of Charles Darwin, toured a great deal of Australia and New Zealand. She published *Recollections of a Happy Life* in two volumes, edited by Mrs John Addington Symonds, in 1892, and *Further Recollections of a Happy Life* a year later. A zealous campaigner for women's rights, the American Fanny Bullock Workman, whose speciality was mountaineering, travelled almost as widely as Isabella Bird. She wrote *Algerian Memories* (1895), *Sketches Awheel in fin-de-siecle Iberia* (1897), *In the Ice World of The Himalayas* (1900), *Through Town and Jungle* (1904), *Icebound Heights of the Mustagh* (1908), *Peaks and Glaciers of Mun Kun* (1909), *The Call of the Snowy Hisper* (1910) and *Two Survivors in the Ice Wilds of the Eastern Karakoran* (1917).

Prominent among the other adventurous ladies of the period are Annie R. Taylor, Mrs Alec Tweedie, Isabella Robson, May French Sheldon, Annie Hore, Mary Kingsley and Kate Marsden. Some work has been done on the subject of these writers, but a great deal more remains to be done. Their works are still available, sometimes at bargain prices because the impressive achievements they record have never been properly recognised. Works by or about these ladies to look out for include *The Victorian Mountaineers* (1953) by Ronald Clark, *The Explorers* (1962) by G. R. Crone, *Hints to Lady Travellers* (1889) by Lillian Campbell Davidon, *A Summer Ride in Western Tibet* (1906) by Jame Duncan, *Life of Mary Kingsley* (1932) by Stephen Gwynne, *To Lake Tanganyika in a Bath Chair* (1886) by Annie Hore, *Mary Kingsley* (1957) by Cecil Howard, *The Life of Kate Marsden* (1895) by Henry Johnson, *Travels in West Africa* (1897) by Mary Kingsley, *On Sledge and Horseback to Outcast Siberian Lepers* (1893) by Kate Marsden, *Victorian Lady Travellers* (1965) by Dorothy Middleton, *Two Lady Missionaries in Tibet* (1909) by Isabella Robson, *Through Finland in Carts* (1898) by Mrs Alec Tweedie, *This is Your Home: a Portrait of Mary Kingsley* (1956) by Kathleen

Queen Victoria's recommendation for On Sledge and Horseback to Outcast Siberian Lepers *by Kate Marsden (The Record Press, London 1893).*

Balmoral Castle.
October 27 1892

Victoria R.I.

The Queen has taken a deep interest in the work undertaken by Miss Marsden amongst the lepers and desires to recommend her to the attention and consideration of any persons

EGYPT
PAINTED AND DESCRIBED
BY
R. TALBOT KELLY

LONDON
ADAM & CHARLES BLACK
1912

PARIS
AND ITS
ENVIRONS
WITH
ROUTES FROM LONDON TO PARIS

HANDBOOK FOR TRAVELLERS
BY
KARL BAEDEKER

WITH 66 MAPS AND PLANS
NINETEENTH REVISED EDITION

LEIPZIG: KARL BAEDEKER, PUBLISHER
LONDON: GEORGE ALLEN & UNWIN LTD., 40 MUSEUM ST., W.C. 1
NEW YORK: CHAS. SCRIBNER'S SONS, FIFTH AVE. AT 48TH ST.

1924

Wallace, and *India and Tibet* (1910) by Frances Younghusband.

Some bookmen seek to represent the whole of a continent, or, indeed, the world, through a series of publications from the same house—a type of collecting which falls somewhere between 'travel' and 'topography'. Most of such series were published as travel guides. Of these, Baedekers are by far the most popular, particularly in Germany where there are dealers who touch nothing else. Many Baedekers—the guides to Italy, Belgium, the Rhine and Switzerland, for example—are extremely common and very cheap, but Russia, a detailed handbook from Tzarist times, currently fetches £20. The guides to Egypt and Syria are so esteemed in the Middle East that they sell for several times their European prices, and Egyptian collectors are willing to part with £25 for the volume describing the Nile steam cruises. Other guides, like Murray's Handbooks and Black's Colour Handbooks are also beginning to rise in price: Black's *Egypt* and Belgium are very common, but *Moscow* and *China* sell for £10 and £6 respectively. In Britain there is still quite a demand for the *Highways and Byways* series, *Britain in Pictures* and the *Nooks and Corners* series.

The first great English topographical work was *Britannia* by William Camden. A survey of the English counties, with engraved maps, it was published, in Latin, in 1586, with six reprints by 1610. The seventh edition, which appeared in 1612, was the first English translation, by Philemon Holland. Several more editions, with improved maps, followed regularly until a new translation, by Richard Gough, was published in 1789, to be reprinted in 1806. The 1610 edition of Camden now sells for more than £500, while a good nineteenth century copy will probably be worth three figures.

American topography begins with the Columbus letter, *Epistola de Insulis nuper inventis* (Barcelona, 1493), of which only one first edition is known, continuing through extensive accounts of the New World written by a number of Spanish travellers, until the early English language portraits of colonial life like *A Generall Historie of Virginia* (1624) and *A Description of Newe England* (1616), both by the John Smith who married Pocohontas. First editions of these two books have been sold at recent auctions for £7500 and £2500 respectively. The first book printed in America was *The Whole Books of Psalmes,* commonly known as the Bay Psalm Book, produced in 1640 by the brothers Stephen and Matthew Daye, with their father Stephen, in Cambridge, Massachusetts under the auspices of the president of Harvard College.

The English and American town and county histories of the seventeenth, eighteenth and early nineteenth centuries are a rich source of topographical material. These surveys, generally with descriptions and illustrations of local antiquities, were often subscription books with the names of the sponsors printed at the beginning. The prices of such books vary greatly, according to the accuracy of the text and the number and quality of the engraved illustrations. Most of these books may be expected to fetch more than £30, but a good example will be worth significantly more. The enlarged, 1730 edition of *The Antiquities of Warwickshire* (1656) by William

An example of American Topography: the only known copy of the first account of Daniel Boone.

THE
ADVENTURES
OF
Colonel DANIEL BOON,
One of the firſt Settlers at KENTUCKE:
CONTAINING
The Wars with the Indians on the *Ohio,*
Yrom 1769 to 1783, and the firſt
Eſtabliſhment and Progreſs of the Set-
tlement on that River.

Written by the Colonel himſelf.

TO WHICH ARE ADDED,
A
NARRATIVE
OF THE
CAPTIVITY,
AND EXTRAORDINARY
ESCAPE
OF
MRS. FRANCIS SCOTT.
An Inhabitant of Waſhington-County Vir-
ginia; *who after the Murder. of her
Huſband and children, by the* Indians, *was
taken Priſoner by them; on the 29th of
June,* 1785.

NORWICH:
PRINTED BY JOHN TRUMBULL.
M,DCC,LXXXVI.

Dugdale, for instance, has been sold at auction for £150, and is likely to increase in value. Dugdale (1605–1686) was Garter King of Arms, and wrote many other books, including *The History of St Paul's Cathedral* (1658). The two-volume edition of 1730 was expanded from the original 854 page folio, and incorporates a series of splendid double page views.

The most rapidly appreciating topographical books in the English trade are the early nineteenth century local histories with steel engraved illustrations. Many of these have been pulled apart by dealers for the sake of the plates they contain. Richard Ackermann's illustrated histories of the great public schools and universities are, perhaps, the most famous books of this type, but a number of other works produced between 1820 and 1840 like Bally's *Hanoverian Scenery,* Allan and Wright's *Lancashire Illustrated,* and Bartlett's *The Holy Land* and *Canadian Scenery,* once moderately priced volumes available in most second hand bookshops, have now become scarce and valuable, sometimes selling for hundreds of pounds. Collectors of illustrated topographical books should bear in mind that views of towns tend to be worth much more than pictures of the countryside or country houses. It is essential to consult books of reference to make sure that a volume has a complete set of plates. The best work is in the three volume catalogue of the Abbey collection, but Shelton on Atlases and Tooley on colour plate books, for instance, provide a useful introduction. Collectors should also be aware that steel engraved books with the illustrations overlaid on thin paper are not nearly so valuable as those printed directly on the thick paper because the colouring is inferior.

Another nineteenth century development was the growth of local history and archaeological societies, which, often under the direction of the vicar, catalogued local antiquities and, in some cases, began the excavation of Roman and Celtic sites. The published proceedings of these societies can form the nucleus of a valuable local history collection. Although individual volumes can usually be picked up for a pound or two, complete sets can be very valuable. Thus, volumes 1–81 of the Transactions of the Cumberland and Westmoreland Local Historical Society now fetch about £350. Early numbers need not be the rarest—volumes produced in war time, or issues which were unexpectedly popular at the time of publication, can be most difficult to find.

The growth of interest in industrial archae-ology has created an enormous demand for nineteenth century trade catalogues, posters, railway timetables and other printed matter associated with Victorian technology, while the first telephone directory ever published was recently offered for sale in New York at 4000 dollars. Charles Wood of Woodstock, Connecticut, Blackwell's of Oxford and William Duck of Hastings are all specialists in technological literature, and, indeed, Mr Duck has recently sold a large collection of books on the subject of sewers.

Poetry and fiction have also enjoyed a major topographical boom, and even the work of major authors can be more expensive where there is a local connection. Robert Frost is especially collected in Vermont, Thomas Hardy's books fetch far more in the West of England than elsewhere, and the Brontes do well in the bookshops of Yorkshire. Collectors will find Lefevre's *Guide to the Regional Novels of the British Isles* useful, but even a minor book with a strong topographical emphasis will command a high price in its own area. Thus, Hesba Caine's *The Manxman,* which sells for a few pence on the mainland, is worth several pounds on the Isle of Man. Francis Brett Young's *The House Under the Water* fetches £4 in Radnorshire, but is of no interest anywhere else. 'Q' and Silas Hocking are greatly esteemed in Cornwall, W. Riley in Yorkshire, Allen Raine in Wales and Mrs Linnaeus Banks in Manchester. To a lesser extent, biography and minor poetry also increase in value through local association. The two volume biography of World War I general Sir Henry Wilson, who was assassinated in connection with the Ulster problem, sells for about £8 in Ireland, but next to nothing in England. First editions of the work of Bernard Barton, the Suffolk poet, and the Rev Hawker of Cornwall now fetch as much as £50 in their respective areas, Frances Nicholson is now in demand in Yorkshire and Macgonigall naturally sells for higher prices in Dundee than anywhere else.

For the collector of travel or topographical books, reference books — catalogues, bibliographies, checklists and chronologies—are a must. The books listed in bibliographies form the basis of price setting in the trade, so that a book not included in a list of sources can turn out to be a valuable find. Information about reprints of major texts can be found in the catalogue of a national library like the British Museum or the Library of Congress.

Children's Books

CHILDREN'S books form a huge and very important field of literature, which is instrumental in shaping minds, leaves long-lasting if not indelible impressions and, at its best, is of value to readers of almost any age. They are often the most beautifully written, the least self-conscious and the best illustrated books, as well as containing much that is of interest to the social historian.

Where, then, does the children's book begin? American collectors will doubtless point to their *New England Primer*, which probably began to make life just that bit less pleasant for New England schoolboys in the late seventeenth century. The earliest surviving copy is a single example. Printed in 1735, it was bought at an auction in 1893, for twelve cents, by a Pennsylvania teacher who sold it in 1903 for $2,500. The copy is now in the Huntington Library at San Marino, California. English collectors might get excited about Comenius's *Visible World* (1658), probably the first picture book used in schools. Collectors everywhere talk with longing about horn books, which were used for elementary teaching from the sixteenth to the early eighteenth century. A wooden back, shaped rather like a hand mirror, held a sheet of paper printed with the alphabet, numerals and the Lord's Prayer and covered with a thin translucent plate of horn. Horn books, though sturdy, were not things that people would have troubled to keep. Authentic examples are extremely rare and, because each one is different, they are comparatively easy to fake. If you are offered a 'genuine' seventeenth-century horn book at a modest price of $1,500, make a polite excuse unless you are an expert or a rich gambler.

But the *New England Primer, The Visible World,* horn books, catechisms and moral advice for the young, however interesting and quaint, were designed to cast the child in the rigid mould of its parents; they are books for children, not children's books. A children's book must be illustrated, if not with pictures then with fantasy, and it must supply the raw material for imagination. Some moralising and a ration of information are inevitable and can be accepted, but only when scope and stimulus for imagination are also provided. The book which sets out self-consciously to educate children more often indoctrinates them.

The earliest books which conform with this definition are the eighteenth-century chap books. A surprising number of these have survived. The comic books of their day, they were frowned upon in respectable homes. The chap books were produced by small printers and circulated in thousands by means of the pedlar's pack. By providing popular literature in a popular form, they contributed much to the survival of fairies, giants and all the better sorts of creature, including of course the dragon.

Among the best of the early chap books were those produced by John White of York. His *Jack and the Giants* and *Red Riding Hood* are good exciting stuff. However, the woodcuts

From an early chap-book, Jack and the Giants, *produced by John White of York.*

Lecture on Matter & Motion.

Above: *another John White chap-book,* Two Children in the Wood. Left: *frontispiece of John Newbery's* The Newtonian System of Philosophy, *'Adapted to the Capacities of young Gentlemen and Ladies'* (1761).

are crude, and White (like many of his contemporaries) did not hesitate to use the same wood block many times. To get as much mileage as possible out of them made sound business sense and was in the best traditions. Thus, Robin Hood pops up in *Two Children in the Wood.*

Probably the most important date in children's books is 1744, the year in which John Newbery began publishing juvenile books in London. His aim was to educate but he seems to have escaped the worst adult characteristics and his first book, *A Little Pretty Pocket Book,* was full of pictures of games and could be bought on its own for sixpence, with a ball or pincushion for eightpence. His books were entertaining and occasionally went so far as to mock the solemn adult world. In 1761, he published *The Newtonian System of Philosophy,* the substance of six lectures read to the Lilliputian Society by Tom Telescope . . . Newbery obviously cared about

Right: *William Blake's frontispiece for* Songs of Innocence.

FOR QUEEN AND KING

or the LOYAL 'PRENTICE

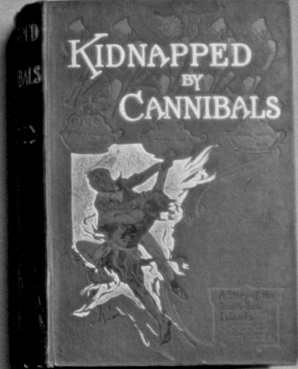

KIDNAPPED BY CANNIBALS

A Story of the South Sea Islands.

IN THE GRIP OF THE SPANIARD

FIRST IN THE FIELD

GEORGE MANVILLE FENN

those who would read his books. He had his blocks specially cut for each job and even used the occasional copper-plate engraving. His typography was clear and attractive and his books were covered in brightly coloured papers. The escape from oppressive morality, of which Newbery's work marks the beginning, was to be a long struggle that continues to the present day. The popularity of his books coincided happily with the start of Thomas Bewick's influential career.

The earliest books, produced long before the time of Gutenberg, had been printed from engraved wooden blocks. As printing developed, wood engraving became more and more sophisticated, reaching a high point in the sixteenth century with the work of Dürer. But in the seventeenth century, copper engraving began to develop and, by the eighteenth century, the art of wood engraving had declined until wood blocks were only considered fit for broadsides and children's books. The decline was reversed in 1779 with the publication of an edition of *Gay's Fables*, illustrated by a virtually unknown artist, Thomas Bewick. Bewick, born in 1753, was the son of a Northumberland farrier. At the age of fourteen he was apprenticed to a firm of engravers in Newcastle. He seemed destined to follow the main trade of his employers, engraving moulds for clay pipes and plates for coffins, but beauty was in his bones. In his *Memoir*, he speaks of leaving home, 'I can only say my heart was like to break, and as we passed away, I inwardly bade farewell to the whinny wilds, to Mickley Bank, to Stobcross Hill, to the water banks, the woods, to particular trees and even to the large hollow old elm . . .' His deep love of the countryside was to be reflected nostalgically in nearly all his work.

Although most of Bewick's work illustrated and redeemed serious adult books, an early commission had been for engravings to the *New Lottery Book of Birds and Beasts*, a charming children's book published in 1771. There, his pictures almost make a pleasant task of learning the alphabet. His later work includes the *General History of Quadrupeds*, his *History of British Birds* for Thomson's *Seasons* and Burns's *Poems*. These were fine books and his pictures would have

A wood-engraved tailpiece by Thomas Bewick.

interested children even if they had not begun to find their way into children's books, largely because of Bewick's fondness for the tailpiece. These whimsical decorations, scattered generously through all his books, exceed even his full-page topical engravings in beauty. They have appeared in countless children's books, officially and unofficially. *History of the Robins* by the horrifying Mrs Trimmer, a moralist of the first order, had some Bewick tailpieces in its thirteenth edition in 1821. In spite of its promising title, the book was a blatant piece of propaganda in which Mrs Trimmer attempted to make decorous children do kind things to creatures (persons understood) of the lower orders. Even Mrs Trimmer is saved by Bewick, whose engravings of robins, bird-nesters and country scenes give ample stimulation to the dullest imagination. But for each similar advance there was an opposite reaction. We find, particularly at the end of the eighteenth century, a definite move against the introduction of romance into children's literature. Richard Edgeworth, father of the novelist Maria, Maria herself and their friend Thomas Day, all of whom were admirable and fascinating characters, had developed theories, combining utopian idealism and moral realism and based on the philosophy of Rousseau. Romantic witches, fairies, giants and other interesting characters were classified as prejudicial nonsense. Even that paragon of initiative and self-reliance, Robinson Crusoe, was vaguely suspect as it was felt that his adventures might inspire an undue wanderlust.

Some of the major triumphs of the period can still be found occasionally, and are worth looking out for. *Original Stories* (1791) by Mary Wollstonecraft is illustrated by William Blake. The illustrations, though not as lively as those of *Songs of Innocence*, have a certain mystery. Blake

CHAP. XXIII.

Charity. — Shopping. — The diſtreſſed Stationer. — Miſchievous Conſequences of delaying Payment.

AS they walked in ſearch of a ſhop, they both determined to purchaſe pocket-books; but their friend deſired them not to ſpend all their money at once, as they would meet many objeΩs of charity in the numerous ſtreets of the metropolis. I do not wiſh you, ſhe continued, to relieve every beggar that you caſually meet; yet ſhould any one attraΩ your attention, obey the impulſe of your heart, which will lead you to pay them for exerciſing your compaſſion, and do not ſuffer the whiſpers of ſelfiſhneſs, that they may be impoſtors, to deter you. However, I would have you give but a trifle when you are not certain the diſtreſs is real, and reckon it given for pleaſure. I for my part would rather be deceived

With Reps moſt majeſtic the Snail did advance,
And he promis'd the gazers a minuet to dance:
But they all laugh'd ſo loud that he drew in his head,
And went in his own little chamber to bed.

Left: *a page from Chapter XXIII of* Original Stories from Real Life; *'with Conversations calculated to regulate affections, and form the mind to truth and goodness' by Mary Wollstonecraft (A New Edition, London 1796, printed for J. Johnson, No. 72 St Paul's Churchyard').* Above and above right: *two pages from* The Butterfly's Ball *'with the Grasshopper's Feast—London: printed for J. Harris, Corner of St Paul's Churchyard, Jan. 1st 1807'.* Right: *from 'The Travelling Companion' in* Hans Andersen's Fairy Tales *translated by Mrs H. B. Paull with original illustrations (Frederick Warne & Co., London 1897).*

was one of the first writers to call attention to the injustices of child labour. William Roscoe published an exquisite series of little books. The first, *The Butterfly's Ball*, set the pattern of fantasy and gaiety without any moralising. Published in 1807, it was very quickly followed by Mrs Dorset's *The Peacock at Home*, *The Lion's Masquerade* and many others. Mrs Dorset's two titles sold 40,000 copies each. They were illustrated by prominent artists like William Mulready and coloured, ironically enough, by a production line of children, each responsible for one colour.

At about this time, toy books in cleverly contrived cases began to appear. These were children's books in cases which were disguised as a large book, a miniature bookcase, a pirate's treasure chest and so on, in an interesting adaptation of the old idea of the travelling library. The books were attractively produced, and the case often gave an air of mystery. Early examples are rare and usually expensive, but the practice has been continued sporadically, and examples from the

late nineteenth or early twentieth century can occasionally be bought for under £50.

Children's books then entered a period of fairly rapid improvement which has continued almost uninterrupted to the present. In the 1840s, one of the founders of the Victoria & Albert Museum, Sir Henry Cole, working under the pseudonym, Felix Summerly, began a series of children's books which have often been hailed as a milestone in juvenile publishing. The concept was fine. The highest standards of typography; excellent paper and attractive bindings were used; the illustrators were nearly all members of the Royal Academy. This series, the *Home Treasury*, alas, was conspicuously lacking in imagination. Unfortunately, the defect became increasingly common—children's books which represented lavish expenditure in terms of production, illustration and text often contained little of the

Then, as ev'ning gave way to the shadows of night,
Their watchman, the Glow-worm, came out with his light.

quality production techniques were applied. Since this series, there have been many thousands of beautifully produced books. At their worst, these are rather patronising; at their best, they are fine examples of coordinated artistic efforts.

Generally speaking, however, this was a period of reaction against the aim of 'amusement with instruction'. A high point was reached with the first publication in English of the stories of the brothers Grimm. The Grimms' *German Popular Stories*, with George Cruikshank's illustrations, appeared in 1824. The beautifully presented tales of Jacob and Wilhelm Grimm represent the beginning of a scientific collection and study of folklore. The brothers adopted a systematic approach to collecting and painstaking analysis of their findings in order to amass an accurate record of folk tales. In 1846 the publication of *Wonderful Stories for Children*, the first English translation of Hans Christian Andersen, marked the firm establishment of fantasy in children's literature.

Fun and even naughtiness were actively encouraged in such books as *Holiday House* (1839) by Catherine Sinclair. But possibly the finest achievement was Edward Lear's *Book of Nonsense* (1846). This gentle, proud and humble, impossibly human person has perhaps done more for children and adults than any other author. What

Nevertheless they got safely to the boat, although considerably vexed and hurt; and the Quangle-Wangle's right

foot was so knocked about that he had to sit with his head in his slipper for at least a week.

charm and mystery of the many cheaper, less polished but more imaginative children's books. The *Home Treasury* is, however, important and worth collecting, if you can find these twelve volumes, the first children's books to which high

'*Violet, Slingsby, Guy and Lionel*' from Nonsense Songs, Stories, Botanies and Alphabets *by Edward Lear (Frederick Warne & Co., London 1871). Illustration to 'The Story of the Four Little Children who went round the world'.*

Edward Lear; above: 'The Dong with a Luminous Nose', from Laughable Lyrics: 'A Fourth Book of Nonsense Poems, Songs, Botany, Music &c. *(Frederick Warne & Co., London 1877).*
Below:

> 'There was a Young Lady whose chin
> Resembled the point of a pin;
> So she had it made sharp, and purchased a harp,
> And played several tunes with her chin.'

From The Book Of Nonsense *(Frederick Warne & Co., London 1846).*

is there which can excel the sublime nonsense of Mr Lear? His early career was spent in zoological and anatomical illustration. The fine ornithological work is very much sought after. In 1832, Lear came under the patronage of the Earl of Derby at Knowsley, and produced the magnificent plates for *The Knowsley Menagerie.* It is said that his *Book of Nonsense* was produced to amuse his patron's grandchildren. While they undoubtedly provided the stimulus, it seems as if nonsense became a very necessary safety valve for Lear, a prodigious and compulsive worker. In 1837, he left England to devote himself to the production of landscapes. Even in his early sixties he was able to do a six months' tour in India, sending home 560 drawings, nine sketch books and four journals. His compulsive work habits form only part of a personality whose many idiosyncracies found expression through his nonsense. And what superb stuff it is. Writing of his need for a regular income, he talks of asking for the position of 'Painter Laureate, and Grand Peripatetic Ass and Boshproducing Luminary'.

Lear's nonsense, while amusing, demonstrates a real sense of humanity, as well as an acute sense of the ridiculous. He points no morals and gives himself no airs. Perhaps his strength is best expressed in his own self-portrait:

> How pleasant to know Mr Lear!
> Who has written such volumes of stuff!
> Some think him ill-tempered and queer,
> But a few think him pleasant enough.
>
> His mind is concrete and fastidious,
> His nose is remarkably big;
> His visage is more or less hideous,
> His beard it resembles a wig.

> 'There was a Young Lady whose bonnet
> Came untied when the birds sate upon it;
> But she said, "I don't care! all the birds in the air
> Are welcome to sit on my bonnet."'

From The Book of Nonsense.

> 'There was an Old Person of Bangor
> Whose face was distorted with anger,
> He tore off his boots, and subsisted on roots,
> That borascible person of Bangor.'

From The Book of Nonsense.

I have loved him since I was seven, when I read, in the introduction to an omnibus of his nonsense, that he hated getting his toenails cut. First editions of his work are very rare. A collector may be lucky enough to stumble upon an unidentified copy; otherwise, when they appear, they are very expensive. Hundreds of editions have appeared, with illustrations by Lear or other artists. These could make up a collection in their own right, or form the basis for a more comprehensive collection representing the development of nonsense literature.

Earlier, and outside the realm of nonsense, there had been two great American writers: Washington Irving and James Fenimore Cooper. Irving's *Sketch Book*, which appeared in 1819, contained one of the earliest and best American fairy stories, *Rip Van Winkle*. Cooper's *The Last of the Mohicans* (1826) and *The Deerslayer* (1841) rapidly became popular on both sides of the Atlantic. Together with Irving's tale, these stories for older children were marked by the first romantic treatment of American folk lore and improved quality of expression in American children's books. In America, there also remained a strong tendency to inform. Samuel Goodrich, writing under the name of Peter Parley, churned out a regular flow of potted biography, history,

John Tenniel: 'The Cheshire-Cat and the Queen's Croquet Ground' from Alice's Adventures in Wonderland *by Lewis Carroll (Macmillan & Co., 1865).*

science, geography and natural history. His *Tales of Peter Parley about America* (1827) is a typical example. Fairly soon, there were several dozen Peter Parleys scribbling in Europe as well. Theirs were popular books, although they were generally very stodgy. The Rollo books, produced by Jacob Abbot, were a similar and even more popular series.

At the height of the fashion for Peter Parley and Rollo the first of a long tradition of very sentimental books appeared. Susan Warner's *The Wide, Wide World* and *Queechy*, both produced in the 1850s, were popular tear jerkers. They were closely followed by that terrible prig Elsie Dinsmore, introduced by Farquharson, writing under the pseudonym Martha Finlay, in 1868. Elsie became the heroine of twenty-six thoroughly sentimental volumes, and this is probably her only claim to fame.

Alice in Wonderland (1866) and *Alice through the Looking Glass* (1872), published in England, provided a foundation for the modern tradition of the fairy story. They are also responsible for the final and complete victory over moral and instructive tales. Lewis Carroll (Revd. C. L. Dodgson), possessing a remarkable affinity with

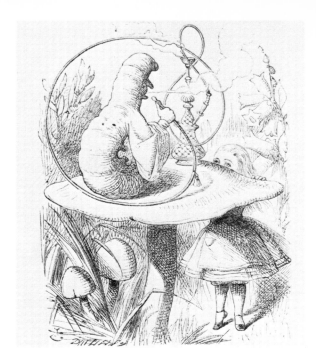

children, produced pure fantasy with a touch of Lear's brand of nonsense. John Tenniel's illustrations, despite the author's attempted interference, were serious drawings of very funny situations, increasing the fun. When copyright on the Alice books expired, numerous editions appeared with illustrations by many artists. Only Arthur Rackham's Alice equals Tenniel's illustrations; none surpass them.

A spate of great children's books of a different type had been appearing in America. Nathaniel Hawthorne's *A Wonder-Book for Boys and Girls* (1852) and *Tanglewood Tales* (1853) provided endless enchantment and created a new interest in myth. Louisa M. Alcott's *Little Women* was published in 1868 and has fascinated girls ever since. Boys have been equally well provided for with *The Adventures of Tom Sawyer* (1876) and *The Adventures of Huckleberry Finn* (1884) by Mark Twain (Samuel Clemens). It would be impossible to measure the influence of these books in America, and they have been extremely popular in Europe. Contemporary with these two books were the works of Howard Pyle, fine examples of historical fiction and folk-lore for children. Another American book of the period was *Nights with Uncle Remus* (1880) by Joel Chandler Harris.

The publication in England of *Black Beauty: the Autobiography of a Horse* (1877) was followed by the development of a tradition of animal stories, which still exists very strongly. Rudyard

Top left: '*The Frog-Footman*';
Top right: '*The Caterpillar and Alice*';
Above: '*The Trial of the Knave*';
Illustrations by John Tenniel for Alice's Adventures in Wonderland.

AUNT JO'S SCRAP-BAG.

JIMMY'S CRUISE IN THE PINAFORE,
ETC.

By LOUISA M. ALCOTT,

AUTHOR OF "LITTLE WOMEN," "AN OLD-FASHIONED GIRL," "LITTLE MEN,"
"HOSPITAL SKETCHES."

BOSTON:
ROBERTS BROTHERS.
1879.

Above: Aunt Jo's Scrap-Bag *by Louisa May Alcott (Roberts Brothers, Boston 1879). Above right:* 'This is the picture of the Animal that came out of the sea and ate up all the food that Suleiman-bin-Daoud had made ready for all the animals in all the world': *illustration to* 'The Butterfly that Stamped' in Just So Stories *written and illustrated by Rudyard Kipling (Macmillan & Co., 1902). Right:* 'This is the picture of the Cat that Walked by Himself, walking by his wild lone through the Wet Wild Woods and waving his wild tail' *illustration to* 'The Cat that Walked by Himself' in Just So Stories.

Kipling's *The Jungle Book* was published in 1894, and *The Second Jungle Book* in the following year.

Adventure stories, such as *Coral Island* (1857), became very popular in the second half of the nineteenth century. The height was reached with Robert Louis Stevenson's *Treasure Island* (1883) and *Kidnapped* (1886). *Treasure Island* is all that is excellent in boys' adventure stories. It was written very quickly, yet it demonstrates a mastery of narrative which is seldom equalled in children's literature.

Flourishing at the same time were the great illustrators, Walter Crane, Kate Greenaway and Randolph Caldecott, creators, with the printer Edmund Evans, of the classic children's picture books. Earlier pictures were either the product of artist-engravers like Bewick, artists like Tenniel, who drew on the wood, or artists whose drawings were copied by the engraver. Edmund Evans changed all this. In the early stages, he copied the paintings of illustrators, printing

'The Ploughboy in Luck' from The Baby's Opera: *'A Book of Old Rhymes with New Dresses' by Walter Crane (1877), and dedication for* The Baby's Bouquet: *'A Fresh Bunch of Old Rhymes and Tunes arranged and decorated by Walter Crane'.*

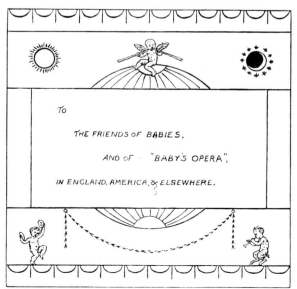

his wood blocks with the colours used by the artists. Later, he persuaded Crane, Greenaway and Caldecott to work with him. This resulted in related adaptations in technique which gave us the children's picture book *par excellence.* Later developments facilitated the printing of such pictures, but despite the technical constraints of Evans's process very few illustrators have managed to excel these three.

Walter Crane's work demonstrates a strong Art Nouveau influence and sometimes fails to come to life. His *The Fairy Ship* (1869), *The Baby's Opera* (1877), *The Baby's Bouquet* (1879), *The Baby's Own Aesop* (1886) and *Flora's Feast* (1888) are beautifully decorative. Kate Greenaway was gentler and had a greater feeling for children than Crane. Her *Under the Window* (1878), *A Day in a Child's Life* (1881), *Mother Goose* (1881) and *Marigold Garden* (1885) are exquisite examples of the children's picture book at its best. Unlike Crane, who filled every available space with decoration, she used white space with great effect. Her imagination and technique are superb. If printed today, her books would be prohibitively expensive; as many as nine separate colour printings were used for the edition of 20,000 of her greatest book *Mother Goose*. Kate Greenaway's enormous influence is demonstrated by her effect on children's fashion. Ruskin, who was very fond of her work, had urged her to paint more realistically, showing real children as they really dressed. Ten years later, children dressed as she had painted them.

Randolph Caldecott had closer affiliations with Bewick. He had grown up in the countryside of the west of England and his work shows it. His first illustrations were for Washington Irving's *Old Christmas* (1875) and *Bracebridge Hall* (1876). After the appearance of his *John Gilpin* and *The House that Jack built* in 1878, he produced at least two new books a year until his death in 1886. As well as the countryside, his work reflects much of society. While he had similar tastes to those of Kate Greenaway in clothing his picture-children, they were not quite as angelic as hers and often displayed a first-rate mischievousness.

Sixteen years after Caldecott's death, there began a series of books which probably rank as high as any in their attraction for children and for collectors. Beatrix Potter's career as an authoress and illustrator of children's books began accidentally. For that matter, the writers of many of the best children's books became authors by

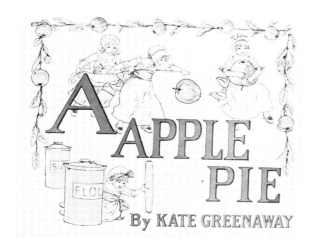

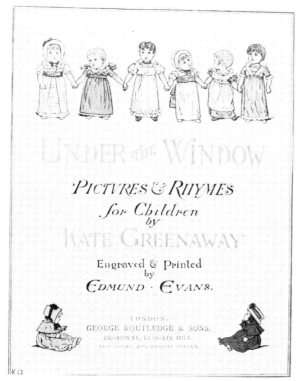

Left: *two examples of Kate Greenaway's illustration.* Above: *announcement for* A Sketch-Book *by Randolph Caldecott (George Routledge & Sons, 1883).*

accident. In the case of Beatrix Potter, however, greatness was very much thrust upon her. In 1893, she had written a letter to Noel Moore, the son of her former governess. She was shy, having grown up in a very strict Victorian family with no companions. Her letter begins: 'My dear Noel, I don't know what to write to you so I shall tell you a story about four little rabbits . . .' Such was the beginning of Peter Rabbit and, shortly afterwards, a series of books which have delighted children everywhere. *The Tale of Peter Rabbit* was privately printed in 1900 and published in 1902. Like her original letter, it was illustrated by the writer. Indeed, the text and illustrations are so closely related that any other pictures are inconceivable. The popularity of Beatrix Potter's little books, all still in print, makes a list superfluous. On her own admission, she did not find illustration easy, but she approached the task with an incredible dedication and remarkable powers of observation. In other circumstances, she might have achieved fame as a water-colourist. While creating an unmistakable atmosphere, her pictures are as accurate as they are attractive. The animals may be dressed in charming costume, but they are definitely drawn from life. The same concern for accurate observation, blended with romanticism, is shown in her writings. These ingredients, together with an essentially child-like simplicity in her view of the world, give Beatrix Potter's books continuing popularity in practically every language.

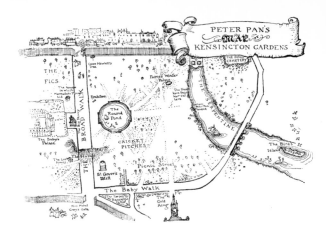

Eastwood Dunkeld
Sep 4. 93

My dear Noel,
I don't know what to write to you, so I shall tell you a story about four little rabbits whose names were—

Flopsy, Mopsy, Cottontail and Peter

They lived with their mother in a sand bank, under the root of a big fir tree.

Left: *the original letter telling* The Tale of Peter Rabbit *written by Beatrix Potter in 1893.* Above: *the end-papers of* Peter Pan in Kensington Gardens *by J. M. Barrie with drawings by Arthur Rackham (Hodder & Stoughton, 1906).*

The glorious tradition of nonsense founded by Edward Lear and perfected by Lewis Carroll reached a new peak shortly after the turn of the century with the creation of *Peter Pan*. This is one of the finest pieces of fantasy in the English language. There is fine poetry here, too. The curious bibliographical history of *Peter Pan* presents a challenge to collectors. J. M. Barrie introduced Peter in a book for adults, *The Little White Bird* (1902); the first six chapters were reissued under the title *Peter Pan in Kensington Gardens* (1906). This first appearance of Peter in a children's book has the added attraction of superb illustrations by Arthur Rackham. Peter Pan also appeared in a play adapted from the original story and produced in 1904, though not published until 1928. However, several story versions were published between 1911 and 1940. Barrie published his own version, *Peter and Wendy*, in 1911, Daniel O'Connor's appeared in 1914, and Mary Byron produced two versions, one in 1929 and one in 1940. Perhaps the strongest point in Barrie's story is the appearance of fantasy and nonsense below the surface of a perfectly normal and orderly world. Lewis Carroll's magnificent fantasy world was a separate one somewhere at the end of a rabbit's burrow. The fantasy world of Peter Pan, however, exists within the experience and comprehension of most children, but is transformed by the magic of night. Only when I grew older did I realise the possibility of Alice's world, because I began to recognise the Wonderland characters as I met their likenesses. Peter's world, on the other hand, is immediately possible in the mind of any child, given the imagination and the necessary ingredient of night-time. The theme of a fantasy world just below the shallow surface of ordinary life is not new. The ancient fairy stories all use it. Indeed, Irish mythology explains it neatly by granting immortality to a defeated race, the Tuatha de Danaan. These magic people became known as the Sidh or fairies and continue to live quite happily throughout Ireland just a few feet below ground. But, while the theme was not new, its application certainly was. Unlike the traditional fairy stories, where principal characters are invariably archetypal, Barrie's tales were peopled by new creations, very much alive, in a straightforward setting.

The nonsense plus fantasy tradition established by Lear and expanded by Carroll was wedded to the fairytale tradition by Barrie. This set the pattern for a number of great children's books which, in their turn, expanded the tradition by further exploiting the natural sympathy between children and animals. This sympathy had always been present in children's stories but took on a new dimension with the publication of Kenneth Grahame's *The Wind in the Willows* (1908). This must surely be the loveliest nature story in any language. Here, the curtain of everyday is drawn back, and the world of the river bank is revealed complete with otters, badgers, toads, moles, water-rats and others who talk and behave in a thoroughly human fashion. The story is all the more convincing because these creatures are normally seen only for a brief instant in real life before they disappear to Toad Hall, or some equally probable but invisible hiding place.

The animal story next found an exponent in Hugh Lofting. *The Story of Doctor Dolittle*, published in America in 1920, is a crazy, exciting world full of remarkable adventures in which the good Doctor talks with all sorts of animals. Doctor Dolittle's conversation with animals was convincing and amusing, but A. A. Milne's treatment of the theme introduces a delicate wit which is unsurpassed. In *Winnie-the-Pooh* (1926), a very ordinary subject, a boy with a teddy bear, is treated with such mastery that it will continue to charm and amuse children and adults alike as long as teddy bears continue to have their ears chewed.

In America, the production of children's books really got into full swing in the early part of this century. In 1922, Frederick Melcher, editor of *Publishers' Weekly*, established the annual Newbery Medal for the most distinguished literature for children. In 1924, *The Horn Book Magazine* devoted to children's books was begun. The Caldecott Award for the best picture book was founded in 1938. These all reflected a tremendous interest and exercised great influence. The lists of good children's books published in England and America became so large from the 1920s that it is impossible to do justice to the subject. For complete listings, reference should be made to the various excellent bibliographies. The very popular Mary Poppins stories by P. L. Travers began to appear in the 1930s. They are *Mary Poppins* (1934), *Mary Poppins comes back* (1935), *Mary Poppins opens the door* (1944) and *Mary Poppins in the Park* (1952). *Paul Bunyan* (1924) by Esther Shephard was the first collection of American tall stories. Significant American contributions to fantasy and the fanciful were: *Rootabaja Stories* (1922) by the poet, Carl Sandburg; *500 Hats for Bartholomew Cubbins* (1938) by Dr Seuss (Theodor Seuss Geisel);

From 'Eeyore Loses a Tail' in Winnie the Pooh *by A. A. Milne, with decorations by E. H. Shepard (Methuen & Co., 1928).*

Rabbit Hill (1944) by Robert Lawson; Carolyn Bailey's *Miss Hickory* (1946); *Twenty-one Balloons* (1947) by William Pene du Bois, and *Charlotte's Web* (1952) by E. B. White. All were highly original and most of them won Newbery Medals. In Britain, one of the most interesting developments has been the rise of the Puffin paperbacks. One of the less fortunate aspects of the children's book has been the growth of the Enid Blyton industry.

Having passed quickly over the last forty years in which so much has been published, we reach the end of a rapid and very personal survey of the history of children's books. Textbooks are not mentioned simply because a line had to be drawn somewhere, and because they belong more properly to the history of educational publishing. With few exceptions, I know of no textbooks which have either provided amusement for children or inspired their imaginations. Another omission has been the huge range of boys' adventure stories. Many of these are for boys who have passed the stage of childhood; the Sherlock Holmes stories among them. Others, like Henty, are the subject of more specialised works which are currently available. Henty particularly is the subject of a regrettable nostalgia cult. His books, of which there were a great many, certainly contained an enormous amount of historical and geographical information but they also suffer from their political bias in favour of the great and glorious Empire. The Empire was great but its glory was sometimes questionable and Henty's propagandist role is an unfortunate throwback to the days of Mrs Trimmer.

The greatest omission in this chapter and one which I regret is the failure to do justice to the vast wealth of children's books which have appeared in other languages. At the end of this chapter are listed a number of references which will be of use to the collector contemplating collecting books in other languages.

Children's books, in most cases, were used by children and consequently it is not common to find copies in pristine condition. Many of the great books have also been collected for many years, and it is only by paying high prices or searching very patiently that they can be collected. In many cases, it may be advisable to accept good copies regardless of edition. Collecting standards are subjective and will change as a collection grows. Many books on book-collecting advise the collector to accept nothing but a mint copy of the book in the original state of its first edition. This reduces books to the level of antiques. It is better to have a slightly worn copy of a good book than to have none at all. Signs of use, provided they are not extreme, should add to the interest of a book. The second edition may be an improvement on the first. Do not set your sights too high or you may end up with little money and few books.

The first problem—there are many more—in collecting, is deciding what to collect. Unless you have a definite objective, visit as many bookstores as you can. Consult the specialist section of a directory of booksellers—you will find one in your local library—and write requesting catalogues. Catalogues, usually free, give an indication of what is available and the going market prices. Talk to booksellers, librarians and other collectors. When you have an idea of what is available, then you can decide what to collect.

Collecting all editions of a particular title or author is a popular approach but is perhaps somewhat sterile. By far the most satisfying is the thematic approach. Choose or invent a theme and build your collection to demonstrate it. Your theme could be anything from the development of children's book illustration, through such interesting areas as the desert island or the long sleep in children's literature. The possibilities are endless and some might be easier than others. Certainly, if your collecting aim is to show the development of fantasy in children's books, you have chosen a central theme which will need a lot of work. To demonstrate the theme of the desert island, however, offers fascinating possibilities and will not involve huge expenditures unless you resolve to have a first edition of *Robinson Crusoe*. This kind of approach to collecting offers endless interest and the opportunity to break new ground, with the added bonus that you have a nice Ph.D. package in the end, if such considerations are important. All collecting, however, involves considerable self-discipline. Without discipline, the collection shows a remarkable tendency to acquire a mind of its own and set off in all sorts of directions. This leads inevitably to huge book monsters which, while charming and very interesting, have a propensity for spreading from room to room, strangling all other interests and driving out all before them. Such was the fate of the greatest collector of all time, Sir Thomas Phillips, whose wife left him when she could no longer find the bed—it was buried under boxes of mediaeval manuscripts. And if all this sounds too involved or energetic for you, then the final criterion is what you like. Any collection should, above all things, provide enjoyment.

Victorian Fiction

THE Victorian age was marked by an enormous upsurge of demand for books, reflecting rapid increases in the population as a whole, and in the literate section of it in particular. The annual production of new books, which had remained stable at around 850 in the period 1802–27, climbed to 2,530 by 1853, and went on increasing until by 1880 the figure stood at more than 8,000. By far the greatest demand was for fiction, and as well as the literary giants of the period 1837–70, hosts of lesser writers, of wildly varying quality, arose to minister to the new popular readership. From the point of view of book production, the story was of rapidly expanding technical progress; stereotyping, mechanical type founding (by 1860), and mechanised binding (after 1870) ushered in the

age of true mass production. The three volume novel, priced at ten and sixpence per volume, remained the standard form for first publication until 1894—its prestige, and its price, had been established in the second and third decades of the century by the extraordinary popular success of Walter Scott, the prototype of the Great Novelist, hailed by critics and public alike, and regarded as much as a prophet and sage as a writer. From about 1830 onwards, however, radical innovations in publishing occurred in the form of uniform series of reprinted editions of living authors, which for the first time brought the works of successful writers to the public in a single volume of handy format, at a price that was a fifth of that of the three-volume edition. Genuinely popular publishing had arrived. Later developments were to bring the price down even further, until the appearance of the yellow-back

A ticket for Mudie's Select Library.

MUDIE'S SELECT LIBRARY,

(LIMITED.)

30 TO 34, NEW OXFORD STREET.

BRANCH OFFICES, { 241, BROMPTON ROAD, S.W.
{ 2, KING STREET, CHEAPSIDE, E.C.

SUBSCRIPTION.

One Guinea Per Annum and upwards

in 1853, priced usually at one shilling and six-pence, heralded the transformation of popular readership into mass readership in the modern sense. In the first twenty years of cheap series publishing, attempts were made to challenge the rule of the three-volume novel by providing original titles in the cheap one-volume form, but these attempts failed in the face of the power of the circulating libraries like Mudie's and W. H. Smith's, who charged subscriptions on each volume lent, and who therefore stood to make more from a three-volume novel. Such was the ability of the libraries to create best-sellers that publishers capitulated to them, and the single-volume reprint became the means of further exploiting established successes, until the libraries themselves brought the day of the three-volume novel to an end by substantially reducing, in 1894, the price they were prepared to pay to publishers.

The age was remarkable as much for the variety as the quantity of its bibliographical output. It is easy to forget that in the 65 years during which Queen Victoria reigned English society changed more rapidly, and more funda-mentally, than ever before. The near-revolu-tionary period of the hungry forties gave way to the dazzling prosperity of the fifties and sixties, with its great consolidation of middle-class values. This in turn prefigured the growth of the British Empire to the point at which British power dominated two-fifths of the world's population. All these changes may be found reflected in the books that Victorians read. In a general introduction to collecting in Victorian fiction, no apology should be necessary for an indication of the scope of what was produced, since it is this that provides enormous oppor-tunities for the collector. It is precisely because fiction remained the universally popular art-form throughout the nineteenth century, that it is possible to represent virtually any Victorian social attitude by a fiction collection. From politics and economics to the niceties of etiquette, from crime to the details of domestic furniture—all is encompassed in the billions of words turned out so indefatigably by the many hundreds of novelists who wrote between 1837 and 1903.

Collectors entering this field should be familiar with Michael Sadleir's *Nineteenth Century Fiction* (1951), if only because this detailed and scholarly catalogue of a collection made largely in the 1930s still largely determines the prices paid for first editions of many nineteenth century novels. The collection (now in the possession of the University of California, Los Angeles) covers the fashionable novelists of the so-called 'Silver-fork' school during the period 1825–40; extensive author collections of Bulwer Lytton, and Trollope; early series publications, notably Bentley's Standard Novels (1st series 1831–55); yellow-backs between 1853–75; and three-volume novels between 1860–98. It also contains a collection of anonymous Londiniana—periodi-cals, chap books, night-life guides, crime sheets published in and about London. Sadleir was able to make his collection comparatively cheaply because by 1930, the first editions of the major Victorian writers—Scott, Dickens, Thackeray, Borrow, the Brontes, George Eliot, Meredith, Gissing, R. L. Stevenson and Hardy—were already sought after and charted. This is even more the case today, even with great writers of the second rank, such as Trollope, Charles Kingsley and Mrs Gaskell. What is more, Sadleir's own work has had much the same effect in establishing values for the first editions, and even the first single-volume editions of the authors listed in his catalogue. Forty-five years of serious collecting in nineteenth-century litera-ture have made rarities of many categories of books, particularly the three-volume novels, which were already hard to find in good condi-tion after the damage which they suffered at the hands of library borrowers. The new collector may do best by looking, not for first editions, but for reprints, and even for second or third editions of reprints, providing that they are complete and in good condition. The time is fast approaching when any of the books mentioned in this chapter, which at present can be picked up in reprint form for anything up to a few pounds, will rise considerably in value. This chapter represents the popular aspect of Victorian taste—the literary giants have been left out not be-cause they were not popular, but because their value has been so definitively established that a glance through a random selection of booksellers catalogues would be a more practical guide to their present prices and availability. The general categories of books which follow relate to themes which may be represented by books or authors outside Sadleir.

The first category is the legacy of the Gothic romance. This, conventionally a tale of unspeak-able crimes committed in a setting of nightmarish horror, was the fashionable reading of the late eighteenth and early nineteenth centuries. Al-

MARIA MARTEN;

OR,

THE RED BARN.

MARIA MARTEN'S LAST VISIT (IN MAN'S CLOTHES) TO THE RED BARN, WITH A VIEW OF THE VILLAGE OF POLSTEAD.—P. 249.

LONDON:
WILLIAM NICHOLSON AND SONS,
20, WARWICK SQUARE, PATERNOSTER ROW, E.C.,
AND ALBION WORKS, WAKEFIELD.

One of the many nineteenth-century versions of The Red Barn.

though eclipsed by the more virile historical romances of Walter Scott, the Gothic novel reappeared in more populist form during the 1840s as the lurid 'penny dreadful'—a coarse melodrama of guilt and retribution published in weekly numbers at a penny a time, clearly aimed at a working-class readership. One of the most enterprising and successful of the many impresarios of cheap literature was the Chartist and radical G. W. M. Reynolds (1814–79) who published dozens of titles in weekly penny numbers during the forties and fifties, as well as a newspaper *Reynolds' Weekly News*, established in 1840. Possibly his most famous titles are *The Mysteries of London* and its sequel, *The Mysteries of the Court of London*, which were serialised over the incredibly long period of eleven years until 1856. Both were reprinted in book form several times. The taste for crude sensation remained a persistent undercurrent of Victorian conscious-

ness throughout the century, always more frankly expressed among the lower classes, where it showed itself. as a prurient interest in the 'street-literature' accounts of contemporary murders, and the so-called 'dying speeches' and 'confessions' of the murderers themselves. In 1831, the firm of Bennet published *The Red Barn: A Tale, founded on Fact*, by William Maginn, which was an adaptation of a street publication of 1828, *The last dying Speech and Confession of William Corder*. Maginn's book was reprinted and dramatised many times during the century. Similarly, *The Awful Disclosures of Maria Monk*, was first published in 1837, and can still be found in later Victorian reprints. By far the greatest number of reprinted editions, however, fell to *Ambrosio: or The Monk* (1797) by Matthew Gregory Lewis (1775–1818) — who became known as 'Monk' Lewis on the strength of it. This tale of Gothic terror in the grand manner, chronicling the treacherous and licentious crimes of a debauched monk, and culminating in the dramatic intervention of the Devil who rescues

TAKING THE VOW.

AWFUL DISCLOSURES

OF

MARIA MONK,

ILLUSTRATED WITH 40 ENGRAVINGS.

AND THE

STARTLING MYSTERIES

OF A

CONVENT EXPOSED!

Philadelphia:
T. B. PETERSON, 101, CHESTNUT STREET.

An American edition of the Awful Disclosures of Maria Monk, *first published in 1837.*

him from execution, only to dash out his brains on a rock, was subsequently republished in Ireland, France, Spain and Germany, in a variety of editions and formats, including dramatised and even operatic adaptations, until the middle of the century. The market for sensation, however, was not confined to the newly literate industrial working classes. The rise of the circulating libraries, such as Mudie's, which was established in 1842, created a wide demand for fiction among the middle classes. The fact that its founder, Charles Edward Mudie, was known to have decided views about what was and was not suitable for decent families to read, allowed the increasing body of subscribers to regard reading novels as at worst a harmless addiction, the material for which had been vetted at source and pronounced fit for human consumption. By 1862 Mudie's, now moved to new premises in New Oxford Street, had a stock of over 309,000 volumes, of which more than 165,000 were

works of fiction. Given Mudie's Dissenting views it is at first surprising that the staple fare of his subscribers should have been stories of implicit sexual irregularities, crimes, disasters and treachery. Frank Smedley (1818–66) satirised such novels in *Harry Coverdale's Courtship* (1855) when Alice Coverdale '. . . opened a parcel of books from the library, and began upon a new novel by that very talented lady, Mrs Bluedeville, and read how a fair and gentle girl, brought up by a select coterie of fiendish relations, and subjected from infancy to a series of tortures sufficient to have expended the stoutest negro, developed under these favourable circumstances into a perfect Houri of Paradise, with the additional attraction of possessing the mind, manners

Right: *unpublished illustration by Charles Robinson.*

THE ENCHANTMENT
OF DON QUIXOTE

and devotion of an old Divine of the Church of England.'

The attraction of the Mrs Bluedevilles, however, was that the evildoers depicted in such loving detail came to satisfactorily bad ends, while their victims, almost exclusively innocent girls, were shown to have been purified by suffering—the best possible training for Victorian marriage. Thus the appetite for sensation was satisfied within the bounds of propriety—indeed, given the limitations imposed upon the middle class women of the time, it was probably the best that Mr Mudie's lady readers could hope for. M. E. Braddon, and her rival, Mrs Henry Wood are excellent examples of the type of manufacturing novelist who supplied the great majority of the books so eagerly consumed by Mudie's subscribers. Both authors were consistent bestsellers, both were enviably prolific writers. Mary Elizabeth Braddon's output was indeed almost prodigious, in the ten years after her first success, *Lady Audley's Secret* (1862) she wrote over twenty more. A typical example is *John Marchmont's Legacy* (1863), an intense story of a woman's revenge on her stepdaughter, who has married the man they both love. After a serious accident to the husband, the stepdaughter is kidnapped, and the husband, now recovered, is led to believe her dead. At the moment that he is to marry again, the plot is unmasked, and the guilty cousin, who has been planning to seize the inheritance, sets fire to the ancestral home, only to perish in the flames. The majority of her work was published by John Maxwell (whom she married in 1874), and produced in three-volume format according to the prevailing custom, and later reproduced as a yellow-back. By the eighties, M. E. Braddon was being referred to in publisher's advertisements as 'Queen of the Circulating Libraries'. The early first edition titles are rare, *Lady Audley's Secret* excessively so, but it is possible to find Maxwell single volume reprints, and the Simpkin Marshall 'Stereotyped' and the 62-volume 'Author's' Editions reprinted in one-volume series during the 1880s: some editions list her titles, numbering one to fifty-six, published by that firm to date.

Although Mrs Henry Wood was older than

Miss Braddon, the years of her success were contemporary with her. Mrs Wood's second novel *East Lynne* (1861) was her first best-seller, running first of all as a magazine serial, and later adapted (also with acclaim) for the stage. The main situation of the novel is one of almost unbearable pathos, a divorced wife re-entering her husband's home disguised as a governess in order to nurse her own child, and dying there, finally (if belatedly) forgiven. The celebrated line 'Gone! Gone! And never called me Mother!' has justly entered the folk heritage, a fact which is the best possible indication of the extent of Mrs Wood's popular success. She wrote over 40 novels, the majority of them published in three volumes by Bentley—apart from *East Lynne*, the most popular proved to be *The Channings* (1862) and its sequel *Roland Yorke* (1869), a pair of novels set in a cathedral town, concerning the ups and downs of two well-bred families, the one a model of Christian piety, the other feckless and irresponsible. *Mrs Halliburton's Troubles* (1862) also achieved considerable success—its sensational elements are limited to the accidents that befall a middle class family, and the emphasis lies on the

Left: 'The Enchantment of Don Quixote' by Walter Crane: an outline proof, hand-coloured, for Don Quixote Retold by Judge Parry (Blackie & Son, 1900).

WITHIN THE MAZE.

A Novel.

BY

MRS. HENRY WOOD,

AUTHOR OF "EAST LYNNE."

IN THREE VOLUMES.
VOL. III.

LONDON:
RICHARD BENTLEY AND SON,
NEW BURLINGTON STREET.
1872.

[*All Rights Reserved.*]

129

patient endurance with which the mother accepts her troubles. After Mrs Wood's death in 1887, Bentley started on the publication of a new edition (in one-volume form) of her novels, bound in scarlet or apple green: this series was continued when the firm was bought by Macmillan in 1897, and a set could be collected at the present time, though some titles are becoming rather difficult to find.

That Mrs Wood should have written stories of domestic life, interspersed with a great deal of pious moralising, as well as her more avowedly sensational novels shows that, as an extremely competent commercial writer, she was perfectly aware of a counterstrand to sensationalism which existed within the great middle class readership. A strong revival in religious sentiment and practice had begun in the 1840s, directed largely at the squalor and greed of an industrialist, materialist society. Both High and Low Church inveighed against the social evils of the time, but in different ways: the High Churchmen, led by figures like Charles Kingsley and John Keble,

demanded a spiritualisation of society, while the Fundamentalists and Dissenters propagandised the virtues of self discipline through pamphlets and tracts chiefly exhorting the lower classes to enlist in the fight against the degrading influence of drink. Both streams met in the exaltation of the Christian family ideal. Such sentiments were the foundation of the successful career of Charlotte Mary Yonge (1823–1901), whose most famous book *The Heir of Redclyffe* (1853) achieved a potent blend of High Church Anglican piety, virtuous family life and idealised romance. The author was the highly educated and extremely devout daughter of a country squire; for a while she was the pupil of Keble himself, who at the time was the vicar of a neighbouring

Right: *title page illustration for a twentieth-century edition of Charlotte M. Yonge's* The Chaplet of Pearls *(Macmillan & Co., 1903).* Below: The Heir of Redclyffe *by Charlotte M. Yonge, illustrated by Kate Greenaway (Macmillan & Co., 1888 edition).*

"She lifted from her cot her little one."—Page 459.

THE

HEIR OF REDCLYFFE

BY

CHARLOTTE M. YONGE

ILLUSTRATED BY KATE GREENAWAY

London
MACMILLAN AND CO.
AND NEW YORK
1888

The Right of Translation is Reserved

parish, and she was greatly influenced by his teachings. Few books, if any, have ever achieved the immediate acclaim accorded to this story of the doomed, passionate Sir Guy Morville, the youthful hero, whose struggle to live according to the highest ideals of duty and devotion provided a spark of inspiration that united all the most human and optimistic elements in Victorian society in admiration. Miss Yonge wrote more than 150 books during the course of a long life: among her works are many stories for children, moral tales in historical settings, beginning in 1854 with *The Little Duke* (often reprinted in recent years), the events in which take place in Normandy during the reign of Richard the Fearless (943–53). She also wrote a series of family chronicles, starting with *The Daisy Chain* (1856). Most of her fiction titles can be found in Macmillan blue cloth 'Uniform Editions' from the 1880s to the early 1900s with, occasionally, a two-volume second edition, and (uncommonly) a first. Among the most difficult titles to find (1855) are her very early works, such as *Abbey-church* (1844), *Kenneth* (1855) and *The Castle Builders* (1859). She also wrote a good deal of non-fictional works of history and biography, including a *History of France* (1879) and a *Life of Hannah More* (1888). When she became a governor of a Girl's High School in Winchester during the eighties she produced a pamphlet *Religious Education of the Wealthier Classes*, emphasising the role of the parents in the religious education of children. Her last book, *Modern Broods: or Developments Unlooked for* (1900), provides a

fascinating codicil to the spiritual preoccupations of the mid Victorian period: in the very different climate of the *fin de siècle* Miss Yonge, in the persona of maiden aunt, speaks her views and criticisms of a modern generation of girls Her own faith undimmed, she is troubled by the religious, emotional and social confusions which bedevil the contemporary equivalents of the youthful and idealistic girls which people her earlier books.

There were other women writers deeply concerned to instil the values of a Christian life into their readers: Mrs Craik (1826–87) who, as well as *John Halifax, Gentleman* (1856), wrote *A Life for a Life* (1859) and *A Noble Life* (1866); Grace Aguilar, whose first book *Home Influence* (1847) ran to several editions, and was followed by *The Mother's Recompense* (1851), as well as a number of other domestic tales under the title of *Home Scenes and Heart Studies*. Charlotte Maria Tucker, under the pseudonym A.L.O.E. (A Lady Of England), wrote almost a hundred somewhat heavily moral stories, many written after her arrival in India as a missionary in 1875. A large number of her books (mostly published by Nelson) are still to be found, often in their original pretty gilt decorated cloth bindings; quite a number of reprinted titles, bound in a later style of pictorial cloth, are also available, for example, *Flora* (1858), *Claudia* (1869), *The Rambles of a Rat* (1857), and *Pride and His Prisoners* (1860). All the profits from her books were donated to charities, mostly missionary societies.

Running parallel with the literary effusions of Victorian high-mindedness were the directly propagandist pamphlets, tracts and 'uplifting tales', designed as a sort of spiritual first-aid for the working classes, and particularly for children, and advertised by their publishers with a sanctimonious smugness completely devoid of self-consciousness. Take for example, this extract from an 1883 catalogue issued by S. W. Partridge and Co.:

> 'British Workman' Series of Tracts, Containing interesting Stories in Temperance subjects, for the Working Classes. 32pp and glazed cover 2d. each.

There are still a great number of these Temperance and Moral Tales to be found: usually fairly small, slim volumes in dark green, blue or brown cloth with decorated covers lettered (and often scrolled) in gilt. In really good condition they are attractive examples of contemporary binding styles, and their advertisements for other publications of a similar kind convey the full flavour of complacent Victorian do-goodery. The best known temperance writer was probably the American T. S. Arthur, whose *Ten Nights in a Bar Room* (1854) fulminates against strong drink with true revivalist gusto. He wrote several more tracts in similar style, among them *True Riches; or, Wealth Without Wings* and *Life's Crosses*.

Women contributed strongly to such literature, usually under sisterly *noms de plume*, such as 'Brenda' and 'Pansy', but the case of 'Hesba Stretton' (a pseudonym for Sarah Smith 1832–1911) is more interesting. Her book, *Jessica's First Prayer* (1867), sold over a million and a half copies, and subsequent titles dealt with the plight of poor children in big cities: these 'Street Arabs' (a nickname much used in sub-titles of the period) were the raw material for Fagin's gang in 'Oliver Twist', and lived on to serve in Sherlock Holmes' Baker Street Irregulars. *Alone in London* and *Pilgrim Street* (a story of Manchester life) are typical.

However much we may deride the simple remedies offered by the Victorians for deep seated social ills, it should never be forgotten that they were but one aspect of a sense of genuine shock at the equally genuine horrors routinely suffered by the poor and underprivileged. The elements of deepening social consciousness and criticism that appear in the novels of Benjamin Disraeli, George Eliot, Elizabeth Gaskell, Charles Dickens and Charlotte Bronte are woven into profound, sometimes unanswerable, questions about the reality and aspirations of society in nineteenth century England. For the majority of middle class Victorians, such complexities were unwelcome, what they wanted was a clear identification of the oppressed and abused as a preliminary to framing some equally clear-cut measure for charitable relief. Such minds responded easily to the pathos of starving women and children, less so to such apparently self-induced problems as drunkenness or aversion to work. The impact of *Uncle Tom's Cabin* (1852), was undoubtedly increased by the stark distinction it drew between the oppressed and the oppressor; it became a formidable weapon in the hands of Abolitionists, and met with enormous and truly popular success on both sides of the Atlantic. Its author, the American Mrs Harriet Beecher Stowe, was fêted in England, and in an account of her visit written

'Eva and Uncle Tom in the garden', illustration from Uncle Tom's Cabin *by Harriet Beecher Stowe.*

after her return to America, described her delight at finding that the book was as famous among the poorer classes as it was with the great. She wrote slavery novels, for example *A key to Uncle Tom's Cabin* (1852), and *Dred* (1856), as well as a series of novels about New England, including *The Minister's Wooing* (1859) and *The Pearl of Orr's Island* (both of which can be tracked down in first editions); none of her other works, however, achieved a success comparable with her most famous book. In contrast, there were two mid-century novelists who openly rebelled against the prevailing morality, whether directly expressed, as in the works of Miss Yonge, or served up with sensational trimmings by Miss Braddon or Mrs Wood. George Alfred Lawrence (1827–76) deliberately reversed the values of the Oxford Movement's 'muscular Christianity' in *Guy Livingstone* (1857), in which extravagantly muscular young bucks exult in a cynical Byronic amorality, interspersed with episodes of reckless physical courage. His affectation of wickedness, however, seems thin and contrived before the

genuine passion and opulent intensity of 'Ouida' (Mlle Loiuise de la Ramée, 1839–1908), who published her first novel *Held in Bondage* in 1863, and at once achieved a *succès du scandale* which drew the whole weight of critical outrage upon her head. Young, imaginative, naive and impossibly romantic, Ouida wrote of a gorgeous world of almost Oriental luxury, in which beautiful heroines, scornful of shame and virtue, abandoned themselves to the capricious embraces of magnificent aristocratic blackguards, supermen whose wealth, physique and intellect alike were of uniformly heroic proportions. She went on to write over forty other such novels, the most vigorous of which were published during the sixties and seventies; although universally condemned for their 'immorality' her books were the secret delight of huge numbers of readers. Such was the demand, indeed, that even the 'select' volumes of Mudie's library were forced to admit her as a companion—although the more respectable of Mudie's subscribers might guiltily hide the evidence of their addiction from visitors, or agonise over the dreaful possibility of their being seen by the children. The novels of Ouida's most prolific period (1863–*c*1880) were reprinted

many times up until the end of the century and beyond, and it would be possible to collect all her titles in this form.

The thirty years that culminated in the heyday of Miss Braddon, Mrs Wood and Ouida had seen revolutionary changes in the form in which books were published and provide a fascinating area for collecting. Binding styles had evolved from the paper boards, or wrappers, in which books were issued, and sent by wholesalers to customers who would have the volumes bound to their own specifications. Although the practice of issuing books, especially novels, in wrappers survived well into the fifties, experiments in the introduction of cloth bindings had begun in the mid twenties, notably by Archibald Leighton, and techniques for gold blocking (by 1832) and blind blocking (by 1837) cloth in suitably commercial quantities were speedily developed until by 1837 Messrs Saunders and Otley produced fine decorated bindings for some of their illustrated editions of Captain Marryat's novels. The 1840s saw polychrome bindings, in both cloth and leather, rich effects being achieved by hand-colouring and the use of coloured paper overlays, produced by firms like J. S. Evans,

Three title pages from different series of novels published from the 1830s onwards.

Remnant & Edmonds, Westley & Clarke, Bone & Co., and Leighton himself. Examples of such bindings will be expensive, whereas the frequently ornate mass-produced bindings of the period 1880–1900 are readily available at modest prices. Such productions, however, were the coffee table books of the time. From the point of view of popular publishing the crucial innovation of the period was the introduction of the single-volume cheap reprint.

In 1831, following the lead of other reprint publishers mainly dealing in serial form, Henry Colburn and Richard Bentley began their series of *Standard Novels,* producing recent titles in complete form and (a very important point for the period) in uniform bindings, initially of glazed white linen with paper labels. The first was Fenimore Cooper's *The Pilot,* published in February 1831. The Series is very significant from the collector's point of view: as Michael Sadleir points out (*XIX Century Fiction,* Vol. 1), in reprinting living authors the publishers were able to claim justifiably that the texts were 'finally approved by the authors'.

The *Standard Novels* were immensely suc-

cessful; the First Series ran from 1831 to 1855 and numbered around 126 titles. During this period, four variations in binding were used. The partnership was dissolved in 1832: the first nineteen volumes up to this time have an imprint on the title page bearing both names (variously described); and from Number 20, the imprint R (or Richard) Bentley (late Colburn & Bentley) was used, with variations.

A large number of the titles were reissued, and there were many offshoots of this first series of early reprint publishing. Colburn set up in opposition to Bentley and produced his Modern Novelist series from January 1835. Blackwood of Edinburgh entered the field in 1841, with his first series of Standard Novels, 'straight' reprints which included John Galt's *Annals of the Parish,* Michael Scott's *Tom Cringle's Log* and *The Cruise of the Midge* and J. G. Lockhart's *Valerius,* described as 'A New Edition, Revised'. Four different issues, each with an individual binding style, were produced by the end of the 1860s. In

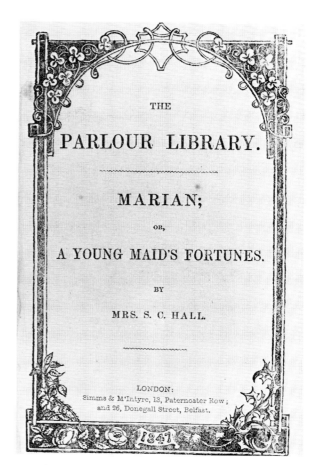

BLACKWOOD'S

STANDARD NOVELS.

VOL. VIII.

———

THE CRUISE OF THE MIDGE.

———

WILLIAM BLACKWOOD AND SONS,
EDINBURGH AND LONDON.
M.DCCC.XLII.

THE

PARLOUR LIBRARY.

MARIAN;

OR,

A YOUNG MAID'S FORTUNES.

BY

MRS. S. C. HALL.

LONDON:
Simms & M'Intyre, 13, Paternoster Row;
and 26, Donegall Street, Belfast.

1847

the meantime, he had the enterprising notion of producing volumes of stories selected from his family publication, Blackwood's Magazine, and began the first series of these *Tales from Blackwood* in 1858. A year later, Bentley, not to be outdone, produced the first of his *Tales from Bentley*, selected from Bentley's Miscellany, a popular magazine which had the distinction of Charles Dickens as its first editor. Bentley's series ran for a considerably shorter time than Blackwoods and is extremely uncommon. An early reprint, in good condition, of any of the early Standard Novels or their derivatives is worth adding to a collection. The best source of reference is undoubtedly *XIX Century Fiction*.

The important point to bear in mind is that the Standard Novels were offered at six shillings, sometimes five, for each volume, compared with the bulk of contemporary fiction offered in three volumes at 31s 6d. At least, that was the situation in 1845, before two enterprising Belfast publishers, formerly printers, radically altered the cheap fiction reprint market. In February 1846, Simms & McIntyre issued the first volume of The Parlour Novelist, which was to appear monthly. Their advertisement describes 'A series of Works of Fiction by the most celebrated authors' and claims:

'Under this title, the Publishers intend to issue a series of Tales, Novels and Romances, by the most distinguished authors.

Each work will, with a few exceptions, be comprised in one neat duodecimo volume of about 320 pages, a size suitable either for the travelling carriage or the library, and will be printed in a style which can bear a comparison with any of the series now in course of publication.

The majority of the works selected for publication are either copyright editions, on the purchase of which a considerable sum has been expended, or translations from the French and German languages by competent persons.

Keeping in view the style of production, this may be pronounced the cheapest series of novels which has ever been offered to the public.'

The price for this 'cheapest series' is quoted as 2s in wrappers, 2s 6d in cloth.

Among the fourteen titles in this first series were a translation of *The Commander of Malta* by Eugene Sue and a reprint of Jane Austen's *Mansfield Park*. A number of different binding forms appears to have been used.

Simms & McIntyre brought off another *coup* in April 1847, with their Parlour Library, at the phenomenally low cost of 1s in boards and (shortly afterwards) 1s 6d in cloth. By the end of 1849, both Bentley's and Colburn's reprint series, having already been reduced to 3s 6d, were further reduced to 2s 6d; and other reprint publishers who had lately joined the market were also forced to cut their prices.

The original series of the *Parlour Library* ran to almost 300 volumes up to 1863; Simms and McIntyre sold out their interest in 1853. Among the series are a number of original first editions, for example Charles Lever's *Maurice Tiernay* (1854) and *Sir Jasper Carew* the following year, and Mayne Reid: *Hunter's Feast*, also 1855.

The cheap single-volume reprint, selling at less than ten per cent of the cost of a three-volume edition, was barely established when it received an additional boost from the rapid expansion of railway travel, and the consequent creation of an entirely new market for cheap, easily portable light reading. This, together with the breakthrough achieved by Simms and McIntyre, inspired Routledge to produce his *Railway Library* starting in 1849: popular fictions at 1s and 1s 6d. The series began as an open, though unacknowledged, imitation of *The Parlour Library*; but in the early 1850s, W. H. Smith began to take over the leases of railway bookstalls and the trashy cheap weeklies that had previously been sold over their counters were replaced by neatly arranged, and widely advertised, 'approved' popular fiction. Mr Routledge's new reprint series exactly fitted the bill: though, of course, other competitors quickly entered the field. At first, the cloth bindings were almost identical with the *Parlour Library*'s conventional decoration. And then a process was developed that resulted in a particularly eye-catching design, and was cheap to produce: the 'Yellowback'. This is a small 8vo volume with decorated glazed paper-covered boards, usually with a yellow background; and with a pictorial front cover depicting a dramatic moment from the novel itself. Yellowbacks have been popular with collectors for many years; their distinctive covers are par-ticularly attractive, but they were never very strongly bound and are therefore difficult to find in good condition. However, they were produced in vast quantity by various publishers up to the end of the century, and can still be found. Among them are first editions as well as reprints of popular titles and translations of works not previously published in English.

The series also reproduced a very great number of American titles. In the booming fiction market of the 1850s, English copyrights became scarce as publishers jealously guarded the rights to reprint their popular authors. Cheap reprint publishing was already well under way in America, and so a vast source could be tapped for marketing in England: names like Fenimore Cooper, Washington Irving and Longfellow; and, later, Bret Harte, Mark Twain and many others.

New publishers, new series, more yellowbacks, more writers: by the end of the 1850s the book trade was thriving. Non-fiction yellowbacks were also printed; not only Victorian railway travellers, but a larger public than ever was being catered for.

In Germany, Bernhard Tauchnitz began printing his 'Collections of British Authors' in 1841 with Bulwer Lytton's *Pelham* and by the end of the following year had added twenty more titles including three by Captain Marryat and one by G. P. R. James. His aim was to establish international copyright, as he saw the advantage of moving into the Continental market with cheap reprints of English and American books in 'copyright editions'. A copyright agreement with Britain was at last agreed in 1846. The firm of Tauchnitz went from strength to strength, enjoying close personal contacts with many of its authors and by the early years of the twentieth century had published almost 4,000 volumes.

The format of the series is distinctive, if not distinguished: small, buff paper wrappers, clearly marked with title, author and volume number. Sometimes, Tauchnitz in later editions retained and used the original title page and date, which makes for bibliographical confusion. The advertisements on the back cover are often the only clue to the date and the fact that the volume is a reprint.

In 1839, Catherine Sinclair had written a story called *Holiday House* which, justifiably, became a very great success. It was about two children who behaved in a natural, uninhibited

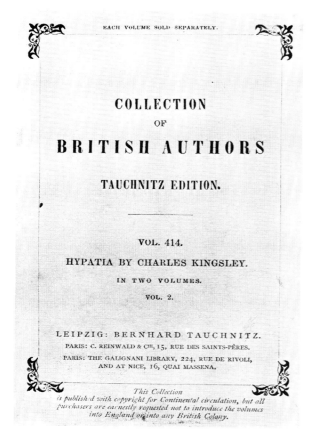

COLLECTION

OF

BRITISH AUTHORS

TAUCHNITZ EDITION.

VOL. 414.

HYPATIA BY CHARLES KINGSLEY.

IN TWO VOLUMES.

VOL. 2.

LEIPZIG: BERNHARD TAUCHNITZ.

PARIS: C. REINWALD & Cᴵᴱ, 15, RUE DES SAINTS-PÈRES.

PARIS: THE GALIGNANI LIBRARY, 224, RUE DE RIVOLI,
AND AT NICE, 16, QUAI MASSENA.

From Charles Kingsley's Hypatia *in the 'Collection of British Authors' published by Tauchnitz.*

way, and was a complete contrast to the moralising, often priggish tales served up by parents to their children. From over twenty novels written

by Captain Frederick Marryat from 1822 to 1848, three were intended for children: *Masterman Ready* (1841), rather didactic in tone, *The Settlers in Canada* (1844) and *The Children of the New Forest* (1847). The latter two are still read and enjoyed by children, of course, but by the middle of the century very little else had been written specially with a juvenile audience in mind until adventure stories for boys, written with realism and spirit, began to flow from the pens of W. H. G. Kingston and R. M. Ballantyne.

Kingston was a businessman with a great love of the sea inherited from his father. After some journalistic work in Portugal connected with his business, he wrote two adult novels, and then turned in 1851 to the first of his very many action-packed adventure stories, *Peter the Whaler*. After this, his output was truly prolific, averaging three or four titles each year. He travelled round the world in his own yacht, wrote travel books, translated *The Swiss Family Robinson* into English (1879), as well as a number of Jules Verne's novels. His well-known boys' stories include *Salt Water* (1857), *Washed Ashore* (1866), *The Wanderers* (1876), and *Arctic Adventures* (1882): and the quartet of adventures through the ranks *The Three Midshipmen, The Three Lieutenants, The Three Commanders* and *The Three Admirals,* written between 1862 and 1877.

His contemporary, R. M. Ballantyne, wrote his first full length novel in 1856 based on his own experiences with The Hudson Bay Company: *Snowflakes and Sunbeams* (quickly reverting to its sub-title *The Young Fur Traders* after the first

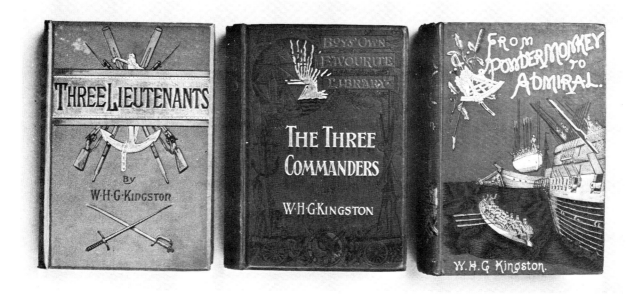

Above: *illustration by D. H. Friston for* The Three Lieutenants; or, Naval Life in the Nineteenth Century *by W. H. G. Kingston, the first of three novels written between 1862 and 1877 (Griffith Farran Okeden & Walsh, London).* Left: *frontispiece of Kingston's* From Powder Monkey to Admiral; A Story of Naval Adventure. Right: *frontispiece and other illustrations from* Poste Haste; A Tale of Her Majesty's Mails *by R. M. Ballantyne, (James Nisbet & Co., London 1881).*

few editions.) This was the story of a boy's adventures with the hunters in the backwoods of northern Canada. The success of this book prompted *Ungava: a tale of Esquimaux Land* (1857). During the 1860s, Ballantyne wrote several adventure stories written from personal observation: for example, *The Life Boat* (1864) after a spell on Goodwin Sands, *The Lighthouse* (1865), *Fighting the Flames* (for which he spent a period of time serving with the London Fire Brigade in order to ensure authenticity) and *Deep Down*, a tale of the Cornish mines (1868).

In America, Edward S. Ellis created a best-seller in *Seth Jones, or The Captives of the Frontier*, in 1860, following the publication of a number of stories in the English equivalent of the 'penny weeklies', which in the States were known as 'dime novels'. From then on, he produced a

large number of titles in book form, mostly about Red Indians, animal-hunters and cowboys; for example *Lost in the Rockies, Redskin and Scout* and *Two Boys in Wyoming*.

Mayne Reid started writing adventure stories for boys in 1852 after his first two books, *The Rifle Rangers* and *The Scalp Hunters*, based on his experiences in the United States Army in Mexico, had proved very popular with younger readers though he had not specifically intended them for them. In all he wrote over seventy stories, mainly on the theme of Red Indians versus pioneers in the West: titles such as *The Bush Boys* (1856), *The Giraffe Hunters* (1867) and *The Free Lances* (1881).

The field of Victorian boys' adventure stories is a vast one: in the 1860s the way was paved for writers like Robert Louis Stevenson, Rider Haggard and Rudyard Kipling.

One of the most 'collected' boys' adventure writers is G. A. Henty (1832–1902) whose first editions fetch very high prices. He served as a war correspondent in several Colonial campaigns and in India, and began his writing career as early as 1867 (unsuccessfully) with novels intended for adult reading. He began, much more successfully, to write adventure stories for boys based on his own experiences in 1871 with *Out on the Pampas*. Then followed ninety or more titles, among them *With Lee In Virginia, Through the Sikh War, With Clive in India, With the Allies to Pekin*. It is not difficult to understand how he illuminated the history lessons, particularly of colonial development, for the schoolboys of the eighties and nineties.

These Victorian adventure stories are often difficult to find in good condition: an indication, probably, of how well read they were. First editions of stories written in the sixties and seventies are uncommon, and often very rare indeed; but their popularity was great, which means that the publishers reprinted, often several times. Publishers like Nelson and Blackie became especially involved in the realm of juvenile literature, and the standard of their decorative bindings and illustrations was very high. The richly coloured cloth boards, decoration and gilt lettering and 'olivine' (that is, green-coloured glazed) edges to the pages of a Henty first edition published by Blackie & Son in the 1880s is particularly fine to see and handle; and is representative of the craft

Right: *illustrations from G. A. Henty's* With Clive in India; Facing Death, *and* For the Temple.

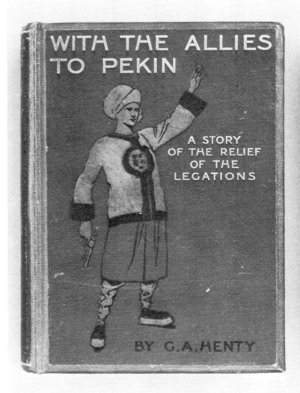

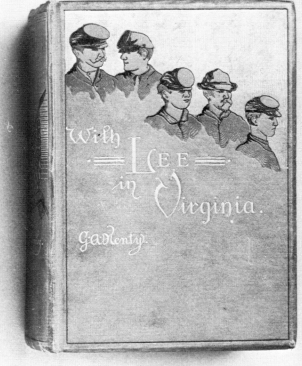

Blackie & Son's Illustrated Story Books

HISTORICAL TALES BY

G. A. HENTY

Won by the Sword: A Tale of the Thirty Years' War. With 12 Illustrations by CHARLES M. SHELDON. Crown 8vo, cloth elegant, olivine edges, 6s.

In this story Mr. Henty completes the history of the Thirty Years' War, the first part of which he described in *The Lion of the North*. His hero has ample opportunity for gratifying his love of hazardous enterprizes and adventures.

"As fascinating as ever came from Mr. Henty's pen."—*Westminster Gazette.*

"Full of sieges, of the smoke, the din and the dust of battle."—*Standard.*

- A Roving Commission: or, Through the Black Insurrection of Hayti. With 12 page Illustrations by WILLIAM RAINEY, R.I. Crown 8vo, cloth elegant, olivine edges. 6s.

Mr. G. A. Henty

The hero of this story takes part in some of the principal engagements in the revolt of the slaves of Hayti against their French masters at the end of last century, and is able to rescue many of the unfortunate French colonists from the infuriated blacks. He also does good service against the pirates who infested the West Indian seas at that period.

"A stirring tale, which may be confidently recommended to schoolboy readers."—*Guardian.*

"A singularly lucky and attractive hero, for whom boy readers will have an intense admiration."—*Standard.*

[46] [1] A

and workmanship (and expense) that went into the creation of a Victorian novel binding. Even the cheaper reprints with pictorial covers in bright clear colours are still eye-catching, and deserve to be collected.

In the whole area of Victorian book collecting, these bindings, in good bright condition, with the text and illustrations firmly sewn in, are the copies to look for and buy.

The firm of Blackie also gained fame throughout the century as educational publishers, and led in the field of 'Reward' books, the Victorians being enthusiastic prizegivers. In fact, such was the cult that one finds by the 1880s that certain publishers (among them R.T.S.) were inserting an already-printed Prize Label on an inside flyleaf.

Clearly, not all boys intent on reading their adventure stories filled their bookshelves (or emptied their pockets) on these splendidly-bound volumes. Several of the writers mentioned (and others, like George Manville Fenn) contributed to various magazines and periodicals designed for boys. The most famous of these was

the *Boy's Own Paper* which began its career in 1879, under the editorship of George A. Hutchison, and published by the Religious Tract Society. Contributions included articles on sport, and very often the first appearance of many of the stories of well established writers such as Henty. Later in the century, both Jules Verne and Conan Doyle contributed to the B.O.P. Copies can still be found, although it is becoming increasingly difficult to locate those earlier than 1900. The Religious Tract Society (RTS) republished in book form a number of 'the more popular and useful Papers and Stories' (to quote from their advertisement of 1885) which had appeared in the *Boy's Own Paper* in their series The Boys' Own Bookshelf.

Two other popular and successful boys' papers were *Chums,* which began in 1892, and *The Captain*, with its distinctive cover designed by John Hassall, launched in 1899. *The Captain* specialised in the boys' school story, and called itself "A Magazine for Boys and 'Old Boys' ".

It is generally supposed that *Tom Brown's Schooldays* in 1857 heralded the arrival of the public school in fiction. In fact, at least two tales

Below and above right: The Boy's Own Annual, *Volume X, a collection of* The Boy's Own Paper.

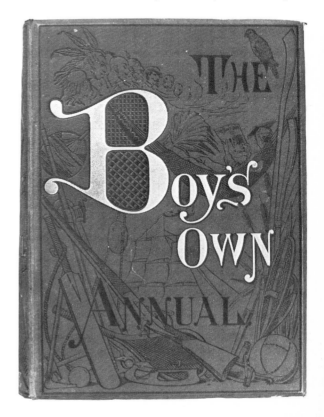

No. 456.—Vol. X.   SATURDAY, OCTOBER 8, 1887.   Price One Penny.

HARRY TREVERTON:
A STORY OF COLONIAL LIFE.
By LADY BROOME.

CHAPTER III.—"BUT YOU GO."

"An uncommonly neat swag."

with a similar theme were published well in advance of this bestseller. One is particularly rare, and would be a joy to find. In 1796, the second edition of a series of tales by Maria Edgeworth was published, and contained a story called *The Barring-Out*, which has all the essential ingredients: the feud between two strong schoolboy characters and their followers, the settling of the issues without loss of face. Another is Harriet Martineau's *The Crofton Boys*, published in 1841, sixteen years before the publication of *Tom Brown*. Other famous titles followed, including Farrar's *Eric; or, Little By Little* and its successor, *St Winifred's or, The World of School*; there were also the more rakish adventures of Jack Harkaway (written by Bracebridge Hemyng) published in serial form by 1871 (and later in America). The copy of *The First of June*, or *Schoolboy Rivalry*, illustrated here, has a preface dated 1858: this is the *twenty-first* edition, published by Routledge and undated, and written by the Reverend H. C. Adams. Listed among his previous titles are *Schoolboy Honour*, *Tales of Charlton School*, *The Boys of Westonbury*, and others: clearly he had produced tales in the same genre before, somewhat didactic perhaps, but certainly *The First of*

Seymour proposes Mertoun as Captain.—p. 15

THE

FIRST OF JUNE

OR

SCHOOLBOY RIVALRY

BY THE

REV. H. C. ADAMS, M.A.
VICAR OF DRY SANDFORD:
EDITOR OF "THE CHERRY STONES," AND AUTHOR OF
"SIVAN THE SLEEPER," ETC. ETC.

TWENTY-FIRST EDITION.

WITH ILLUSTRATIONS BY ABSOLON

LONDON
GEORGE ROUTLEDGE & SONS
BROADWAY, LUDGATE HILL
GLASGOW AND NEW YORK

SCHOOL DAYS
AT
SAXONHURST

BY 'ONE OF THE BOYS'

EDINBURGH: A. & C. BLACK
1867

June is about schoolboys and, very largely, about a cricket match.

There is also illustrated a near-fine copy of *Schooldays at Saxonhurst* being the first edition, dated 1867, with its authorship attributed to 'One of the Boys'. A later edition of 1873 proved this to be Percy H. Fitzgerald, though the story itself leaves one guessing about which school is portrayed.

The 'golden age' of the public school story was the period from the nineties to the First World War, when a great number of them were published with a high standard of pictorial and often gilt-decorated binding and illustrations to the text. Successful writers include Talbot Baines Reed with *The Fifth Form at St Dominic's*, Andrew Home *(From Fag to Monitor)*, John Finnemore (the '*Teddy Lester*' stories) and many more, among them P. G. Wodehouse, whose early stories appeared in a number of magazines. His first full length work was *The Pothunters* which first appeared in a publication called *The Public School Magazine* in 1901: and several more were serialised in *The Captain,* for example *Mike: A Public School Story,* one of his most entertaining in this *genre*. This was published in book form a year later (in 1909) by A. & C. Black.

It is interesting, too, that many famous writers wrote a public school story when otherwise they wrote in quite different areas: Ian Maclaren with *The Young Barbarians* in 1901, Rudyard Kipling's *Stalky & Co.* (written in 1899 with a very unsentimental approach), Horace Annesley Vachell with *The Hill,* 1905 (about Harrow) and Alec Waugh's *The Loom of Youth* (Sherborne). These books, of course, have a distinctly autobiographical flavour.

Girls' school stories were rare until later in the century when the emphasis in stories for girls had become a little less domestic. None the less Mrs Sherwood wrote *The School Girl* in 1836 and one or two of Mrs J. H. Ewing's titles in the 1880s deal partly with life in a girls' school. Otherwise both these writers are better known for their childrens' stories.

Reading matter for girls was certainly not neglected, however. The publishers' catalogues for the eighties and nineties in particular reflect the number of authors and titles setting out to appeal to the sisters of the *Boys' Own* readers: Blackie, of course, with Bessie Marchant who wrote adventure stories with girl heroines set in countries all over the world (*Three Girls on a Ranch, Daughters of the Dominion,* and so on), Rosa Mullholland and Angela Brazil; R. T. S. and the *Girls' Own Bookshelf,* in its turn reproducing stories from the *Girls' Own Paper*. Evelyn Everett-Green, who lived from 1856 to 1932 (and in her long lifetime produced over 300 novels) was particularly popular as a girls' writer and wrote family stories and historical novels as well as books for adults. Many of her titles were particularly well produced and illustrated, and were published mainly by Nelson and R.T.S. Agnes Giberne, Mrs de Horne Vaizey, L. T. Meade and more supplied a flourishing market, again stretching from the nineties well into this century, with publishers like Nisbet, Chambers, Ward, Lock & Co., and A. & C. Black leading the field in juvenile literature.

Part of the attraction of many of these books is their wide use of really good illustrators like W. Rainey, Paul Hardy, Walter Paget, Cyril Cuneo, Harold Copping, W. S. Stacey and Gordon Browne, who formed a long association with the *Boy's Own Paper* and with Blackie's. So often it is the case that the best-produced edition of a particular title is the one to look for rather than the first edition. Clearly, to have the

Frontispiece by Gordon Browne for Henty's With Lee in Virginia.

story one wants combined with good design and illustration is to have the best of both worlds: Gordon Browne's illustrations to Manville Fenn's *Devon Boys*, or to some of Henty's stories, to take only two examples in one area of fiction, meet this requirement. The cover designs, the stories, the illustrations and, often, the publishers' catalogues on the back pages combine to give one the full flavour of the period.

The 1890s were the Golden Age of another area of fiction publishing, the detective novel. Edgar Allan Poe is acknowledged to be the writer of the first detective story. This was *The Murders in the Rue Morgue*, published in 1841 in the April issue of Graham's Magazine, Philadelphia: a successful periodical edited by Poe himself. The story was of a brutal murder, but, significantly, it also had a hero, Dupin, whose analytical mind solved the crime. The first book edition was published four years later in New York together with two other Dupin tales by Poe: *The Mystery of Marie Roget* and *The Purloined Letter*. Poe knew a great deal about the French police system, and used Paris as the background to his tales.

During the next ten years, the emphasis moved to England, to articles by Charles Dickens

in *Household Words* during 1850 describing the work of the recently formed detective police force in London, and his portrayal of characters in some contemporary novels: for example, Inspector Bucket in *Bleak House* (1853).

The Recollections of a Detective Police-Officer by 'Waters' (William Russell) appeared in 1856: there was at that time a vogue for recounting personal experiences in fictional form, and writing episodes from 'real-life'. The *Recollections* were printed and re-issued in yellowback several times, and were immensely popular, as were several more by Russell and others in the same vein up to about 1870. The fact that they were published so profusely in yellowback reflects the growing popularity of detective-type fiction.

Emile Gaboriau has a serious claim to be counted among detective novelists with *L'Affaire Lerouge*, which began as a serial instalment in a Parisian newspaper in 1866. Four more works he produced may be described as detective fiction: *Le Dossier 113*, *Le Crime d'Orcival*, *Monsieur Lecoq* and *Les Esclaves de Paris*, all first published between 1867 and 1869. Their translations first appeared in England under the imprint of Vizetelly during the 1880s, but are extremely rare. Reprinted editions in book form were published in Britain and America during the nineties.

Meanwhile, in England, Wilkie Collins'

outstanding detective novel *The Moonstone* was being serialised in one of Charles Dickens' magazines (1868), and then published in three volumes later the same year. Joseph Sheridan Le Fanu, an Irish writer, otherwise known for his tales of the supernatural, produced an ingenious detective novel in *Checkmate,* published by Hurst and Blackett, 1871, in three volumes. And here, again, quite apart from the yellowbacks, the binding styles are eye-catching decorated cloth: in the area of detective fiction there are some quite stunning cover designs.

Fergus Home's *Mystery of a Hansom Cab* had a phenomenal success after it first appeared in Melbourne in 1886, and was published in London the following year: copies were avidly sought then as now by collectors, though the work itself is not considered to have any literary merit. The first and early editions (Australian and English) are very scarce indeed. His next two detective novels (Hume having arrived back in London) were *The Piccadilly Puzzle* (1889) and *Miss Mephistopheles* (1890), both published by F. V. White. After that, he changed publishers frequently, but wrote several other detective novels in the course of a prolific career.

The London publication of *Mystery of a*

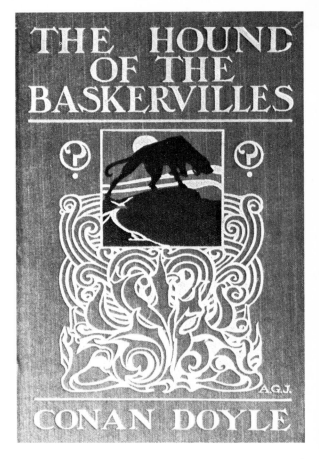

THE MYSTERY OF
A HANSOM CAB

By FERGUS HUME
AUTHOR OF THE LONE
INN—THE MYSTERY OF
LANDY COURT, &c.

377th THOUSAND

WARWICK LANE, E.C.
JARROLD AND SONS
LONDON

Hansom Cab coincided with the introduction of Sherlock Holmes to the public. This was in *Beeton's Christmas Annual* which printed *A Study in Scarlet* in its issue for 1887. The sequence of publication of the early Holmes stories is a little complicated, and is one of serialisation followed shortly afterwards by publication in book form. The second story to appear was *The Sign of Four,* in *Lippincott's Magazine* early in 1890; this was in Vol 45 of the American edition, which became Vol 1 of the special English edition.

In 1891 George Newnes invited Conan Doyle to contribute to his new illustrated monthly, *The Strand Magazine,* as part of his policy of engaging leading writers of the day, among them Dumas, E. W. Hornung and Bret Harte. So began the celebrated series of Sherlock Holmes adventures. After the first twelve stories had appeared by mid-1892, Newnes published them in one volume under the title of *The Adventures of Sherlock Holmes;* similarly, the second collection of tales to appear in *The Strand Magazine,* this time numbering eleven, were published in a companion volume in 1894 as *The Memoirs of Sherlock Holmes.* These were large

SITTING BY THE FIRE, WAS NONE OTHER THAN SHERLOCK HOLMES

Illustration for 'The Man with the Twisted Lip' by Sidney Paget in the 1911 edition of Arthur Conan Doyle's The Adventures of Sherlock Holmes *(Smith, Elder & Co., London).*

octavo volumes bound in blue gilt decorated cloth, and can, with luck, still be found; as also can *The Strand Magazine* issues, bound biannually in pictorial cloth volumes. Other Sherlock Holmes stories in hardback are *The Return of Sherlock Holmes* (1904) which is very rare; and a further three, *The Valley of Fear* (1915), *His Last Bow* (1917) and *The Case Book of Sherlock Holmes* (1927).

Sidney Paget was engaged as an artist with *The Strand Magazine,* and produced the illustrations to the Sherlock Holmes stories from the first series; it was he who created the familiar image of Holmes as a hawk-faced figure with cape and deerstalker.

In America, as early as 1878, Anna Katherine Green had invaded a male preserve and produced an exciting and well-constructed detective novel, *The Leavenworth Case* which has gone into countless reprints. This was very much the best-seller among her writings, but she wrote about thirty more detective stories and also introduced a woman detective called Violet Strange. Other interesting titles are *House of the Whispering Pines* and *The Filigree Ball*. Her books were all published first in the States and then shortly afterwards in Britain.

Three more American women writers in particular remain 'collected' and are well worth reading for their detective fiction. Lawrence Lynch (a pseudonym for Mrs Emma Murdoch Van Deventer) also started to write before the eighties: *A Mountain Mystery* (1886) and *A Dead Man's Step* (1893) are among the titles published in London after their first American editions; Mary Roberts Rinehart wrote *The Man in Lower Ten* and *The Circular Staircase* (1909), and Carolyn Wells *The Clue* and *The Diamond Pin* as well as her critical work, *The Technique of the Mystery Story* in 1913, contributed after the turn of the century.

In Britain, a fictional detective was portrayed by Florence Warden (1857–1929) in *The House on the Marsh* (1884) and *A Prince of Darkness* (1885) and others later. L. T. Meade has already been mentioned as a writer of girls' stories, but the most uncommon and interesting among her titles are those she wrote in collaboration with Clifford Halifax and Robert Eustace (both pseudonyms: one was a doctor, the other a scientist). The early writings appeared as *Stories from the Diary of a Doctor* in issues of *The Strand Magazine* between 1892 and 1895—sometimes coinciding with Sherlock Holmes—but the most sought-after (and rare) is the first edition in book form of *The Brotherhood of the Seven Kings* (1899) written with Robert Eustace, and illustrated by Sidney Paget. The *Strand Magazine* stories were also published in book form in 1894 and 1896 and were followed by other detective titles.

By the 1890s, the number of writers★ attracted to the field of detective fiction was very great. Many of them became better known in other areas of fiction: E. Phillips Oppenheim, for example, during a long life (1886–1946) and prolific writing career, wrote comparatively few detective titles among a huge number of other

★These include the following, with their best-known titles:
Coulson Kernahan, *The Dumpling* (1906) (with a dramatically illustrated front cover by Stanley L. Wood);
Richard Marsh, *The Beetle* (1897);
Gaston Leroux, *Mystery of The Yellow Room* (1907);
E. W. Hornung, The '*Raffles*' stories (starting with *The Amateur Cracksman* [1898]);
E. Phillips Oppenheim, *The Mysterious Mr Sabin* (1898);
Robert Barr, *The Triumphs of Eugène Valmont* (1906);
R. Austin Freeman, *The Red Thumb Mark* (1907) (the first book to introduce Dr Thorndyke);
Jacques Futrelle, *The Thinking Machine* (1907);
Mark Twain, *Pudd'nhead Wilson* (1894) (using the device of fingerprints).

The Yellow Book

An Illustrated Quarterly

Volume II July, 1894

London : Elkin Mathews & John Lane
Boston : Copeland & Day
Agents for the Colonies : Robt. A. Thompson & Co.

Left: *frontispiece by Stanley L. Wood for* The Lust of Hate *by Guy Boothby (1898).* Above: *Aubrey Beardsley's title page for* The Yellow Book *in its first year.*

novels, mostly spy thrillers; and Mark Twain had already achieved prominence with *Tom Sawyer* and *Huckleberry Finn* several years previously.

Some mystery stories come very close to being classed as detective fiction, but purists require a definition. It amounts to this: that a sequence of logical conclusions on the part of a investigator should result in the exposure of the crime or criminal within the framework of the story.

This excludes, for instance, many of the novels of Guy Boothby, an Australian, which feature the cold and compelling Dr Nikola: *A Bid for Fortune* (1895), *Dr Nikola* (1896), *The Lust of Hate* (1898), *Dr Nikola's Experiment* (1899) and *Farewell, Nikola* (1902). These were vividly illustrated by Stanley L. Wood. It also means that the novels of William Le Queux, A. E. W. Mason and Louis Tracy cannot be classed as true detective fiction: the list is a long one and takes us, in fact, beyond Victorian fiction.

In the nineties, the publishing firm of John Lane made two important contributions towards the advancement of the short story and of imaginative new writers. Between 1893 and

1897 he published a particularly attractive and interesting selection of novels in *The Keynotes Series*. Using high quality paper and type and covers of an elegant design, each had on the spine a specially drawn key which is the work of Aubrey Beardsley incorporating the author's initials; in many cases, there was also a title page design by Beardsley. (The American editions, published simultaneously by Roberts Brothers of Boston, have the key symbol on the back cover.) There are thirty-two titles in *The Keynotes Series,*★ and any one of them in good condition is well worth buying.

★Including, up to 1895:
George Egerton, *Keynotes* (a volume of stories), first edition;
George Egerton, *Discords*, first edition;
M. P. Shiel, *Prince Zaleski*, first edition;
Grant Allen, *The Woman Who Did*;
Henry Harland, *Grey Roses and Other Stories*;
Arthur Machen, *The Great God Pan* and *The Inmost Light*, first edition;
Arthur Machen, *The Three Imposters*, first edition.

The Yellow Book, an illustrated quarterly which had a cover design by Beardsley was intended as an outlet for the 'advanced' writers and artists of the day. In the three years of its existence, from 1894 to 1897, it was widely read, and published contributions by Max Beerbohm, Edmund Gosse, Bernard Shaw, Henry James and Oscar Wilde among others, so that in fact it also used established writers as well as new. (It was, however, the resurrected periodical *The New Review* that published the first instalment of H. G. Well's *The Time Machine* in 1895).

Although there is a very great deal of material available on the development of the new writing from the 1880s, parallel developments in the enormous best selling market in fiction by 'popular' writers remain comparatively undocumented.

Some of the bestsellers in vogue were Hall Caine's *The Christian* (1897), George du Maurier's *Trilby* (1895), Ellen Thorneycroft Fowler's novel of Methodist manners and fashionable levity, *Concerning Isabel Carnaby* (1898), which showed the New Woman struggling, and suffering, in the fight to assert her independence, Edna Lyall's *To Right the Wrong* (1893) and the reissues and current novels of the veterans, 'Ouida', M. E. Braddon, Rhoda Broughton and Mrs Henry Wood. One firm of flour merchants in the 1890s offered customers a set of Mrs Wood's novels in exchange for accumulated tokens.

In the same period, the taste for exotic adventure was fed by Rider Haggard's tales of Africa, which began with *Dawn* in 1884, followed by the enormous success of *King Solomon's Mines,* first published in 1886. (The Allan Quatermain stories continued right up to 1920.) Today, Rider Haggard novels are still to be found fairly easily in the Longmans *Silver Library* editions, which were attractively produced and cover an extensive range of his titles. Rudyard Kipling had his first stories of Anglo-Indian life, *Plain Tales from the Hills,* published in 1888. He wrote poems and short stories and was published in both America and England; his adventure story for boys *Captains Courageous* appeared in 1897: *Kim* followed in 1901 and the *Just So Stories* were first published in 1902. There are several collected editions of Kipling's works: the Seven Seas edition published between 1913 and 1926 possibly being the easiest to find in separate volumes.

Anthony Hope wrote his romances of

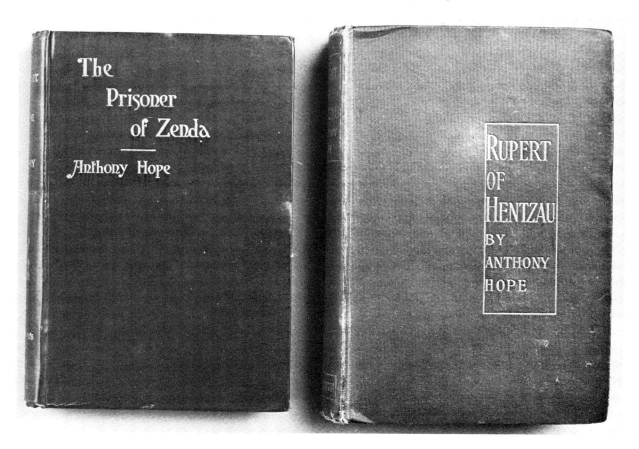

"God Save the King!"

They two then stood at the salute.

Frontispiece and an illustration 'They two then stood at the salute' by Charles Dana Gibson for Anthony Hope's Rupert of Hentzau *(J. W. Arrowsmith, Bristol).*

Ruritania (*The Prisoner of Zenda*, published in 1894) while the enduring popularity of R. D. Blackmore's *Lorna Doone* was reflected in the number of editions reprinted from the late 1880s onwards. Originally published in 1869, *Lorna Doone* has an historical background but mainly illustrated the author's feeling for the West Country and Exmoor in particular. Blackmore wrote also several other tales with backgrounds in other parts of the country: for example, *Cradock Nowell*, set in Hampshire, and *Mary Anerley* in Yorkshire. William Black, a Scottish journalist, became popular with *A Princess of Thule*, set in the Hebrides and Mull. He wrote several other adventure stories with a Scottish background, the last being *Wild Eelin* (1898) set in his native town, Inverness.

These novels were a blend of regional history and invention: entertaining and romantic and, to some extent, informative in their regional background. The challenge to long-held religious beliefs was depicted in *John Inglesant,* written by Joseph Henry Shorthouse in 1881 who himself gave up Quakerism for the Church of England.

This was an immensely successful book, held in great esteem: and the spiritual conflict between faith and agnosticism portrayed in *Robert Elsmere* (1888) brought fame and notoriety, particularly in America, to its author, Mrs Humphry Ward. She was a niece of Matthew Arnold, was brought up in Oxford and became a personal friend of both George Eliot and Henry James. Her next novel was *The History of David Grieve* in 1892, which was about a poor young man and his religious and social problems. By this time, Mrs Ward had become involved in mission work in London, and her portrayal of poverty was intended to effect political reform, by further mobilising and directing the influence she had gained through the success of *Robert Elsmere*. *Marcella* (1894) and its sequel *Sir George Tressady*, two years later, both contained schemes for the improvement of the conditions of the poor.

It is here that a line might be drawn across the end of an era. By 1900, Mrs Humphry Ward had turned from social reform novels of society life; Arnold Bennett, while earning a living writing serials of a popular sensational type, had written his first avowed 'serious' novel, *A Man From the North* in 1898. *The Bookman*, a monthly magazine launched in 1891, was very considerably devoted to novel reviews and news of novelists of the period, and serves very well to illustrate the variety and profusion of writers and their books, and the esteem their readers held for them, by the end of the nineteenth century.

Modern First Editions

MODERN first editions are books collected in the author's lifetime. There is no precise date at which we can start to include the 'moderns' of the past. At the same time, it is important to understand the category, since the values of modern firsts fluctuate more than those of any other class of book. The collector is vulnerable to changes of fashion both in terms of the value of his existing collection and the cost of new acquisitions.

Serious interest in collecting the first editions of contemporary authors began in the 1890s, and the work of many writers and illustrators published during this period is still regarded as modern by collectors today. The term becomes less appropriate as time passes. All the work of much-collected authors, like Henry James, Oscar Wilde, Stephen Crane, Corvo and others who are still favoured, has been published since 1860, and this seems a reasonable, though arbitrary, date to choose if we wish to confine our interest to a definite period. These authors' first publications were: Henry James Jr.: *A Passionate Pilgrim* (1875, Boston, £120)—James is more highly esteemed in England, and the price would be lower in America; Thomas Hardy: *Desperate Remedies* (1871), published anonymously in London, three volumes, £500. (In 1972, it would have been £200); Oscar Wilde: *Ravenna* (1878), Newdigate Prize Poem, Oxford, £40. (Not to be confused with the pirated reprint of 1904, which does not have the college arms on the title page). Stephen Crane: *Maggie: A Girl of the Streets* (1893, Johnston Smith, New York). Ordinary first edition, £30, the rare first issue has fetched $1,900; Frederick Rolfe (Baron Corvo): *Tarcissus: the Boy Martyr of Rome* (1880),

The first edition of A House of Pomegranates *by Oscar Wilde with the design and decoration by Charles Ricketts and C. H. Shannon (James R. Osgood, London 1891) with (above) the title page to one on the stories 'The Young King'.*

published anonymously at Saffron Walden, a twelve-page poem, £250 or more; a fine copy fetched £950 in 1972. Beware of the pirated edition in stiff wrappers, which is worth £5.

There is no doubt a market, somewhere, for every first edition, but the price may not be very high, and the customer may be extremely elusive. Most beginners tend to start off with modern first editions. The average reader or collector has confidence in his powers of critical appraisal. He assumes that his literary taste reflects a knowledge of literature and an understanding of contemporary values and feels instinctively at ease in his chosen field. Having selected modern literature, he will naturally aim for first editions. Although personal literary preferences help little towards an understanding of the market in a commercial sense, this feeling of assurance has much to recommend it for the new collector. If he backs his own judgment and

Left: *title page of* A House of Pomegranates. Below: *the romance* Don Tarquinio *by Frederick Rolfe (Baron Corvo).*

DON TARQUINIO

A KATALEPTIC PHANTASMATIC
ROMANCE

BY
FR. ROLFE
AUTHOR OF "HADRIAN THE SEVENTH," ETC.

LONDON
CHATTO & WINDUS
1905

resists the complex influences of contemporary taste, his chances of achieving his goal—completeness—are greatly increased. As he gains more experience, he will learn the right price to pay for the material he wants. Even if he has backed a loser, in the sense that his requirements are available only at an inflated price, he will know, for example, not to buy Henry Miller's *Tropic of Cancer* (1934), Obelisk Press, Paris (recently signed) at Sotheby's for £459 (1972), when a good copy can be obtained for £125.

The ultimate commercial value of the modern first depends on the lasting literary quality of the work, and collecting plays an important part in the process of appraisal. To have his work collected over a long period of time confers an established literary reputation upon an author as it is an expression of enthusiasm from the audience. This is not to say that well-established authors do not go out of fashion (although there will always be some market for their books), nor that some of them are not still avidly collected (here, the market for their books will be fairly stable), but that first assessments are usually more emotional. It is during this initial period of enthusiasm, which may last many years, that prices are most unstable.

It often happens, for example, that the work of an author is noticed primarily through its relevance to some topical issue rather than its intrinsic value, which may not correspond closely with its sudden reputation. Just as frequently, however, the author remains in relative obscurity within a small but fervent circle of admirers. Certainly, the press and television encourage such movements in fashion. An impulsive review of Basil Bunting's *Briggflatts* (1966), Fulcrum Press, London, in which Cyril Connolly urged the public to buy, beg, steal or borrow a copy, raised the price to £60 for the limited edition almost immediately. The price has since dropped below £10. Similarly, the television serialisations of John Galsworthy's *The Forsyte Saga* (1922 edition, one of 250 signed, £20) and Henry James's *The Golden Bowl* (1904, London, £10) produced an excessive demand for the works of these writers, though in many cases the actual titles were reprinted for those who were unable to wait for the last instalment. Here, television briefly increased interest in authors with a settled reputation.

Responsibility for new cultural trends does not, of course, lie in the mass media alone. This rests with a relatively small number of people at

Black Spring, *the second title by Henry Miller, published by The Obelisk Press (Paris 1936). This French publishing house was responsible for a number of books which were thought to be unsuited to the moral climate of London or New York at the time.*

any one time. It was Tom Pickard, with the Morden Tower poets, who rescued Bunting from obscurity and inactivity (in the 1930s he had been writing for Eliot in The Criterion, among other things), encouraged him to write *Briggflatts* and helped him to reach once more a wider audience. But for them, Cyril Connolly would never have set eyes on *Briggflatts*. Something new and original is usually recognised by a minority unless the social, political and intellectual climate make it more generally acceptable. It is at this point that the press, television and the publishing world hasten to present an already established trend to a wider audience. Clearly, the time to buy is early; the collector must develop a keen response to the changes in taste and ideas of a critical vanguard that is often small in number. His success is a measure of his own foresight, and he frequently has to wait to achieve it. Certainly, if he had bought a copy of Samuel Beckett's *Waiting for Godot* (1952)—first French limited edition of 59 copies, £2,000; first French trade edition £300; first American edition £35; first

English edition £25—he would have acquired a permanent asset. This play has since emerged as a milestone in the history of modern theatre. In France, there is much interest in Ionesco, Adamov, Ghelderode and others who continue the Theatre of the Absurd in the tradition of Jarry, but these writers were already established before *Godot* and, although affected by Beckett, still command good prices. Perhaps Beckett's statement was too final and alien to allow a significant trend to develop in England, for none of the many successful modern English dramatists is seriously collected. It is surprising that a playwright like John Osborne, with an international reputation, whose works are performed all over the world and are acknowledged to have changed the course of British drama is not collected. *Look Back in Anger* (1957), Faber, London, mint in dust wrapper costs £5 and is not easy to sell. Similarly, works by Joe Orton and Tom Stoppard are not collected, although Noel Coward benefits from the quirks of fashion.

The initial upsurge of interest in a new and fashionable movement usually develops into a more discriminating approach. The agreement that gradually emerges about the authors'

relative merits is reflected in a stabilisation of values for their books. (This process is discussed in greater detail later in the chapter, particularly with reference to high priced rarities of otherwise easily obtainable authors.) Some movements are sustained to become recognised and developing strands of art—Surrealism is a good example—while others decline in popularity, leaving some figure of central importance as representative. The publication of W. B. Yeats's *The Celtic Twilight* (1893), London, £35, provided a focus for the Irish literary revival, and the author's subsequent status as one of the greatest lyrical poets of the twentieth century was sufficient to maintain a lasting interest. On the other hand, his followers in the Celtic Twilight group, and later

Below left: *the successor to* Look Back in Anger, *John Osborne's* The Entertainer, *with a photograph by Anthony Armstrong Jones of Laurence Olivier as 'Archie Rice' (Faber & Faber, London 1957).* Below: *title page for a late Cuala Press edition of a Yeats one-act play (Dublin 1934). The Cuala Press was founded as The Dun Emer Press in 1902 by Yeats's sister, Elizabeth. The first book was produced in 1903 and the press ceased publication in 1938.*

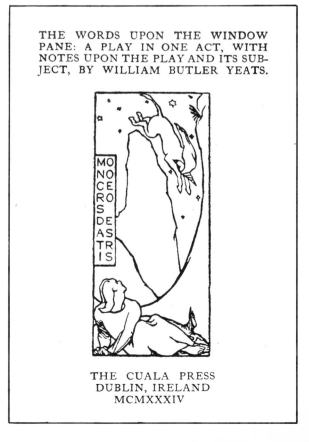

THE WORDS UPON THE WINDOW PANE: A PLAY IN ONE ACT, WITH NOTES UPON THE PLAY AND ITS SUBJECT, BY WILLIAM BUTLER YEATS.

MONOCEROS DE ASTRIS

THE CUALA PRESS
DUBLIN, IRELAND
MCMXXXIV

P·O·E·M·S
BY·LIONEL
JOHNSON

1 8 9 5

LONDON·ELKIN MATHEWS
BOSTON·COPELAND & DAY

THE TINKER'S WEDDING
A COMEDY IN TWO ACTS
BY J. M. SYNGE

MAUNSEL AND CO., LTD.
DUBLIN   1907

the Abbey Theatre, are rather out of fashion. The first editions of 'A.E.', Lionel Johnson, J. M. Synge, Lady Gregory and Padraic Colum, for example, fetch fairly low, though stable, prices. Yeats's first and most valuable book is *Mosada* (1886), Dublin, £500 or more for a separately issued off-print from The Dublin University Review of June 1886, consisting of a hundred copies in wrappers. The original issue of the magazine would fetch over £100. Even the first two volumes of The Dublin University Review, bound without wrappers (1885 and 1886), are worth about £250; they contain no less than eighteen contributions by Yeats. The Cuala Press, Dublin (formerly the Dun Emer Press, Dundrum) editions of Yeats's work currently reach £40 to £70. Though some titles by J. M. Synge are sought after—*Playboy of the Western World* (1907), Dublin, a limited edition of twenty-five, £60, or *In the Shadow of the Glen,* containing *Riders to the Sea,* London 1905, £60 (a limited edition of fifty, New York 1904, costs £250)—the general price range is under £20 for this group of writers, apart from the obvious rarities—limited editions, presentation copies and so on.

The poets of the 1930s provide a similar example, and W. H. Auden has emerged as a doyen of English letters, no longer particularly associated with a movement that has lost ground in a more revolutionary political climate. *Authors Take Sides on the Spanish Civil War* (1937), Left Review, London, in wrappers £40 (not to be confused with the American book of the same title, published in the same year, which contains about a third of the English contributions and is worth £10), might be examined in this context, for the ideological statements of some of the group are scarcely evinced in their subsequent work. Perhaps, too, the New Writing group had so many European affiliations as to make it difficult to pin down. In any event, W. H. Auden, *Poems* (25–45), privately printed by Stephen Spender (under initials S.H.S.) in London in 1928, would fetch £1,500, his *Poems* (1930),

Above left: *a limited edition of 750 copies of* Poems *by Lionel Johnson, a prominent figure in the Irish literary revival of the 1890s.* Left: The Tinker's Wedding: '*A Comedy in Two Acts' by J. M. Synge (first edition, Maunsel & Co., Ltd., Dublin 1907). This was written in 1905 while Synge was also working on* Riders to the Sea *and* In the Shadow of the Glen.

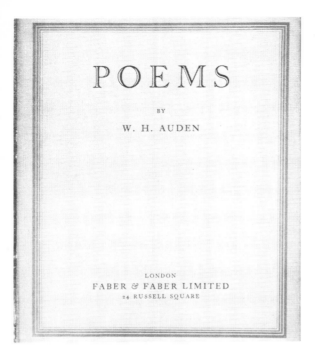

POEMS

BY

W. H. AUDEN

LONDON
FABER & FABER LIMITED
24 RUSSELL SQUARE

Above: Poems *by W. H. Auden, his first commercially published book (Faber & Faber, London 1930). Below: Roy Campbell's* Light on a Dark Horse, *'An Autobiography 1901–1935' with jacket design by Werner Stein (Hollis & Carter, 1951).*

Faber, London, £40, and most of his earlier work, which is relatively easy to find, between £10 and £25. The prices for Lous MacNeice, Spender, C. Day Lewis and Roy Campbell, on the other hand, are dropping. The most collected books by MacNeice are his first novel, published under the pseudonym Louis Malone, *Roundabout Way* (1932), London and New York, £70, and his only limited edition, *The Last Ditch* (1940), Dublin, £30 to £50, in common with most Cuala Press publications. *The Earth Compels* (1938), London, sells for £8 to £10, but the collector may prefer Issue 28 of New Verse (January 1938) containing *Bagpipe Music* for £15. Spender has a few high prices. *Forward from Liberalism* (1937), Gollancz, London (not the Left Book Club edition), only goes for £5, though *Twenty Poems* (1930), Oxford, 75 signed, has fetched £170. Probably, Roy Campbell's most valuable book, apart from his small limited editions, is his autobiography, *Light on a Dark Horse* (1951), London, £10. C. Day Lewis is more collected as the detective writer, Nicholas Blake, and a fine copy of *The Beast Must Die* (1938), London, is worth £25. Of course, we are at exactly the wrong place in time to judge the lasting reputations from this period. George Orwell's *Homage to Catalonia* (1938), London,

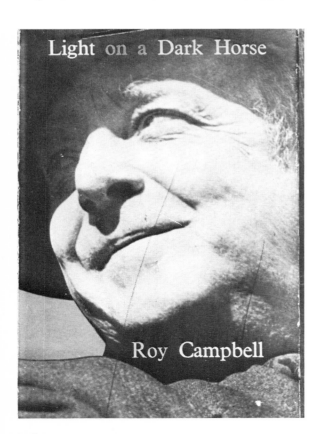

Light on a Dark Horse

Roy Campbell

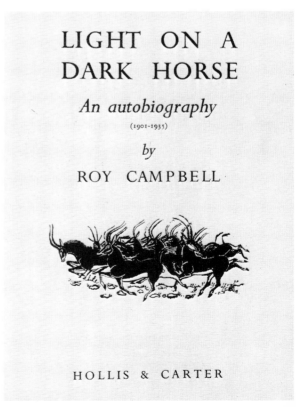

LIGHT ON A
DARK HORSE

An autobiography
(1901-1935)

by

ROY CAMPBELL

HOLLIS & CARTER

Carnegie Art Gallery, Pittsburgh

ROY CAMPBELL (1924)

by AUGUSTUS JOHN, O.M., R.A.

Frontispiece to Roy Campbell's Light on a Dark Horse. *Right: frontispiece photograph of Wilfred Owen for the 1931 edition of* The Poems of Wilfred Owen *(Chatto & Windus, London).*

fine in dust wrapper £75 (£40 without wrapper), still seems rather important, as do *Nineteen Eighty-four* (1949), London, in wrapper £40 to £70 and *Animal Farm* (1945), London, also fine in wrapper, fetching £50 in 1973 and easy to sell a year later at £100.

Typically, of the rebel movements, the writers of the 1950s Beat Generation are still of interest for sociological or nostalgic reasons. *Howl* (1956), San Francisco, which is not scarce, has fetched $70 and is worth, perhaps, £10. *Siesta in Xbalba and Return to the States* (1956), Alaska, signed, has sold for $400 in the saleroom, and the price for Allen Ginsberg alone which reflects the interest in the group and the influence it has had over contemporary literature. *Siesta in Xbalba* epitomises the movement and in fact the rest of Ginsberg is difficult to sell. Other Beat Generation writers now fetch lower prices

and their work is clearly considered less signicant than Ginsberg's. The exaggerated values of the early 1960s relate to the interest in the movement with which they are associated, rather than to their lasting literary contribution.

Nostalgia may also explain the revival of interest in the World War I poets—an interest which has more lately extended to the poets of World War II. The early deaths of Rupert Brooke, from illness, and Wilfred Owen and Issac Rosenberg, in action, provided an emotional inspiration for the collector. However, their output was so small that war poetry is more fashionable as a subject for a collection. Although the works of these poets (Alun Lewis and Sidney Keyes in World War II) are the foundation of such collections, they are not necessarily the most expensive. Authors like Graves, Sassoon, Edward Thomas, Robert Nichols, Blunden, and Masefield may command high prices in a different context. Some authors are sought by different groups of collectors because of their associations with different areas of interest. Robert Graves's *Over the Brazier* (1916), The Poetry Bookshop, London—his first book—has fetched £170 at auction (£80 in the trade), Rupert Brooke's *1914 and Other Poems* (1915), London, £20, and *Poems* (1911), London £30 (inscribed to W. W. Gibson, £320). More collectors are looking for

ISAAC ROSENBERG

COLLECTED WORKS
POEMS · PROSE · LETTERS
& SOME DRAWINGS

H.F.T. from Siegfried Sassoon
Sept 11th 1920.

COUNTER-ATTACK

AND OTHER POEMS

BY

SIEGFRIED SASSOON

AUTHOR OF
"THE OLD HUNTSMAN"

LONDON
WILLIAM HEINEMANN
MCMXVIII

OVER THE BRAZIER
BY ROBERT GRAVES

THE POETRY BOOKSHOP

the Graves than for the Brooke titles. An impressively priced Brooke item is *Lithuania* (1915), The Chicago Little Theatre, with an auction record in 1968 of $6,750. This was a freak price for the first copy to appear at auction for some time; on a rising market two hundred copies were published, and £100 is a more realistic price. Brooke's first work, *The Pyramids* (1904), Rugby printed for private distribution, is safe at £200–400. Other examples in this area are Isaac Rosenberg's *Youth* (1915), London, £25; Wilfred Owen's *Poems* (1920), London, £30–50 (£60 for a copy in dust wrapper—rare in this condition—on a recent catalogue); Sidney Keyes' *The Iron Laurel* (1942), London, £5.

Surrealism is a sustained movement, very much alive today, commanding as good prices as ever. It is no longer thought of as simply a movement, but as an effective approach to artistic and literary expression. During the process of cultural development, artistic movements tend to accumulate and to remain with us, while literary phases with no contemporary relevance fall into obscurity. The French, on the other hand, are still wrapped up in their early achievements in this field and honour Surrealism in a

self-congratulatory and commemorative manner. In this sense, they preserve the idea of trend in much the same way that the members of the Dickens or Johnson Society do in their own field of interest. The three Surrealist manifestos of André Breton are the literary core of the movement. *Manifeste du Surréalisme. Poisson soluble*, (1924), Paris, £110; *Seconde Manifeste du Surréalisme* (1930), Paris, £90; *Les Manifestes du Surréalisme, Suivies de Prolégomènes à un troisième Manifeste du Surréalisme ou non* (1946), Paris, 508 copies, £110. The artistic high spot is Max Ernst's collage novel, *Une Semaine de Bonté* (1934), Paris, 812 copies; five volumes in wrappers, boxed, £650. The periodicals contain the most vital expression of the Surrealist attitude: *Transition* 1–27 (April 1927–Spring 1938), Paris, 27 numbers in 25, £450; *This Quarter* (Surrealist number, Volume 5 no 1, September 1932), Paris, £20; *Minotaure, Revue Artistique et Littéraire* (1–12/13, 1933–39), Paris, 13 numbers in 11,

Left: *frontispiece by Picasso for* Thorns of Thunder: Selected Poems *by Paul Eluard (Europa Press and Stanley Nott, 1936). One of fifty numbered copies signed by the author. Below:* the most influential English Surrealist periodical.

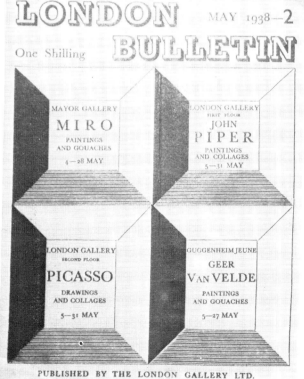

159

£200 for a fine set; *London Bulletin* (1–20, April 1938–June 1940) 20 numbers in 15, £250; *View* (Volume 1 no 1—Volume 7 no 3, 1941–46), New York, 29 numbers in 28, over £300—the early tabloid issues are very scarce; *VVV*, poetry, plastic arts, anthropology, sociology, psychology (1–4, June 1942–February 1944), New York, 4 numbers in 3, £150.

Some movements are too recent to have produced a single representative writer. In the same way that all Surrealists are collected because of the movement's permanent influence on the cultural scene, all writers of a new movement are studied until individuals have been selected by the commentator and collector. Concrete poetry and the Liverpool poets are good cases in point. The Liverpool poets—who were caught up to some extent in Beatles publicity—are up and coming. Unfortunately, the press tends to ignore individuals or groups which cannot be easily fitted into a definable 'scene'. The group would have been exciting to collect in the early stages for they produced much ephemeral material, some distributed free, and privately printed work. Adrian Henri's *Christ enters into the City of Liverpool* (1969, 100), I.C.A., could sell for £10, and Brian Patten's *Little Johnny's Confession* (1969) Fulcrum Press, London for £5. Pete Brown and Roger McGough are also important. Concrete poetry (and its various manifestations) is better established, and perhaps more significant, since it explores the possibility of communication on an entirely new level. The association of literature, graphics and sound is an attempt to synthesise distinct areas of artistic expression. The final outcome for concrete poetry is hard to predict. It may contribute more to graphics and the performing arts than to literature, and the audience should be wide. Ignoring the Brazilian and German exponents, the most important British concrete poets are Ian Hamilton Finlay, Edwin Morgan, Dom Silvester Houédard, John Furnival and Bob Cobbing. *Concrete Poetry: Britain Canada U.S.A.* (1966) published by Hansjörg Mayer, Stuttgart and Corsham, is worth £65; of the 78 copies printed, nearly half are imperfect, for the introduction by Jasia Reichhardt is missing or damaged. Dom Silvester Houédard's *Wall Poem, Sand Rock Tide* (1966), Openings Press (Furnival) is a single sheet, limited to 50+12, and would sell for £25 or more. All John Furnival's folders are severely limited to between 15 and 50 copies, and worth £25 or more. The concrete poetry

magazine *Futura* (1965–68) Hansjörg Mayer, is complete in 26 numbers; each issue is a large folded sheet and devoted to the work of one poet. Complete sets are now difficult to find and would cost more than £30.

Factors other than personal literary judgment, prevailing fashion or press publicity influence an author's rating in the eyes of the collector. An author's death always has a disturbing effect on the market. His prices may fall (sometimes dramatically) or rise, and settle again at an unpredictable level in relation to his former standing. Perhaps interest diminishes when the prospect of further output ceases and the collector can no longer identify with a living author; nor are there new books to stimulate new collectors who would increase the demand for early work. Both Churchill and Eliot prices have suffered in this respect; although one would expect a quick recovery in Eliot's case, and important titles like his first book, *Prufrock and other Observations* (1917) London: The Egoist Ltd, 500 copies printed, £150, or *The Waste Land* (1922), New

Title page and, above right, frontispiece to Ezra Pound: His Metric and Poetry *written anonymously by T. S. Eliot (Alfred A. Knopf, New York, 1917). This was Eliot's second book and was revised by Pound himself, who also compiled the bibliography which closes the book.*

EZRA POUND

HIS METRIC AND POETRY

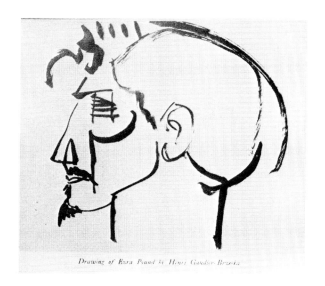

Drawing of Ezra Pound by Henri Gaudier-Brzeska

*Sylvia
Plath*

*The
Colossus
and other
poems*

The Colossus and Other Poems *by Sylvia Plath (Heinemann, London 19660). This was her first published volume and contains ten poems not in the American edition.*

York, £70 (with a dropped 'a' in 'mountain' in some copies) are not affected; indeed a presentation copy of *The Waste Land* to the author's wife made £1,300 auction in 1969. The prices for 'fashionable' authors will suffer permanently. When Ian Fleming died, there was a stampede for his work, caused, no doubt, by the publicity given to the event and the rapid re-publishing of his books, followed by a sharp drop below his original level. His first book, *Casino Royale* (1952), London, will still fetch £40 if fine in the dust wrapper, but no other titles are worth more than a pound or two. In contrast, the circumstances surrounding the deaths of Sylvia Plath, Emily Dickinson, Anne Sexton and others contributed strongly to the esteem in which they are held by collectors.

The publication of a bibliography may affect the market by attracting collectors who like to know what they are looking for and discouraging others who are not stimulated by the challenge of what might be a futile search. The bibliography may reveal the impossibility of completing an author collection. Severely limited items and their whereabouts may be listed. A new collector with serious intentions would pass on to another author after a glance at the Sassoon bibliography (Geoffrey Keynes, London 1962). Eleven of Sassoon's first twelve books (Keynes A1–A12) are in editions of 50 or less. All would be worth three figures. Even A10, *The Daffodil Murderer* (1913) London published under the pseudonym Saul Kain, 1,000 copies printed, costs £70. Genuine rarities and high spots will usually maintain their high values. When a collected author loses favour the commoner material tends to decrease in price. Several authors who are no longer popularly associated with high prices, or who have never been seriously collected, have high priced rarities.*

---

*J. B. Priestley, *The Chapman of Rhymes* (1918), London, £250. (Suppressed by the author);
Arthur Waley, *Chinese Poems* (1916), privately published. Printed by Lowe Bros, £250 or over (Only two copies known);
John Galsworthy, the four titles published under the pseudonym John Sinjohn, *From the Four Winds* (1897), London, *Jocelyn* (1898), London, *Villa Rubein* (1900), London, *Man of Devon* (1900), Edinburgh and London, £70–200;
Arnold Bennett, *The Old Wives' Tale* (1908), London, £60 (£200 for a fine copy with lettering on spine intact);
Sean O'Casey, *Lament for Thomas Asche* (c 1919) by Sean O'Cathasaigh, Dublin, single leaf, poor copy £75. And so on. If you are the sort of person who looks for a 1933 penny you might keep an eye open for these: Robert Frost, *Twilight* (1894)—One copy known, two printed;
Edward Fitzgerald, *Rubaiyat of Omar Khayyam* (1859);
Fergus Hume, *The Mystery of a Hansom Cab* (1886), Melbourne.

THE
COMMON READER

VIRGINIA WOOLF

" . . . I rejoice to concur with the common reader; for by the common sense of readers, uncorrupted by literary prejudices, after all the refinements of subtilty and the dogmatism of learning, must be generally decided all claim to poetical honours."—Dr Johnson, *Life of Gray.*

PUBLISHED BY LEONARD & VIRGINIA WOOLF
AT THE HOGARTH PRESS, 52 TAVISTOCK SQUARE
LONDON, W.C.
1925

LINGUAL EXERCISES
FOR
ADVANCED VOCABULARIANS

by
the author of
"RECREATIONS"
&c

I am not high-minded; I have
no proud looks. I do not exer-
cise myself in great matters
which are too high for me
Psalm cxxxj

❀ CAMBRIDGE
Privately printed at the University Press
MCMXXV

Walter Sickert.

99 *copies printed February* 1925

Top: *a first edition of Virginia Woolf's* The Common Reader, *with the cloth cover decorated by Vanessa Bell.* Left: *a very different work by Siegfried Sassoon, in a private limited edition, and (above) the inscription on Walter Sickert's copy.*

Bibliographies and check-lists are guides to the present state of knowledge and have an air of undisputed authority. But they usually contain inaccuracies, and over-enthusiasm on the part of the bibliographers when confronted with issue points may be disguised by the punctilious, scientific descriptions. On the other hand, the omission of certain editions or works from a bibliography should be regarded with suspicion, for they may not be great rarities. They are less likely to have been overlooked by the bibliographer than to have been purposely excluded as outside his frame of reference.

Some literary forms are much more popular with collectors than others. Poetry has always been more keenly collected and more valuable than fiction. This is partly because poetry as a minority interest is published in smaller editions for an initially more discerning readership. Poetry is never commercial, so that bad poetry has little hope of getting itself into print, whereas the reverse is true of fiction, where the borderlines between successful bad novels and successful good novels are much harder to draw. Poets are almost invariably less productive than novelists and other prose writers, although an interesting exception is the case of Edna St Vincent Millay, very popular and much collected—particularly in America during the 1920s. The popular poet is so rare that it is not surprising that he too is collected. The relationship of dramatists to collectors is also interesting; some, like Beckett, are collected while other important figures are neglected. Often, an unsuccessful play, such as *The Ascent of F6* (1936), by Auden and Isherwood, London, £20 in dust wrapper, will become a collectors' item because of the subsequent reputation acquired by its authors in other fields, and will reach an unrealistic price in proportion to its worth. This is the point at which a collector's enthusiasm for the completeness of his collection may carry him away from the realm of sound judgment or taste: though even here, works may be rescued from oblivion at the most surprising stages. James Joyce's *Exiles* (1918), London, £25, which was a disastrous flop when first produced, was nevertheless keenly collected as a Joyce item, regardless of its supposed lack of theatrical merit. Lately, however, it has been salvaged and brought back to life, very successfully, with two long and critically acclaimed runs. There are other occasions, though, when no case can be made for concealed but lasting importance. Only the dedication of the collector can explain a price of £150 for E. M. Forster's *Alexandria: A History and a Guide* (1922), Alexandria, or a similar price for his notes on Egypt.

It will, by now, have become clear that the variety of first editions and the subjective element in their assessment make this field most difficult to evaluate. Even the layman grasps, in some obscure way, the concept of the first edition, finally translating his sense of its permanence as the original into an idea of value. But most first editions are not valuable—there are too few collectors to absorb the available supply. Nevertheless, there are criteria that go some way towards making possible a relative judgment of values; these standards concern scarcity and desirability. We have looked at the idea of the right author at the right time, and suggested the unknown author selected in advance of his fashion. An impractical exhortation: the £2,000 Beckett was on sale at the theatre on Godot's first night, and we are always wiser after the event.

Scarcity and desirability are usually, but not inevitably, closely interconnected. Johann Schmidt's *Prolegomena to a Personal Reading of a Pamphlet by John Lyly* is undeniably rare since only ten copies were printed, but his mother is the only person on earth who wants one. With collected authors, however, there will be more hopeful customers than copies available and the value of the book will depend upon this imbalance. In absolute terms, the first Shakespeare folio is not a rare book because of the number of copies known to be extant, but such is the demand for the first editions of our national bard that value and rarity part company and a copy of *Comedies, Histories and Tragedies,* 1st folio edition (1623), if you could find it, would cost £25,000 or more. More modestly, let us consider the following: William Golding: *Poems* (1935), approximately 500 copies printed, £50, and Virginia Woolf: *The Voyage Out* (1915), London 2,000 copies, £50. In the cases of both these first books, the limitations, the appeal of the author, and the appeal of the book itself interact to produce (coincidentally) the same value. There is no apparent rational basis for the value, because the vital imponderable—how many customers there are to pay how much—is always unknown.

There has always been a tendency in the first edition market to create artificial scarcity by the production of a limited edition—that is to say an edition in which the actual number of copies printed is specified, and, usually, each one is numbered. Although the limited edition rationalises one aspect of the data about the book and, in this sense, should make evaluation a little less difficult, in fact it introduces new dimensions of uncertainty. A limited edition of 2,000 copies is a common book, far more so, perhaps, than an edition without an 'official' stamp of rarity which may have been published in a smaller number and is less likely to be preserved because it lacks the publisher's 'approval'. The book producer can take this hot-house cultivation for the collector a step further and publish commissioned work, in limited numbers, at his own private press. This activity introduces the factor of quality, since such presses are usually concerned with fine printing and fine book production, so that a further subjective element obtains. Books from private presses like Kelmscott, Eragny, Ashendene, Doves, Gregynog, Nonesuch, Riccardi, and Golden Cockerel—form a hierarchy of their own in addition to the inherent desirability of the work. For example, Yeats in Cuala is worth less than Morris in Kelmscott, but the values change completely in other editions. Similarly, Elizabeth Bowen in Cuala (*Seven Winters*) is worth more than Norman Douglas in

The final page of A Dream of John Ball and A King's Lesson *by William Morris (Kelmscott Press, 1892). The Kelmscott Press was founded in 1891 and ran for seven years, its organizers doing virtually everything for themselves, including hand printing on hand-made paper.*

house, therefore do I forbear to preach it. Yet it shall be preached. ❡ And not heeded, said the captain, save by those who head and hang the setters forth of new things that are good for the world. Our trade is safe for many and many a generation. ❡ And therewith they came to the King's palace, and they ate and drank and slept, and the world went on its ways.

A king's lesson

THE END OF A KING'S LESSON.

kelmscott william morris

This book, a Dream of John Ball and a King's Lesson, was written by William Morris, and printed by him at the Kelmscott Press, Upper Mall, Hammersmith, in the County of Middlesex; and finished on the 13th day of May, 1892. Sold by Reeves & Turner, 196, Strand, London.

123

Lugano, although Douglas is normally more valuable than Bowen. When private presses publish books that are of no interest to the first edition collector, beautiful book production comes into its own.

In the 1930s, publishers tried to sell H. E. Bates in limited editions—the manufactured rarity (a phrase first coined by Basil Blackwell). Though not itself a limited edition, his first work, a pamphlet, *The Last Bread* (1926), sells for only a pound or two. Bates is the classic example of an author whose reputation has been destroyed for the collector by the manufactured rarity. Bates was not sufficiently interesting or controversial to carry the burden of the limited edition. A rarity must come from an author who is already desirable.

Although one must concede the undoubted rarity of extremely limited editions, the value of such works does not usually increase sharply with time (except in instances of reappraisal), since such productions are treated with an immediate respect not necessarily accorded to the ordinary book. The limited edition has no element of the unknown. In the same way, a museum of domestic utensils may lack in sixteenth century cheese-graters but have an abundance of gold plate. Furthermore, there is always the danger that collectors may be alienated if their chosen author produces works in editions too limited to be available to them.

Sometimes there is the added inducement of the author's signature—a manageable feat when the limitation is small. And here we have the beginnings of the logical pyramid that rises to the ultimate original. In a sense, the signed limited edition is the most modest form of direct author involvement—the purely mechanical signing of his name for commercial purposes. The next step up is the presentation copy, which has its own degrees of intimacy. The following sequence of possible presentations and dedications in a book by George Orwell (Eric Blair) published in say 1936, illustrates this:

G.O.

George Orwell. 1942.

Best wishes, George Orwell. 1936.

To John with kindest regards, Eric Blair.

Love, Eric.

When one reaches the higher pinnacles of intimacy, judgment as to relative desirability becomes subjective. Thus T. S. Eliot, *Selected Essays* (1932), inscribed to his wife, fetched £300; the ordinary first edition is worth £5. In any

MURDER
IN THE
CATHEDRAL

by
T. S. ELIOT

FRIENDS OF
CANTERBURY CATHEDRAL
EDITION

Canterbury
H. J. GOULDEN, LIMITED

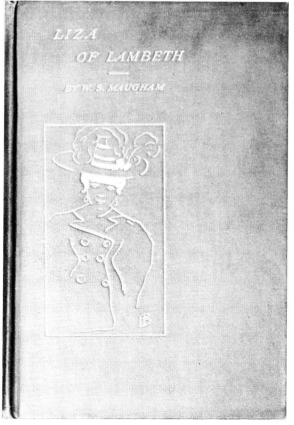

LIZA
OF LAMBETH

BY W. S. MAUGHAM

event, the artificiality of the signed limited edition has less appeal to the collector than the spontaneity of the presentation copy. On the same level as the presentation copy, desirable because of its association with the author, proof copies are attractive because they precede the first edition. They are very limited in number and are sought after in descending order from galley to first proof to revised proof to final proof. Naturally, the proof with the author's own corrections will be the most valuable. The ultimate original is, of course, the author's manuscript or typescript. The field is as unpredictable as the art market, for here, too, we are dealing with unique items and the only general statement possible is that the value of the manuscript corresponds to the importance of the work in the author's canon. One snare—apart from the counterfeit—is the fair copy. Such manuscripts are sometimes put out by authors, perhaps for charity, intended to be sold for what they are, and have considerably less value than the original.

Only a few remaining points can serve as a guide to the relative values of ordinary first editions. Three categories of book within an author collection spring to mind, his first book, his best book and his rarest book. Sometimes the three coincide—most obviously in the case of the one book author—and the rarest is often, but by no means always, the first book. A few more examples of first books may be worth mentioning: W. Somerset Maugham: *Liza of Lambeth* (1897), T. Fisher Unwin, £50; Ford Madox Ford: *The Brown Owl* (1891), A Fairy Story, £50; Edith Sitwell: *The Mother and other Poems* (1915), Oxford, £200; Ernest Hemingway: *Three Stories & Ten Poems* (1923), Paris, £800; [Edmund] E. C. Blunden of Christs' Hospital: *Poems* (1914), Horsham, £250; Joseph Conrad: *Almayer's Folly* (1895), T. Fisher Unwin, £150; E. M. Forster: *Where Angels Fear to Tread* (1905), Edinburgh & London, £60. Many new authors today are published in a fairly large edition, the newness of the author being the publisher's recommendation. Therefore, unfortunately, we may not be sitting on the bargains of the future when we buy all the new novels that come out.

The rarity of a book may be brought about

Above left: *signed copy of T. S. Eliot's* Murder in the Cathedral *(1935). This acting version is the true first publication, preceding the Faber edition.* Left: *the second edition of* Liza of Lambeth, *W. Somerset Maugham's first novel.*

in a number of ways, apart from the obvious numerical element. Graham Greene, for example, disliked the dust wrapper of *The Basement Room,* and it was called in after less than 100 copies had been released. A copy with the rare dust wrapper is worth £200, with the regular wrapper, £30. The classic example is the first edition of *Alice in Wonderland* (1865), £1,200 or more, depending on condition. The printing of the first edition was so bad that Lewis Carroll had the issue withdrawn, giving away a few copies in the meantime. About twenty copies are known to exist. The 1866 edition is worth a little over £100. Lastly, the author's most significant work, if there is one will always command a good price because it inevitably appeals to a wider range of buyers than the modest one-author collector.

The 'highspots' will always be collected, and the novice should be encouraged to concentrate on them before embarking definitively upon an author collection. The bookseller often offers the (over-priced) easy items because he himself is unable to find the highspots, and in the

Youngman Carter's cover design for It's A Battlefield *by Graham Greene (Heinemann, London 1934).*

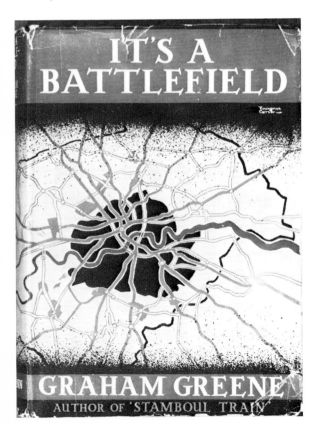

long run the easy items will not become difficult to find but lack significance without the best and the rarest. Incidentally, the best is sometimes the commonest and positive best-sellers need cause no anxiety, because they can always be found at a low price. Typical examples are Joseph Heller's *Catch 22,* Norman Mailer's *The Naked and the Dead,* Carson McCullers' *The Ballad of the Sad Cafe,* Saul Bellow's *Henderson the Rain King,* and Truman Capote's *Breakfast at Tiffany's.* One problem which sometimes crops up for the new collector is whether to collect English or American first editions of a given author. Purists will argue for the first edition published anywhere, whereas others might regard the edition published in the author's own country as the book to possess.★

The question of the inclusion of periodical contributions in author collections is a matter of personal taste. The conventional argument against the inclusion of periodical issues in first edition collections is that the issue, or several issues of a serial publication, containing the first appearance of a work, were never bound as a book. However, it could pertinently be said than an exhaustive collection is the ultimate goal, and as far as the publication in book form is concerned, the modern first edition from small presses published in flimsy wrappers, the broadsheet and the pamphlet which would automatically be included in any true collection might be said to suffer from the same deficiency. In general, values are much higher in the case of the conventional first edition, but with the boom in collecting (i.e. increased demand for a constant product) those of variants of the first editions of collected authors are rising. First edition booksellers frequently include periodical issues in their

★The following books by British authors were first published in America:
Oscar Wilde, *The Picture of Dorian Gray* (1890);
Rudyard Kipling, *Stalky & Co.* (1899);
Thomas Hardy, *Far from the Madding Crowd* (1874);
Charles Dickens, *The Mystery of Edwin Drood* (1870);
Wilkie Collins, *The Woman in White* (1860);
H. Rider Haggard, *She* (1886);
George Bernard Shaw, *Love among the Artists* (1900);
Robert Louis Stevenson, *The Black Arrow* (1888).
The following books by American authors were first published in Great Britain:
Mark Twain, *Tom Sawyer* (1876);
Longfellow, *The Song of Hiawatha* (1855);
Herman Melville, *The Whale* (1851);
Henry James, *Daisy Miller* (1882) and *The Bostonians* (1886);
Nathaniel Hawthorne, *Pansie* (1864).

catalogues at high prices. The first issue of *The Criterion* (October 1922), edited by T. S. Eliot and containing the first appearance of *The Wasteland,* has fetched £26 in the saleroom and regularly sells at £30 to £50 from first edition catalogues. Even more impressively, Conan Doyle's first Sherlock Holmes story *A Study in Scarlet* which appeared first in *Beeton's Christmas Annual* (1887) has fetched £450, and a good copy would sell for up to £1,000. Such exceptional cases make it inevitable that the practice will be extended, and many collectors who seek the gratification of further acquisition will be tempted by contributions to periodicals when their collections are near to completion or the remaining books are very scarce and expensive.

In spite of the relatively low prices that periodical contributions command compared with the conventional first edition, even these are sometimes too high. Volumes 29 and 30 of *The Cornhill Magazine* (1874) containing Hardy's *Far From the Madding Crowd* in twelve instalments, have been offered for £15. In view of the commonness of the periodical in question, this is a very high price indeed. A purchaser would be paying for the bibliographical information. It is self evident that an essay, poem, article or short story published in a periodical and never reprinted book form must inevitably form part of any author collection. There is little point in a collection of, say, Vernon Watkins, which contains no periodicals, for he published only six books and the remainder of his not inconsiderable output is to be found in approximately two hundred separate periodical issues covering over fifty titles. To a lesser degree, this pattern will be true of many poets. Finally, the absence of periodicals in an author collection will frequently exclude the author's first appearance in print e.g. John Keats in *The Examiner,* Yeats in *The Dublin University Review,* George Meredith and Thomas Hardy in *Chambers's Journal,* Dylan Thomas in the *Swansea Grammar School Magazine,* Auden in *The Badger* (Downs School Magazine).

The whole business of forecasting for financial gain is fraught with uncertainty and any advice one might offer as to whom to collect and whom not to collect would probably prove meaningless. However, one may make the following lists (naturally far from exhaustive— indeed random and personal) for the stable author, the falling and the rising.

Stable

Yeats, Joyce and Beckett (still good for the wealthy collector), Hardy, E. M. Forster, Greene, Evelyn Waugh, the Sitwells, Sassoon, Conrad, Corvo, 1890s group (Wilde, Beardsley), Pound, Aldous Huxley, Hemingway, Faulkner, Mary Webb, T. E. Lawrence, Conan Doyle (increasing), Chesterton and other Catholics, William Golding, Philip Larkin, Powys brothers, Pasternak, Nabokov, Lowry, Firbank, Bram Stoker, Gordon Craig, Ford Madox Ford, Gertrude Stein.

Losing ground

Dylan Thomas, Auden, Spender, Day Lewis, MacNeice and other 1930s poets; Eliot; Plath (too many limited editions, and posthumous) and Ted Hughes; Churchill, D. H. Lawrence, Aldington, Norman Douglas; Miller and Durrell (over-priced).

Recommended/Rising

Women writers—Doris Lessing, Iris Murdoch,

Simonetta Perkins, *L. P. Hartley's very scarce first novel (G. P. Putnam's Sons Ltd., London & New York 1925). Putnam also published Hartley's famous trilogy* The Shrimp & The Anemone *(1944),* The Sixth Heaven *(1946) and* Eustace and Hilda *(1947).*

Muriel Spark, Margaret Drabble, Elizabeth Taylor, Edna O'Brien etc.; Bloomsbury group —Leonard and Virginia Woolf, Lytton Strachey; Underground authors, Orwell, Joyce Cary, Charles Causley, L. P. Hartley, Raymond Chandler, Seamus Heaney, Thomas Kinsella; Arthur Waley, J. R. R. Tolkien (these not easy to find); Anthony Powell; 1sts of modern illustrators (irrespective of the literary merits of the works they illustrate)—Kay Nielsen, Mervyn Peake, Rackham, Dulac, Pogany, Greenaway, Harry Clarke, Morris associates. Some authors who fetched high prices in the 1920s and 1930s and dropped out of the market are beginning to appreciate—Wells, Shaw, Bennett, Galsworthy; on the other hand, Kipling, Walpole, Stevenson, and Masefield have not yet.

Some writers elude these categories, they are famous but not seriously collected e.g. C. P. Snow, Kingsley Amis, Brendan Behan, Arnold Wesker. And some authors enter the first edition field in other contexts. Collectors of juveniles will prize the first editions of Henty, Ballantyne and Westerman, while those interested in art criticism will seek Herbert Read, Paul Nash and Roger Fry in firsts. Uniform editions of the collected works of a number of authors whose single works are not in great demand are often of some value. The complete works of any author who has written himself into the body of syllabus literature are the necessary tools for any student of the subject.★

A tendency in modern first edition collecting today—and a realistic one in view of the difficulty of building up a first class collection of a first class author—is that of a collection unified by subject, imprint, or setting, for example. Such thematic collections could well be financially rewarding, and certainly offer more scope to the individualistic and creative inclinations of the collector than does the rigid, circumscribed mould of the author collection. Rational suggestions for such collections would include: World War I poetry; World War II novels; novels with homosexual themes; books about Sherlock Holmes; cinema or theatre background novels; 1890s; the Bloomsbury group; literature with horseracing backgrounds; scientific first editions (Ian Fleming collected these); Utopian literature; privately printed books; books from particular presses (as distinct from private presses) —Hours Press (Nancy Cunard), Hogarth Press (Woolf), Grey Walls Press, Editions Poetry London, John Lehmann, Fantasy Press (Oscar Mellor) etc.; series books such as King Penguins, Tauchnitz editions, Left Book Club (256 titles), Saturday Books, Britain in Pictures, Armed Services Editions (1,324 titles) and so on.

What we have said so far about modern first editions is the tip of the iceberg; one further

The Tauchnitz edition of Orlando *by Virginia Woolf (1929). The 'Collection of British Authors', which began in 1841 had run into over 4,000 volumes by the early twentieth century.*

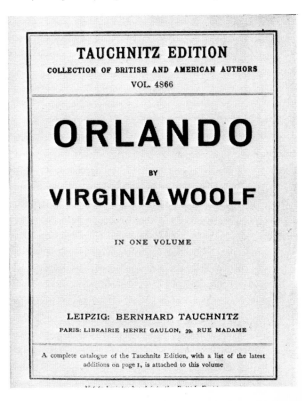

TAUCHNITZ EDITION
COLLECTION OF BRITISH AND AMERICAN AUTHORS
VOL. 4866

ORLANDO

BY

VIRGINIA WOOLF

IN ONE VOLUME

LEIPZIG: BERNHARD TAUCHNITZ
PARIS: LIBRAIRIE HENRI GAULON, 39, RUE MADAME

A complete catalogue of the Tauchnitz Edition, with a list of the latest additions on page 1, is attached to this volume

---

★For example:
Galsworthy, Limited Manton edition, 30 volumes, 1922–36, £100;
Stevenson, Limited Vailima edition, 26 volumes, 1922–23, £150, Tusitala edition, 35 volumes, no date £30;
Kipling, Sussex edition, 35 volumes, 1937–39, Bombay edition, 31 volumes, 1913–38;
Barrie, Kirriemuir edition, 10 volumes, 1913, £30.
Complete works of collected authors are more valuable still:
Conrad. Medallion edition, 22 volumes, 1925–28, £80;
Wilde, Works, 14 volumes, 1908, £100 or more;
Yeats, Shakespeare Head Press, 8 volumes, 1908, £150 or more;
Hardy, Limited Melstock edition, 37 volumes, 1919–20, £250.
(1) H. R. Trevor Roper.
Religion, the Reformation and Social Change (1967) MacMillan, p. 296.

TO A PROUD PHANTOM

ENA LIMEBEER

PRINTED AND PUBLISHED BY
LEONARD AND VIRGINIA WOOLF
AT THE HOGARTH PRESS
RICHMOND
1923

To A Proud Phantom by Ena Limebeer (Hogarth Press, 1923). The Hogarth Press was founded by Leonard and Virginia Woolf in 1917 in Richmond and then moved to 52 Tavistock Square, London, in March 1924. Books produced after Virginia Woolf's death in 1938 are regarded with less interest by collectors.

hazard that lies below the surface (apart from the inherent risks attached to speculation in a volatile market) is the identification of the goods. In general, a first edition can be recognised by the absence of any indication to the contrary, but frequently the information is insufficient or misleading, and bibliographies (or reliable and experienced booksellers) must be consulted. This subject is as enormous as the sum of all bibliographies ever written, and we cannot tackle it here. Suffice it to say that caution is of the essence. The apparent first edition of Walter de la Mare's *Come Hither* (1923) without the publisher's name on the back strip is the second issue—the first state is very rare. *Widower's Houses* (1893) by Shaw, bound in mauve cloth follows the earlier issues in blue and olive-green. The complications are endless, the range of prices may be consider-able. As far as the speculative aspect is concerned, the prevailing world economic climate is making itself felt. Capital is always seeking investment, but the collector who continues with moderns is playing safe. The modern moderns are suffering as well as the unembellished common titles by the better established collected authors. Fine copies in dust wrapper, signed limited editions, presentation copies and other rarities command high prices. Greene's *Stamboul Train* without the dust wrapper is worth £5, with it perhaps £30, inscribed over £100. The intense demand in such restricted areas introduces new levels of unpredictability and it only takes a few wealthy collectors to start collecting the same author to turn the market upside down. This has happened in the case of Hemingway, Betjeman, Hawthorne and also Harold Frederic (surprising though this may seem to some). Beckett has lost ground as wealthy collectors withdraw from the field with complete collections. This period of retrenchment may leave the rest of the field more open to the modest collector, and what he may garner now will be reappraised, for better or for worse, by the changing values and circumstances of the future.

Glossary

ALL PUBLISHED A booksellers' term meaning that, despite appearances, the volume or series described represents the whole work—that a continuation had originally been projected but was never carried out.

ANTIQUA The German name for roman type, occasionally used in English contexts.

ANTIQUE or ANTIQUED BINDING Used of a recent binding on an old book, done in a style appropriate to the book's age; often simulating signs of wear.

ANTIQUE PAPER Used to describe any good-quality paper with a rough surface when used in a modern book.

AQUATINT A process of COPPER-ENGRAVING immensely popular in the years around 1800, in which a finely-powdered resin is spread over the copper plate to provide a porous surface which is then etched with acid. Aquatints are easily recognisable by the vast number of tiny dots which make up the illustration and which appear as toning.

ARABESQUE Any decoration in the form of flowing lines of foliage and scroll-work, fancifully intertwined; originally in an Islamic style.

ARMORIAL BINDING A binding stamped with an owner's coat of arms, usually in gilt.

ART PAPER A modern kind of clay-coated paper, especially suitable for printing HALF-TONE illustrations.

ASSOCIATION COPY A copy with interesting associations, e.g. one which belonged to the author or which shows signs of having passed through his hands, or which belonged to somebody connected with the contents; often loosely applied to a copy which belonged to somebody who was well-known in his own right but who was not otherwise connected with the book.

AUTHORISED EDITION An edition published with the author's consent or, if he is dead, published by someone legitimately and legally possessed of the manuscript or with the consent of the copyright-holder. *See* PIRATED EDITION.

AUTHOR'S BINDING A binding specially done on the author's instructions, on a copy to be given away by him; a very occasional practice, and usually difficult to authenticate.

AUTOGRAPH Any hand-written matter (not necessarily signed by the writer), such as annotations in a book or a letter inserted in it. The term usually implies that the writer is important, interesting or connected with the book.

BACKSTRIP That part of the binding which covers the SPINE and which faces the front when a book is in its normal position on a shelf.

BINDER'S CLOTH A cloth binding, whether new or old, which is tailor-made for an individual copy; as distinct from EDITION-BINDING.

BINDER'S LEAF = FLYLEAF (see ENDPAPER).

BINDER'S TICKET A small printed or engraved label fixed to one of the endpapers of a book, bearing the binder's name. This method of 'signing' a binding went out of fashion some time around the middle of the last century, since when most binders wanting to record their name have used a tiny stamp or PALLET (b).

BINDING COPY Used in booksellers' catalogues to describe a copy which needs rebinding. It usually implies that the inside of the book is clean and sound enough to justify the trouble and expense of this.

BLACK-LETTER 'Gothic' or 'Old English' type-face; the style of type used by the earliest printers, modelled on the handwritings current in western Germany in the fifteenth century. Black-letter type was used almost invariably in Germany until very recent times, but in England, except for special purposes, it was very gradually superseded by roman type in the course of the sixteenth century.

BLEED The area of an illustration which extends outside the finished page size of a book: a bled illustration is one which runs to the edge of the page without a margin.

BLIND-STAMPING, BLIND-TOOLING Blank impressions made by the binder's tools on the binding of a book, i.e. impressions not highlighted by ink or gilt.

BLOCK-BOOK A book printed entirely from incised wooden blocks instead of from units of metal type; especially one of those printed during the fifteenth century in Europe, or in the Orient over a much longer period. In China, at least, this manner of printing (known as Xylography) was practised long before the invention of movable type; and some European block-books were probably produced at least thirty years before its invention in the West, but surviving early examples have been extremely difficult to date.

BOARDS (a) The solid sides of a book, distinguished from the material covering them; used in this sense only if the solid material is worthy of special note, e.g. 'calf over oak boards'.

(b) More loosely, a book's solid sides including both the base and the covering material together; as in the phrase 'boards detached'.

(c) Used to describe a binding of straw-board covered simply with plain paper, the sort of binding in which most books published between about 1770 and the 1830s were temporarily encased when they were first distributed. 'Original boards', where they have survived on a copy, are often highly prized.

BOLTS The folds at the outer margins or FORE-EDGES of the leaves of a sheet folded in OCTAVO, before they have been trimmed by the binder; sometimes used also of the folds at the HEAD and (when they occur) at the TAIL of the pages.

BOOK-LABEL A label indicating a book's past or present ownership, usually fixed to one of the front ENDPAPERS, and smaller and simpler than a a bookplate. It will often bear just the owner's name.

BREAKER or BREAKING COPY An illustrated book which is so seriously imperfect, or in such poor condition except for some or all of the plates, that it seems fit only for dismemberment for the sake of preserving the plates separately.

BROADSHEET or BROADSIDE A whole sheet of paper printed as a single page, not folded to form a GATHERING of a book. This format was commonly used, for example, in the seventeenth and eighteenth centuries for printing official proclamations and popular ballads.

CAMBRIDGE BINDING A style of calf binding in which the centre of each cover is occupied by a large vertical rectangular panel mottled or sprinkled, within which is another smaller panel left plain. The origin of the term is obscure.

CANCEL See pp. 45–6. The sheet, or part of a sheet, which is removed in cancellation is called the CANCELLANDUM or CANCELLAND; that which replaces it is known as the CANCELLANS (or simply CANCEL).

CASE (a) In printing by hand: the receptacle in which type is kept, and from which the compositor takes it, letter by letter, when composing. Traditionally it is in two parts, with the layout governed by strict convention, the upper part occupied in the main by capital letters (hence the term UPPER-CASE for these) and the lower by minuscule or small letters (hence LOWER-CASE).

(b) The covering of a CASED book.

CASED Having a prefabricated cover (usually of cloth), into which the book has been fixed by machine. Since modern books are almost invariably made in this way, the word 'bound' applied to a late nineteenth- or twentieth-century book normally means 'cased'; but the use of the latter term implies a strict distinction between 'cased' and hand-tailored 'bound' books.

CATCHWORD The first word of the following page printed at the foot of each page of a book, normally in the right-hand corner below the bottom line of the text. You will find them in most books printed between the sixteenth century and the close of the eighteenth, and towards the end of this period they were sometimes known as 'direction-words'. Their principal use was as a guide to the printer when he was arranging the pages of type in position on the press, and they are a useful aid to the collector in checking the completeness and continuity of the text.

CATHEDRAL BINDING A style of binding used on some English and French books of the early nineteenth century, in which each cover is decorated with a unified Gothic architectural design.

CHAIN-LINES In books printed on hand-made paper: the more widely-spaced of the mesh of semi-transparent lines visible when the paper is held up to the light, produced by the wires in the bottom of the paper-maker's mould. The more closely-spaced lines which cross them at right-angles are called WIRE-LINES. Since chain-lines almost always run parallel to the shorter side of the sheet of paper, the direction which they take on the page is the surest indication of FORMAT: in a QUARTO book (in which the sheets have been folded twice) they will be horizontal, in a FOLIO (one fold) or an OCTAVO (three folds) they will be vertical. Chain-lines are sometimes artificially produced in machine-made paper by running it between special rollers while still damp.

CHAPBOOK Any small pamphlet of an educational, moral or sensational nature, especially those which in the eighteenth and early nineteenth centuries were sold by hawkers or 'chapmen' instead of by the organised book trade. Ballads, transmogrified history and a repertoire of stock folk-tales were their staple matter. Because of their size, fragility and cheapness, a relatively small number of chapbooks have survived.

COCKLING An unhappy condition (a) of paper, when its surface becomes bumpy and uneven as a result of exposure to damp or to inconstant temperatures; or (b) of bindings, warping for the same reasons or because the PASTEDOWNS have been cut or fixed unskilfully without allowing for the effects of drying-out.

COLLATION (a) The arrangement of GATHERINGS in a book, as expressed by a statement of the sequence of SIGNATURES found in it.

(b) The process of establishing the completeness or incompleteness of a copy by checking the continuity of the signatures.

(c) The comparison of the text of different EDITIONS of a book, or of two or more copies of the same edition.

COLLOTYPE A highly sophisticated photographic process used for reproducing illustrations. Briefly, it involves projecting a photographic image on to a sheet of glass thinly coated with sensitized gelatine; the gelatine hardens in proportion to the strength of light passing through the negative, and the plate is then flooded with glycerine and water. The relative hardness of the gelatine on each part of the plate regulates the amount of moisture retained, and this in turn regulates the amount of ink which each part will hold. The process has been perfected to achieve great subtlety of tone but it is very expensive, especially since one plate will only last for about 1,000–2,000 impressions. Its most successful application is in modern fine art books.

COLONIAL EDITION Used to describe any separate issue, usually in a cheaper style of binding and often on cheaper paper, of a late nineteenth- or early twentieth-century novel, specially produced for export to the Empire and usually printed in the same run as the regular copies.

COLOPHON The name given to the IMPRINT of a book when (as in most books printed before the middle of the sixteenth century) it appears on the last leaf instead of on the title page. The colophon has been artificially revived in the products of certain rather precious PRIVATE PRESSES of the present century.

CONJUGATE 'Joined together'; said of two leaves which, if traced into and out of the SPINE of the book, are found to form a single piece of paper.

CONTEMPORARY Applied to binding or manuscript annotations in a book means contemporary with the book, not 'present-day'. The term generally has to be used fairly loosely, since exact contemporaneity of binding or of handwriting cannot usually be proved; if the style of binding looks as though it originated within a few years of the date of the book, it seems reasonable to call it 'contemporary'.

COPPER ENGRAVING or COPPER LINE-ENGRAVING The basic method of printing an illustration from an engraved plate, in which the design has been incised with an engraving-tool or burin. Ink is wiped on to the surface of the plate and pressed into the incisions with a 'dabber'; the surplus ink is removed (sometimes leaving a little to give toning; in this case it is not strictly line-engraving) and the plate is pressed on to the dampened paper.

CORRIGENDA = ERRATA.

'COTTAGE' or 'COTTAGE-ROOF' STYLE. A style of binding widely used in England during the second half of the seventeenth century and the first half of the eighteenth, in which a central rectangular panel on each cover is surmounted by a triangular or rhomboid gable, repeated upside-down beneath the foot of the panel.

COUNTERMARK In hand-made paper; an additional WATERMARK found in the centre of one half of the sheet, the principal watermark being in the centre of the other. Often it consisted of the maker's initials.

CROPPED Said of margins which have been so ruthlessly trimmed in binding that the edges of the text or of illustrations have been sliced off.

CRUSHED MOROCCO See MOROCCO.

CUL-DE-LAMPE The French word for TAIL-PIECE; sometimes used, rather affectedly, in English contexts.

DECKLE The edge of a sheet of hand-made paper, which is always slightly uneven. In some kinds of modern machine-made paper, rough edges are artificially produced in order to create an ornamental 'hand-made' effect.

DENTELLE (French, = 'lace') A decorative border, usually of gilt leather, round the edge of the PASTEDOWN; strictly, incorporating a lace-work pattern, but the word is now applied more freely. When the border is quite undecorated, it is called a TURN-IN.

DIAPER (a) On leather bindings, gilt or BLIND decoration in the form of 'a small pattern indefinitely repeated, often in the form of lozenges and triangle containing conventional flowers' (J. B. Oldham, *Shrewsbury School Library Bindings* [1943]).

(b) On cloth bindings, lozenge grain produced by crossing sets of diagonal parallel lines.

DICED Of leather, as used in binding: BLIND-STAMPED or ruled with crossing diagonal parallel lines so as to produce a pattern of lozenges. RUSSIA is the commonest leather to be treated in this manner.

DIRECTION-LINE A line at the foot of a page, below the text, containing the SIGNATURE and

CATCHWORD, where either is present. Where the two are on different levels, the direction-line is taken to be the lower of them.

DIRECTION-WORD = CATCHWORD.

DISBOUND   Used of a copy which shows signs (e.g. remnants of leather on its SPINE) of having been in a binding, but is so no longer. This state is most often represented by pamphlets which have been bound together in a volume and later split up.

DIVINITY CALF   A kind of smooth, brownish calf commonly used in the middle of the nineteenth century for binding theological and devotional books. Use of the term generally implies mild distaste.

DOCTORED   A booksellers' term; = SO-PHISTICATED.

DOUBLURE   A PASTEDOWN of leather, instead of paper, found in some fine (especially French) bindings.

DROP-HEAD TITLE or DROPPED-HEAD TITLE   A heading to any section of a book (or, appearing on the first page of the text, to the whole book) positioned a little distance below the top of a page, above the text.

DRY-POINT   A variety of LINE-ENGRAVING in which the design is incised on a plate, not with a burin but with a special needle called a *dry-point* which is pulled instead of pushed, so as to leave the 'burr' or waste metal in the incisions.

DUODECIMO   The FORMAT in which twelve pages are printed on each side of the sheet of paper, which is then folded four times to form a GATHER-ING. When used loosely to indicate size, 'duodecimo' describes any book measuring between about $6\frac{1}{2}''$ by $4\frac{1}{2}''$ and $4''$ by $2\frac{3}{4}''$. Usually abbreviated to '12mo', and pronounced (but not usually written) as 'twelve-mo'.

DUST-JACKET or DUST-WRAPPER   A detachable folded paper wrapper, usually printed and often illustrated, covering the binding of a modern book and issued with it on publication.

EDITIO PRINCEPS   Latin for 'first edition'; used especially for the first appearance in print of a classical text in the early days of printing.

EDITION   'Edition' means all those copies of a book which were printed from the same setting of type. If the type, once set up and used for printing some copies, is stored so that further copies of the book can be printed later, or if (e.g.) ELECTRO-TYPE or STEREOTYPE plates are used and stored for this end, the later copies will be of the same edition but of a different IMPRESSION. In the case of modern books, collectors and booksellers often (though bibliographers would insist on more precise

distinctions) add lustre to a first impression (and denigrate later impressions) of a book by calling it 'the first edition' even though it may not have the sole right to be so described. The problems of defining 'edition' and 'impression' in relation to books printed by modern methods are discussed in four-teen very complex pages of Fredson Bowers's *Principles of bibliographical description* (Princeton, 1949, pp. 379 ff.). Professor Bowers defines ISSUE as 'the whole number of copies of a form of an edition put on sale at any time or times as a consciously planned printed unit' (op.cit., p. 40). Thus the FINE-PAPER COPIES of a book, in instances such as those discussed on pages 40 and 41, even though they may have been published at the same time as the ordinary copies, constitute a separate issue. So too, for example, do the copies of certain books published simultaneously, or nearly simultaneously, in different FORMATS (which may be their only point of difference).

EDITION-BINDING   Binding by some form of mass-production (nearly always of CASED books), ordered and paid for by the publisher or distributor. As a general practice it has long since superseded individual binding for the customer.

EDITION DE LUXE   Any sumptuously produced EDITION, especially if it consists of a strictly limited number of copies (see LIMITED EDITION). In a more specialised sense the term is used sometimes of a number of copies printed in a more lavish fashion than, but usually at the same time as, the ordinary copies of an edition.

ELECTROTYPE   A modern printing process, in which a thin wax mould is taken from the original type-face and a delicate coating of copper is applied to this mould by electrolysis. The mould is then backed up by pouring in lead alloy, to produce a durable plate which can be printed from. Electrotype plates normally produce a more precise facsimile of the original type than STEREOTYPE.

EMBLEM BOOK   A book with emblematic or allegorical pictures of a moral, religious or educational nature, accompanied by an explanatory text (often verse) as an inseparable complement to them; especially one of those produced in very large numbers and in great variety all over Europe in the sixteenth and seventeenth centuries.

ENGRAVING   *See* COPPER-ENGRAVING, DRY-POINT, MEZZOTINT, PROCESS-EN-GRAVING, STEEL-ENGRAVING, STIPPLE-ENGRAVING.

ENDPAPER   Any of the pieces of paper immediately inside the covers of a book, not forming part of the GATHERINGS which make up the body of it. The endpaper which is pasted to the inside of the cover is called the PASTEDOWN, while the leaf facing it is known as the FREE ENDPAPER or FLYLEAF.

ERRATA Errors noticed after a book has been printed. If they are noticed before the printing of the PRELIMS is completed (usually the last part of the book to be printed) there may be room for a corrective list there. Otherwise they may be corrected on an extra leaf or a little slip TIPPED IN. Sometimes further errors are found after this has been done and after some of the copies have been issued to the retailers, and so you will find some copies with a more extensive errata-list than others.

ET INFRA (Latin, 'and below') Used occasionally in describing a collection or set of books which are of different SIZES, e.g. in an auction lot. The largest size is stated and the smaller sizes are inferred: e.g. '12 vols., 8vo *et infra*' means that some of the books are OCTAVO and the others (probably) DUO-DECIMO.

EX-LIBRIS (Latin, 'out of the books of . . .') A bookplate, BOOK-LABEL or stamp indicating a book's past or present ownership. EX-LIBRIS COPY is a rather apologetic term used in some booksellers' catalogues to describe a copy in which such features are obtrusively present.

EXPLICIT A repetition of the title and/or of the name or initials of the author (or scribe), copied from the manuscript from which the book was printed and appended to the COLOPHON.

EXTENDED Used of a leaf which has been given a new inner margin, because the old one had become frayed or otherwise damaged after the leaf had become detached. *See also* INLAID (a) and RE-MARGINED.

EXTRA-ILLUSTRATED Used of a book which has had additional plates added to it, often cut out of other books, either by a private owner or by a bookseller. If this is done to any considerable extent in one volume, the extra leaves required usually necessitate complete rebinding. See GRANGERISED.

FILLET A straight line, or two or three parallel straight lines, usually gilt and on leather, made by the impression of a binder's tool which consists of a wheel with one or more raised bands on its rim.

FLYLEAF *See* ENDPAPER.

FLY-TITLE (a) An extra title-page, usually elaborately engraved or in some other way illustrated, immediately before the conventional title-page.

(b) A separate title-page introducing a distinct section of a book. But (a) is the more usual meaning.

FOLIATION Numbering by leaves, i.e. on one side of the leaf only, instead of by pages. This practice preceded PAGINATION and is found in most books printed before about 1590. The leaves of the very earliest printed books, however, were not numbered at all.

FOLIO (a) The FORMAT in which two pages are printed on each side of the sheet pf paper, which is then folded once (parallel with the shorter side) to form a GATHERING (or part of a gathering, since a number of sheets are very often folded one within another). Often abbreviated to 'fol.' or, by bibliographers, to '2°'. When used loosely to indicate SIZE, 'folio' implies a tallish, narrowish book of anything more than about 11″ by 8″, on analogy with the likely result of folio folding.

(b) A single leaf of a book or manuscript.

FORE-EDGE The edge of a book furthest from its SPINE.

FORE-EDGE PAINTING Any painted decoration on the FORE-EDGE of a book. Most examples of this are English and date from the nineteenth or late eighteenth centuries, after the celebrated Edwards family of binders, of Halifax in Yorkshire, who perfected the technique. The painting is done while the edges of the leaves are very slightly fanned out, and they must be fanned out again for the picture to be seen properly. Fifteenth- or early sixteenth-century fore-edge paintings are also found occasionally.

FORMAT Strictly, the number of times each sheet of paper has been folded in the construction of a book; loosely (and especially applied to modern books), 'format' is used to mean simply 'size'. See DUODECIMO, FOLIO, OCTAVO, QUARTO, SIXTEEN-MO.

FORREL (*Forel* seems to be a more old-fashioned spelling.) A binding material, usually off-white and thinner even than PARCHMENT, produced by further splitting the split sheepskin from which parchment is made. It is still sometimes used for cheap rebinding.

FOUNT (sometimes pronounced 'font') A complete set of any particular type, containing letters, figures, punctuation marks, etc.

FOXING Discoloration of paper taking the form of brownish-yellow spots.

FRENCH-FOLD A sheet of paper with four type-pages printed on one side only and folded into four without cutting the HEAD. The inside of the sheet is therefore completely blank.

GATHERING A sheet of paper (or two or more sheets together, or sometimes half a sheet) folded to form a single group of leaves in a book.

GAUFFERED or **GOFFERED EDGES GILT EDGES** decorated with an embossed pattern.

GOUGE. In the decoration of leather bindings: a

curved line or segment of a circle, or the tool used in impressing it.

GRANGERISED = EXTRA-ILLUSTRATED. From James Granger (1723–76), who first encouraged the practice by publishing in 1769 a *Biographical history of England* with blank leaves for the insertion of portraits, etc., to be collected by the purchaser.

GRAVURE = PHOTOGRAVURE.

GUARDED Of an illustration:
(a) not an integral part of a GATHERING but pasted at its inner edge to a specially prepared STUB. This is a common way of fixing in plates which have had to be printed separately from the text or which are on a different kind of paper.
(b) = TISSUE-GUARDED.

HALF BINDING A style of binding in which the SPINE and corners of a book are covered in a different material from that which covers the remainder of the sides; thus HALF CALF, in which the spine and corners are in calf while the rest of the binding may be of cloth, HALF MOROCCO, HALF VELLUM, etc. If there are very large corner-pieces in the same material as the spine, the book is said to be in a THREE-QUARTER BINDING (THREE-QUARTER CALF, etc.). If only the spine is in a different material, not the corners, the book is in a QUARTER-BINDING.

HALF-TITLE A leaf before the title-page bearing the title of the book, sometimes in a shortened form and usually without the author's name or any other details.

HALF-TONE Used of any illustration which includes varying intermediate tones between black and white.

HEADLINE A line of type at the top of a page, above the text, containing for instance the page-number and the RUNNING-TITLE.

HERBAL A book containing the names, descriptions and (usually) illustrations of herbs, or of plants in general, with their useful applications.

HISTORIATED Decorated with figures of men or animals; used of prominent initial letters or borders in manuscripts or early printed books.

HORN-BOOK 'A leaf of paper containing the alphabet (often, also, the ten digits, some elements of spelling, and the Lord's Prayer) protected by a thin plate of translucent horn, and mounted on a tablet of wood with a handle' (*Shorter Oxford English Dictionary*). Horn-books seem to have been a very common aid for children between the sixteenth and the early eighteenth centuries, but an extremely small number have survived to the present day.

IDEAL COPY 'A book which is complete in all its leaves as it ultimately left the printer's shop in perfect condition and in the complete state that he considered to represent the final and most perfect state of the book. An 'ideal copy' contains not only all the blank leaves intended to be issued as integral parts of its gatherings but also all excisions and all cancellans leaves or insertions which represent the most perfect state of the book as the printer or publisher finally intended to issue it' (Bowers, *Principles of Bibliographical Description*, p. 113).

ILLUMINATION Coloured or gilt decoration, in the form of tracery or miniature illustrations, applied by hand, especially to the margins or prominent initial letters in manuscripts or very early printed books.

IMPENSIS (Latin, 'at the expense of') In the IMPRINT OR COLOPHON of an early book, this word precedes the name of the publisher or of whoever took financial responsibility for the printing.

IMPOSITION The laying-down of pages of type in position ready for printing, in such a way as to ensure correct sequence when the sheet of paper is folded.

IMPRESSION *See* EDITION.

IMPRIMATUR (Latin, 'Let it be printed') A formula signed by a licenser of the Press, either religious or secular, authorising the printing of a book. This authorisation is often printed on a separate leaf which is then called a LICENCE-LEAF.

IMPRINT The statement (normally at the foot of the title-page) of the place and date at which the book was printed, usually with the name of the printer and/or publisher. *See also* COLOPHON.

INCUNABLE (strictly, INCUNABULUM; plural INCUNABULA) Any book printed before 1501; from the Latin *cunae*, a cradle: hence, a book dating from the infancy of printing.

INDIA PAPER A very thin, strong, opaque paper, often used for printing Bibles and other books which require a large number of pages in small bulk; first made by the Oxford University Press in the late nineteenth century in imitation of the imported paper after which it is named.

INLAID (a) Used of a leaf which has had all four margins renewed.
(b) In a binding: used of a piece of leather or other material which is sunk into a surround of another material, so that the two surfaces are continuous.

INTAGLIO (Italian, 'engraving') A blanket term covering any method of reproducing illustrations (or, for that matter, letters of text) from the recesses in an incised surface, e.g. COPPER-ENGRAVING, DRY-POINT, MEZZOTINT, STIPPLE-ENGRAVING.

INTERLEAVED Bound with printed leaves alternating with blank ones, which have been inserted for the owner to make his own notes.

ISSUE *See* EDITION.

JUVENILES Children's books. Not to be confused with *juvenilia,* works written when their author was very young.

LAID DOWN = MOUNTED (b).

LAID PAPER Paper showing CHAIN-LINES and WIRE-LINES produced by the wires in the base of the mould in which it was made.

LAMINATED Of damaged or frail leaves: strengthened by a coating of tissue on each side, ironed on under heat.

LAW CALF Smooth, beige calfskin used particularly (though less so nowadays) for binding law books.

LETTERING-PIECE A leather label on the BACKSTRIP of a book, giving its title, etc.

LIBRARY EDITION A tolerably handsome EDITION, especially of an author's collected works in several volumes, well-printed in a large, easily readable type and published at some considerable expense.

LICENCE-LEAF A leaf, usually at the beginning or end of a book, bearing an IMPRIMATUR.

LIMITED EDITION An EDITION which is strictly limited to a certain number of copies (which is usually stated; see LIMITATION NOTICE) and which will not be republished in the same form.

LIMITATION NOTICE A statement of how many copies of an EDITION or ISSUE have been printed; usually found at the beginning or end of a book published in a LIMITED EDITION.

LINE-ENGRAVING *See* COPPER-ENGRAVING.

LINING-PAPER = PASTEDOWN

LININGS Used to describe the endleaves of a book when they are not of paper (see ENDPAPER) but of some more opulent material such as watered silk. When the PASTEDOWN is of leather it is called a Doublure.

LINOTYPE A modern technique of printing, using a machine which sets type in solid lines ('type-bars' or 'slugs') instead of by single letters; generally used in printing newspapers.

LITHOGRAPHY An important SURFACE PROCESS for printing illustrations, which exploits the natural antipathy of grease and water; invented by the Bavarian experimenter Alois Senefelder in 1786. On a stone surface which has an equal receptiveness to both water and grease, a design is drawn in a greasy substance, either crayon (called 'chalk') or ink, and the unshaded parts are moistened; the design is then transferred to a greasy roller (the wet areas resisting transference) from which it can be printed. Derived variants of the process are transfer lithography, by far the commoner of the alternative methods, in which the design is made first on a grained 'transfer paper' from which it is transferred to the stone (the process of drawing straight on to the stone is called 'auto-lithography'); offset lithography, in which the design is transferred from the stone to the printing paper via a sheet of rubber; photolithography, which uses a grained zinc plate on which a design has been printed from a photographic negative; and chromolithography, or lithography in colour, using a different stone or plate for each of the composite colours.

LITHOTINT A variety of LITHOGRAPHED illustration with a yellowish tint, often with highlights showing as patches of white, widely used in books of topographical views published between about 1810 and 1840.

LONGITUDINAL LABEL A feature which has survived in quite a large number of English books printed during the third quarter of the seventeenth century. It consists of the title, printed vertically in large type, on an otherwise blank leaf at the beginning or end of a book. It was evidently intended to be removed and used to serve some external function, though nobody has been able to say with any confidence what that was; but the fact that (so far as we know) no longitudinal label has ever been found anywhere but in its original position suggests that the function was probably a temporary one connected with identification and display on a bookseller's shelves.

LOWER-CASE *See* CASE (a).

MADE-UP COPY *See* SOPHISTICATED COPY.

MARBLED Stained to a pattern resembling the graining of marble. MARBLED PAPER, often used for ENDPAPERS and for the sides of bindings, seems to have originated in Moslem countries, and was probably first made in Europe by the French bookbinder Macé Ruette in the 1620s; the marbling effect is achieved in the course of sizing, by using a comb to spread colourings on the surface of the SIZE in which the paper is dipped. Ruette may also have been the first to produce MARBLED CALF by combing acid on to it. Marbled paper and marbled calf began to be used in England during the late seventeenth century. MARBLED EDGES (i.e. of the leaves) are a post-1800 feature.

MEZZOTINT A highly-skilled technique of engraving in which the plate is first uniformly roughened, and then smoothed out in parts to the required design. Tones of subtly varying depth can be achieved by this process, the roughest areas of the plate retaining the most ink.

MINIATURE (a) A small hand-painted illustration, of the sort which embellishes many manuscrips and some early printed books.

(b) A very small book, say smaller than 3″ by 2¼″, representing a rather debased taste of the nineteenth century. Such books are now often collected for no other quality than their diminutive size.

MISBOUND Used of a leaf or leaves, or a whole GATHERING, wrongly folded or misplaced by the binder. The term does not imply that anything is actually missing.

MONOLINE = LINOTYPE.

MOROCCO Originally, high-quality North African goat-skin leather; later used of any goat-skin, easily recognisable by its pronounced graining. The variety with the most prominent grain, and usually highly polished, is LEVANT MOROCCO, originally made of the skin of the Angora goat from Turkey (now more often from South Africa); HARD-GRAINED MOROCCO describes a variety with an even, closely-grained surface, from whatever source; and NIGER MOROCCO, from West Africa, is a very soft leather with an irregular grain, tending to vary considerably in texture from one part of a book's cover to another. CRUSHED MOROCCO (rolled or ironed so that the grain, while still fairly easily visible, can only just be felt by the fingers, and usually given a high polish after binding) is perhaps the most sensually engaging of all leathers; while STRAIGHT-GRAINED MOROCCO is as recognisable as its name suggests.

MOUNTED (a) Used of an illustration which is not printed on the leaf itself but is pasted to it, either along one edge of the plate or over its whole back.

(b) Of a badly damaged leaf: backed with strengthening paper so as to halt the deterioration and to hold in place what is left. The first and last leaves of a book are the most vulnerable and will often, in old books, be found treated in this way. The process is obviously unsuitable for leaves printed on both sides, since one side or the other will be covered over; but it was occasionally used regardless, before the more modern remedy of LAMINATING was developed.

NATURE PRINTING A technique of printing an illustration, e.g. of a flower, leaf or insect, from an impression made by the object itself. The object is squeezed between a copper plate and a lead plate, so that it leaves an impression on the lead. The process has been used, very occasionally, since the eighteenth century.

NOT SUBJECT TO RETURN A formula in a bookseller's or auctioneer's catalogue indicating that the book described is either imperfect or suspected of being so, and that the usual guarantee is therefore suspended. 'W.a.f.' ('with all faults') means the same.

NUMBERS For 'publication in numbers' see PARTS.

OCTAVO The FORMAT in which eight pages are printed on each side of the sheet of paper, which is then folded three times (first parallel with the shorter side, then with the longer, then again with the shorter) to form a GATHERING. Applied loosely to indicate size (especially of a modern book), 'octavo' describes any book between about 6½″ by 4½″ and 10½″ by 7½″. Usually abbreviated to '8vo'.

OFFSET (a) An unpleasant browning effect caused by the transfer of ink from an illustration (or, occasionally, from text) on to the opposite page. It usually occurs under damp conditions and can be guarded against by the insertion of tissue paper (see TISSUE-GUARDED).

(b) See LITHOGRAPHY.

OPENING Two pages which face one another when a book is open.

OPEN SHEET = BROADSHEET.

PAGINATION Page-numbering. See also FOLIATION.

PALLET In bookbinding, any self-contained abstract decorative device (or the tool used to make it), e.g. of a foliate design, used to fill one of the panels on the BACKSTRIP of a book. A NAME-PALLET is one which includes lettering (such as for the title on the backstrip) instead of mere abstract decoration.

(b) A small stamp indicating the binder's name (in gilt or ink or BLIND), usually impressed at the extreme lower edge of one of the PASTEDOWNS or DENTELLES. Since the middle of the last century this has been the usual way for a binder to sign his work; see also BINDER'S TICKET.

PARCHMENT A thin writing or binding material made from the inner or lower layer of a sheep-skin, not (like SKIVER) tanned but de-greased in a special way as in the manufacture of VELLUM, for which it is sometimes used as a cheaper substitute. It is not a good material for binding, as it is very liable to rub and tear.

PARTS 'Publication in parts' is the usual term for the publication of a large and popular work in instalments, in some form distinct from the book form in which it was subsequently published; especially used of certain mid-nineteenth-century novels which were published in weekly, fortnightly or monthly parts intended to be bound together later. Some eighteenth-century books were published in a rather similar fashion and were usually described as 'issued in numbers'.

PASTEDOWN · *See* ENDPAPER.

PHOTOGRAVURE   A modern process of reproducing illustrations, very cheap to use if a large number of copies are to be printed, e.g. in magazines. The picture is printed photographically on a copper cylinder together with a closely-ruled screen of crossed lines. When the picture is etched with acid on to the cylinder, the spaces in this grid create a large number of tiny pits in the copper surface, shallow for the lighter ones and deep for the darker ones, which give the finished illustration a characteristic dotted or stippled effect.

PIRATED EDITION   An EDITION published without the author's consent; or, if he is dead, published by someone who is not legitimately or legally possessed of the manuscript or without the consent of the copyright-holder.

PLANOGRAPHIC PRINTING = SURFACE-PRINTING *See* COLLOTYPE and LITHOGRAPHY.

PLATE-MARK   The impression made in the paper by the edge of the metal plate used for printing ENGRAVINGS.

POCHOIR   The French name for a technique perfected in some fine French illustrated books of the 1930s. It consists of hand-colouring a printed illustration using water-colours, a brush and a set of stencils (either of metal or of celluloid).

PRELIMS   (short for 'preliminaries')   The preliminary part of a book, consisting of the title-page, front endpapers and any prefatory matter such as half-title, frontispiece, table of contents, foreword, etc.

PRESS-MARK   'In libraries, a mark or number written or stamped in or on each book, and also given in the library catalogue, specifying the room, book-press, book-case, shelf, etc., where the book is kept' *(Shorter Oxford English Dictionary)*.

PRIMARY BINDING   When an EDITION of EDITION-BOUND books appears in more than one style of binding, the earliest style (where priority can be established) is called the PRIMARY BINDING and subsequent ones SECONDARY BINDINGS.

PRIVATE PRESS   A printing house which prints books which it chooses to publish, not books which another publisher pays it to print; and it usually distributes its products itself, either to SUB-SUBSCRIBERS or directly to retail booksellers, by-passing the usual publishing channels. Most modern private presses specialise in LIMITED EDITIONS.

PRIZE BINDING   A nineteenth- and early twentieth-century style of binding in leather, using gilt, such as was suitable for a copy which was to be given as a school prize. The term is sometimes used of a copy which does not show signs of having been bound for this precise purpose.

PROCESS-ENGRAVING   A blanket term covering any method of reproducing illustrations more technical than simple engraving, e.g. COLLOTYPE, LITHOGRAPHY, PHOTOGRAVURE.

PROVENANCE   The pedigree of a book's previous ownership. It can often be established by means of bookplates, inscriptions, library-stamps and bindings.

PUBLISHER'S CLOTH   The original cloth on any book in an unadulterated EDITION-BINDING.

QUARTER-BINDING, QUARTER-CALF, etc. *See* HALF-BINDING.

QUARTO   The FORMAT in which four pages are printed on each side of the sheet of paper, which is then folded twice (first parallel with the shorter side, then with the longer) to form a GATHERING. Applied loosely to indicate size and shape, 'quarto' describes any book of a squarish appearance, by analogy with the likely result of quarto folding. Usually abbreviated to '4to' or by bibliographers to '4°'.

QUIRE   A quantitative term denoting twenty-four sheets of paper; also used to mean 'GATHERING' (from the late Latin *quaternum*, a group of four sheets folded in folio to form eight leaves), but to avoid confusion this usage is best avoided.

RAISED BANDS   Horizontal ridges across the BACKSTRIP of a book, under which are the cords on to which the GATHERINGS are sewn. Some CASED books also have raised bands on the backstrip, purely for ornament and to give an effect of genuine binding.

REBACKED   Used of a book which has been given a new BACKSTRIP because the old one has become detached or loose, in part or in whole, or because GATHERINGS have become loose. If the old backstrip has become detached but remains whole, it can often be mounted on the new one.

RECTO   A right-hand page. The back is called the VERSO.

REGISTER   (a) The exact adjustment of type-pages back-to-back when printing the second side of the sheet, so that when the sheet is folded all the margins will be correct.
  (b) In printing in two or more colours, the positioning of one colour in its correct relation to the rest.
  (c) See REGISTER-LEAF.

REGISTER-LEAF In many fifteenth- and sixteenth-century books, a leaf (usually at the end) giving a list of the SIGNATURES, to indicate to the binder the number and 'order of GATHERINGS which make up the book.

RE-JOINTED Strictly, this applies to a book of which only the joints on either side of the SPINE have been renewed (because they were weak or broken), keeping the old BACKSTRIP in its original state. But the term is misleadingly used in some booksellers' catalogues to describe books which have been REBACKED with whole or part of the old backstrip mounted on the new one.

ROAN A kind of soft sheepskin, of poor quality, used as a cheap substitute for MOROCCO from the end of the eighteenth century onwards. Its surface tends to tear, and the joints of roan books split easily.

ROLL or ROLL-TOOL A binder's tool having a continuous or repeated design round the edge of a wheel, which makes a continuous impression when rolled along over the leather.

ROUGH-GILT Used of a copy in which the edges of the leaves have been decorated with gilt without having first been trimmed smooth.

RUBRIC A heading such as a DROP-HEAD TITLE printed (or written) in red. RUBRICATED, when describing manuscripts or early printed books, generally means that prominent initial letters are also coloured in red, usually by hand; or, sometimes (as in many seventeenth-century books), that borders or the lines of type on the title-page are ruled in red.

RUNNING-TITLE The title of a book recurring, often in an abbreviated form, above the text on each page (or on each OPENING).

RUSSIA An attractive leather, made from cowhide impregnated with birth-oil (the smell of which lingers with it for some long time) to give it a smooth, rich finish. It was especially popular with English binders during the last years of the eighteenth century and the first part of the nineteenth, and is often found DICED. It is not a durable leather and when, as very often, it starts to crumble at the joints it is almost impossible to repair.

SECONDARY BINDING *See* PRIMARY BINDING.

SEME (French, 'sown' or 'scattered like seed') Of bindings: sprinkled or dotted with small ornaments.

SEXTO-DECIMO *See* SIXTEEN-MO.

SHAKEN Said of a book 'which is no longer firm in its covers, and in which perhaps particular GATHERINGS are coming loose; a state which one imagines could be induced by holding a book up by its two covers and shaking it.

SHAVED Not quite CROPPED; with the leaves trimmed so that the edges of some letters of type have been lost, but no more.

SIGNATURE A letter (or other mark) found at the foot of (at least) the first leaf of a GATHERING; serving as a guide to the binder in arranging the gatherings and perhaps in folding them. They also enable the collector to check the completeness of a copy. The signatures usually follow an alphabetical sequence omitting either *i* or *j*, either *u* or *v*, and *w*; then if necessary doubling to *Aa*, *Bb*, etc., and trebling (and so on) in long books. Typographical marks such as ★ and † are very commonly used as signatures in the PRELIMS.

SIGNED BINDING *See* BINDER'S TICKET and PALLET (b).

SINGLETON A single leaf not CONJUGATE with any other leaf that survives in the book.

SIXTEEN-MO (strictly 'sexto-decimo'; whence the '–MO') The FORMAT in which sixteen pages are printed on each side of the sheet of paper, which is then folded four times (first parallel with the shorter side, then each time at right angles to the previous fold) to form a GATHERING. Loosely applied to indicate size, 'sixteen-mo' describes any book between about 4″ by $2\frac{3}{4}$″ and $2\frac{3}{4}$″ by 2″. Usually abbreviated to 16mo.

SIZE (a) For sizes of books, see DUODECIMO, FOLIO, FORMAT, OCTAVO, QUARTO, SIXTEEN-MO.

(b) A gluey substance with which some kinds of paper are treated in the course of their manufacture. When leaves of a book are WASHED the size inevitably comes out, and the paper has to be further washed in size to restore it.

SKIVER A very poor, thin kind of leather, from the underside of a sheepskin, hard to distinguish from ROAN.

SOPHISTICATED COPY A copy which has been tampered with in some way, either in respect of its construction or of the type, so that it is in part a fake. The term is applied, e.g., to such occasional horrors as a copy of a late EDITION which has a first-edition title-page inserted; or a copy whose imperfections have been met by leaves extracted from another copy (not necessarily of the same edition); or a copy of which some part is supplied in facsimile with the aim of passing as the original.

SPINE That part of a book where the GATHERINGS are sewn or glued together, out of sight under the BACKSTRIP; but the term is often used to mean the backstrip itself.

SPRINKLED Ornamented with small black dots; either on a binding (especially of calf) or on the edges of the leaves.

STABBING A manner of sewing used for the GATHERINGS of certain very thin books: the thread is sewn through sideways, i.e. from the front to the back of the book, generally ¼″ or so from the SPINE.

STEEL-ENGRAVING As COPPER-ENGRAVING, but using a steel plate instead of a copper one. Steel provides a more durable surface than copper but in terms of economy cannot compete with LITHOGRAPHY, by which it was superseded in the third quarter of the nineteenth century after some forty years of fashionable life.

STENCIL COLOURING See POCHOIR.

STEREOTYPE A modern process of printing in which, once the type is set up, sheets of moistened paper are beaten down on to it to produce a kind of papier-mâché mould, from which it is possible to cast solid plates of type-metal which can be stored and re-used indefinitely. Stereotype was invented by a certain Edinburgh goldsmith, William Ged, in or soon after 1725; but though he printed two or three books by the process in his later years, it was not used to any great extent or commercial advantage until after its reinvention at the beginning of the nineteenth century.

STIPPLE-ENGRAVING A technique of engraving by small dots instead of lines, used especially in the eighteenth century; it provided a toning effect suitable for, e.g., copying oil-paintings. It was sometimes referred to as 'the English manner'.

STUB The narrow strip of inner margin which remains when a leaf has been cut out from a book, or when an additional leaf has been inserted with an extra width of inner margin to allow it to be sewn in.

SUBSCRIPTION, PUBLICATION BY A frequent procedure in the publication of expensive books, particularly in the eighteenth and early nineteenth centuries. The number of copies printed was limited, more or less strictly, to the number of prospective customers who had responded to notices of impending publication and (usually) paid part of the price in advance. Occasionally in the eighteenth century some small representative sample of the work was first published separately as a specimen for subscribers. A list of the subscribers' names was very often printed in books published in this manner.

SURFACE-PRINTING (or PLANOGRAPHIC PRINTING) Either of the methods (COLLOTYPE or LITHOGRAPHY) for reproducing HALF-TONE illustrations by exploiting the relative absorbencies of chemicals applied to the surface of a plate, which does not then need to be engraved.

THREE-DECKER A colloquial term for a nineteenth-century novel in three volumes.

THREE-QUARTER BINDING, THREE-QUARTER CALF, etc. See HALF BINDING.

TIES Ribbons or tapes sewn into the outer edges of the covers of a book, so that they can be tied together over the FORE-EDGE to prevent the covers from warping. Traces of them can be seen on many books bound before the late seventeenth century, but the ties themselves rarely survive for many generations. They are often replaced. The bindings of books from certain rather precious PRIVATE PRESSES of the present century incorporate ties.

TIPPED IN (a) A slightly technical term used of illustrations not integral to the GATHERINGS of a book but pasted in, either at the inner margin or at the HEAD, as extra insertions.
(b) Used of some relevant item, such as an AUTOGRAPH letter from the author, loosely inserted in a book.

TISSUE-GUARDED Of an illustration: protected by a piece of tissue-paper, usually loosely inserted to absorb OFFSET.

TOOLING Decoration impressed by hand on the cover of a book by the binder, using any one of a large number of kinds of small metal tool such as a ROLL or a FILLET.

TRADE BINDING A term used in relation to books printed before the days of EDITION-BINDING (i.e. before c. the 1820s) to describe a binding produced before the book was first sold or distributed, done at the expense of the bookseller and not, as was more usual, done afterwards at the customer's expense and to his taste a trade binding customarily used modest materials but was distinct from the temporary bindings of BOARDS (c) or WRAPPERS. The term relates to a commercial circumstance rather than to any distinct style or styles, and it is always difficult (and usually impossible) to identify a trade binding with any certainty.

TREE CALF A kind of calf commonly used in eighteenth- and nineteenth-century bindings, stained on each cover by the interaction of green vitriol and pearl-ash into a design something like an image of a gnarled oak-tree.

TRIAL BINDING A preliminary specimen of a nineteenth- or early twentieth-century EDITION-BINDING, sent by the binder to the publisher or author for approval. Because of the obvious difficulty of identification, the term is used only in those cases where the sample differs from the style of binding which was finally decided on.

TRIAL ISSUE or TRIAL EDITION An ISSUE

(or, if the type is subsequently re-set for publication, an EDITION) produced in a small number of copies before publication proper, usually for private circulation and to test reaction to the work.

TURN-IN   A strip of the outer covering-material of a binding, folded in so as to form a border round the top, bottom and outer edges of the PASTE-DOWNS. When this border is of leather and decorated, it is usually called a DENTELLE.

TWELVE-MO   *See* DUODECIMO.

UNBOUND   Generally used to mean that a copy is not and never has been in a binding; thus distinct from DISBOUND. The sewing should be clearly visible in an unbound book.

UNLETTERED   Used of a book which does not have its title or the author's name printed or stamped anywhere on the binding. Most books bound in England before the late seventeenth century are unlettered, and cheaper styles of CONTEMPORARY BINDING on eighteenth-century books often include no lettering, though in many cases some past owner has supplied a hand-written label or (in the case of VELLUM bindings) has written directly on the BACKSTRIP.

VELLUM   Calf-skin treated in a special way, degreased but not tanned, so as to produce a binding (or writing, or printing) material of extreme toughness and of a yellow or off-white shade. In binding it can either be used limp on its own or as a covering for BOARDS (a), and can easily be told from PARCHMENT, which has sometimes been used as a cheap imitation of it, by its resistance to scratching.

VENETIAN MOROCCO   An old name for olive STRAIGHT-GRAINED MOROCCO.

VERSO   A left-hand page.

VIGNETTE   (a) Any small representational ornament inserted in a blank space on a page, especially on the title-page or at the beginning or end of a chapter or other division.

(b) In a slightly narrower sense, an illustration not squared off at the edges but shading away into the surrounding paper.

W.A.F. = 'with all faults'   *See* NOT SUBJECT TO RETURN.

WASHED   Leaves of a book which are stained, e.g. with mould, ink or browning, can be washed with certain chemicals to remove the blemishes. Very early or valuable books are sometimes washed merely to give them a 'face-lift' and to restore crispness to the leaves. The job needs technical expertise and is best done by professionals. *See also* SIZE (b).

WATERMARK   A device of semi-transparent lines in a sheet of paper, usually barely noticeable except when the sheet is held up to the light. In the days of hand-made paper the watermark resulted from a pattern of wire in the base of the papermaker's mould; in modern manufacture, it is produced by running the paper while still damp through special rollers. The infinite variety of watermarks found in hand-made paper, and their variable positions, is of immense use in bibliographical analysis and identification. Sometimes, such as in English paper made between about 1790 and 1830, watermarks give the date of manufacture.

WIRE-LINES   *See* CHAIN-LINES. Wire-lines are also sometimes known as *vergeures*.

WOODCUT   Any illustration or device printed from a block of wood, on which a design has been cut in relief. Woodcuts can usually be distinguished very easily from engraved illustrations by the look of the black lines or surfaces, which in woodcuts occupy the whole area of the illustration excisions in the block, while in engravings they represent the excised (or etched) lines only.

WOVE PAPER   (in contradistinction to LAID PAPER)   Paper made by the modern method on a mould in which the wires are too closely-woven to leave any visible impression on the product.

WRAPPERS   Paper covers, which can be plain, printed or MARBLED. Like BOARDS (c), wrappers were commonly used as a cheap temporary binding on books printed during the late eighteenth and early nineteenth centuries, especially on slender books. Wrappers have nothing to do with DUST-WRAPPERS.

XYLOGRAPHY   *See* BLOCK-BOOK.

YAPP   A style of leather binding in which all three edges of each cover have a flap projecting inwards over the edges of the pages; commonly used for Bibles and devotional works since the 1860s, when the style was first employed by a London bookseller named W. Yapp.

ZINCOGRAPHY   A process of printing illustrations, using photography to produce a design in relief on a zinc plate, first developed in Paris in the 1880s. The zinc is coated with emulsion and a photographic negative is printed on it, so that the transparent areas (corresponding to the dark lines or dots in the original) admit the light, which hardens the emulsion where required; the rest of the emulsion is washed off and the plate is then washed in acid which eats away the exposed zinc, leaving the design in *haut-relief*.

Bibliography

General and Historical

Aldrich, Ella V. *Using Books and Libraries.* Prentice-Hall, Hemel Hempstead (1967).

Allen, Agnes. *The Story of the Book.* Faber and Faber, London (1967).

Bennett, Henry Stanley. *English Books and Readers.* Three volume study of the English book trade. Cambridge University Press (1965–70).

Bigmore, E. C. and Wyman, C. W. (eds.). *A Bibliography of Printing.* Holland Press, London (1969).

Block, Andrew. *Book Collector's Vade Mecum.* The Mitre Press, London (1938).

Book Dealers in North America. Sheppard Press, London (1968).

Bookman's Concise Dictionary. F. C. Avis, London (1956).

British Museum. *Bookbinding from the Library of Jean Grolier.* Pamphlet.

Brittain, Robert (ed.). *Booklover's Almanac.* Charles Skilton, London (1970).

Carter, John. *A.B.C. for Book Collectors.* Hart-Davis, London (1968).

Carter, John. *Binding Variants in English Publishing 1820–1900.* Constable, London (1932).

Carter, John. *Books and Book Collectors.* Hart-Davis, London (1956).

Carter, John. *Taste and Technique in Book Collecting.* Private Libraries Association (1970).

Chandler, C. *How to Find Out. A Guide to Sources of Information for All Arranged by the Dewey Decimal Classification.* First edition 1963, fourth revised edition 1974. Pergamon Press, Oxford, New York, Toronto, Sidney, Braunschweig.

Clarke, Adam. *A Bibliographical Dictionary.* Scarecrow Press, Metuchen, New Jersey; Bailey Bros, London (1971).

Clarke, J. H. L. (ed.). *Book Auction Records.* Dawsons Pall Mall, Volume 69 (1963).

Clough, Eric A. *Short-title Catalogue Arranged Geographically of Books Printed and Distributed by Printers, Publishers and Booksellers in the English Provincial Towns and in Scotland and Ireland up to and including the Year 1700.* Library Association (1970).

Coe, G. and Coe, D. (eds.). *The Book Collector's Directory.* G. Coe Ltd., Market Harborough (1968).

Dahl, S. *History of the Book.* Scarecrow Press, Metuchen, New Jersey; Bailey Bros, London (1968).

Diehl, Edith. *Bookbinding, Its Background and Technique.* Kennikat Press, Port Washington, New York; Bailey Bros, London (1967).

Duff, E. Gordon. *Blind-Stamped Panels in the English Book Trade 1457–1557.* Oxford University Press (1949).

Evans, Charles. *American Bibliography.* 13 volumes in 1. Scarecrow Press, Metuchen, New Jersey; Bailey Bros, London (1967).

Glaister, Geoffrey. *Glossary of the Book.* Allen and Unwin, London (1960).

Growell, A. and Eames, W. *Three Centuries of English Book Trade Bibliography.* Holland Press, London (1963).

Halliday, John. *Book Craft and Bookbinding.* Pitman, London (1951).

Haupt, Helmut Lehmann in collaboration with Lawrence C. Wroth and Rollo G. Silver. *The Book in America: History of the Making and Selling of Books in the United States.* Bowker Publishing Co., London (1951).

Howe, Ellic. *List of London Bookbinders 1648–1815.* Oxford University Press (1950).

Joy, Thomas. *The Truth about Bookselling.* Pitman, London (1964).

Madison, C. A. *Book Publishing in American Culture.* McGraw Hill, London (1967).

Mahony, Bertha E., Latimer, Louise P. and Folmsbee, Beulah. *Illustrators of Children's Books 1744–1945. Bookcollecting Course, Wk. 1.* B. F. Stevens and Brown Ltd., The Horn Book Incorporated, Boston (1947).

Mansfield, Edgar. *Modern Design in Bookbinding.* Peter Owen, London (1966).

Middleton, Bernard C. *History of English Craft*

Bookbinding Technique. Hafner Press, New York (1963).

Mumby, F. A. *Publishing and Bookselling; A History from the Earliest Times to the Present Day.* Jonathan Cape, London (1974).

Mumby, F. A. *Romance of Bookselling.* Scarecrow Press, Metuchen, New Jersey; Bailey Bros, London (1968).

Nilon, Charles H. (ed.). *Bibliography of Bibliographics in American Literature.* Bowker Publishing Co., London (1970).

Newton, A. E. *Amenities of Book Collecting and Kindred Affections.* Kennikat Press, Port Washington, New York; Bailey Bros, London (1970).

Orcutt, W. D. *In Quest of the Perfect Book: Reminiscences and Reflections of a Bookman.* Kennikat Press, Port Washington, New York; Bailey Bros, London (1970).

Plant, M. *The English Book Trade.* Allen and Unwin, London (1965).

Plenderleith, H. J. *The Preservation of Leather Bookbindings.* British Museum pamphlet (1970).

Pendred, John. *Earliest Directory of the Book Trade 1785.* Edited with an introduction and appendix by G. Pollard. Supplement to the Bibliographical Society's Transactions No 14 (1955).

Pratt, R. D. *A Thousand Books on Books.* R. D. Pratt, Weston-super-Mare (1967).

Quaritch, B. (ed.). *Contribution towards a Dictionary of English Book Collectors.* Quaritch, London (1969).

Roth, Cecil. *Studies in Books and Booklore.* Gregg International, Farnborough (1972).

Shaffer, K. R. *The Book Collection.* Clive Bingley Ltd., London (1967).

Thomas, A. S. *Fine Books.* Pleasures and Treasures Series, Weidenfeld and Nicolson, London (1967).

Wheale, W. H. J. *Bookbindings and Rubbings of Bindings in the Victoria and Albert Museum, 1894–98.* Holland Press, London (1963).

Walker, Ronald N. (ed.). *Thousand Best Books for Collectors, 1971–72.* P. Weller, Cirencester (1971).

Winterich, J. T. and Randall, D. A. *A Primer of Book Collecting.* Allen and Unwin, London (1967).

Zaehnsdorf, J. *The Art of Bookbinding.* Gregg Press, London (1967).

The Illustrated Book

Bland, David. *History of the Book: Illuminated Manuscript and the Printed Book.* Faber and Faber, London (1969).

Brunner, Felix. *A Handbook of Graphic Reproduction,* Alec Tiranti, London (1962).

Day, Kenneth. *Book Typography, 1815–1965.* Ernest Benn, London (1966).

English Book Illustration 966–1846. British Museum (1965).

Hamilton, Sinclair. *Early American Book Illustrators and Wood Engravers, 1670–1870.* Princeton University Press (1969).

Hardie, Martin. *English Coloured Books.* Kingsmead reprints, London (1973).

Ivins, William M. *How Prints Look.* Beacon Press, New York (1958).

McLean, Ruari. *Victorian Book Design and Colour Printing.* Faber and Faber, London (1963, revised 1972).

Muir, Percy. *Victorian Illustrated Books.* Batsford, London (1971).

Prideaux, S. T. *Aquatint Engraving: a Chapter in the History of Book Engraving.* W. & G. Foyle, London (1968).

Singer, Hans W. and Strong, William. *Etching, Engraving and other Methods of Printing Pictures.* Kegan Paul, London (1897).

Tooley, R. V. *Books Illustrated by English Artists in Colour Aquatint and Colour Lithography: English Books with Coloured Plates, 1790–1860.* Dawsons Pall Mall, London (1973).

Twyman, Michael. *The Techniques of Drawing on Stone in England and France and Their Application in Works of Topography.* Oxford University Press (1970).

Wakeman, G. *Victorian Book Illustration: The Technical Revolution.* David and Charles, Newton Abbot (1973).

Natural History

Agassiz, L., Strickland, H. E., & Jardine, W. *Bibliographia zoologiae et geologiae. A general catalogue of all books, tracts, and memoirs on zoology and geology.* 4 vols. Ray Society, London (1848–54).

Blunt, W. *The art of botanical illustration.* The New Naturalist series, London (1951).

British Museum (Natural History). *Catalogue of the books, manuscripts, maps and drawings.* Compiled by B. B. Woodward and A. C. Townsend. 8 vols. London (1903–40, Reprint 1964).

Dance, S. P. *Shell Collecting: an illustrated history.* London and Berkely (1966).

Freeman, R. B. *The works of Charles Darwin. An annotated bibliographical handlist.* London (1965).

Rohde, E. S. *The old English herbals*. London (1922, Reprint 1972).
—— *The old English gardening books*. London (1924, Reprint 1972).
Roscoe, S. *A bibliography raisonné of the editions of the General History of Quadrupeds, History of British Birds and Fables of Aesop issued in his lifetime*. London (1953, Reprint 1973).
Soulsby, B. H. *A catalogue of the works of Linnaeus . . . preserved in the libraries of the British Museum (Bloomsbury) and the British Museum (Natural History) (South Kensington)*. London (1933).
Stagemen, P. *A bibliography of the first editions of Philip Henry Gosse, F.R.S.* Cambridge (1955).
Wood, C. A. *An introduction to the literature of vertebrate zoology*. Oxford (1931).

Travel and Topography
Abbey, J. R. *Travel in Aquatint and Lithography, 1770–1860*. 2 volumes. Dawsons Pall Mall, London (1972).
Anderson, J. P. *The Book of British Topography*. Satcheel and Co., London (1881).
Baker, J. N. L. *A History of Geographical Discovery and Exploration*. London (1937).
Beaglehole, J. C. *The Exploration of the Pacific*. Pioneer Histories, London (1934).
Beazley, Sir Charles Raymond. *The Dawn of Modern Geography*. 3 volumes. John Murray, London (1897–1906).
Blackwell, Henry. *Bibliography of Welsh Americana*. National Library of Wales, Aberystwyth (1942).
Brebner, John B. *The Explorers of North America 1492–1806*. Pioneer Histories, London (1933).
Burney, Admiral James. *A Chronological History of the Discoveries in the South Sea*. 5 volumes. London 1803–17.
Chubb, Thomas. *The Printed Maps in the Atlases of Great Britain and Northern Ireland, A Bibliography, 1579–1870*. Homeland Association, London (1927).
Cordeaux, E. H. and Merry, D. H. *Bibliography of Printed Works Relating to Oxfordshire*. Oxford University Press (1955).
Ferguson, Sir John Alexander. *Bibliography of Australia*. 7 volumes 1955–70. Angus and Robertson, Sydney and London.
Fite, E. D. and Freeman, A. (ed.). *A Book of Old Maps Delineating American History*. Dover Publications, New York (1970).
Flint, J. E. *Books on the British Empire and Commonwealth*. Royal Commonwealth Society: Oxford University Press (1968).

Fordham, Sir Herbert George. *Some Notable Surveyors and Map Makers of the Sixteenth, Seventeenth and Eighteenth Centuries and their Work*. Cambridge University Press (1929).
Grierson, P. (ed.). *Books on Soviet Russia 1917–42*. A. C. Hall, Twickenham (1969).
Handlin, Oscar (ed.). *This Was America: True Accounts of People and Places, Manners and Customs as Recorded by European Travelers to the Western Shore in the 18th, 19th and 20th Centuries*. Harvard University Press (1970).
Heawood, Edward. *A History of Geographical Discovery in the Seventeenth and Eighteenth Centuries*. Cambridge University Press (1912).
Heard, J. N. and Hoover, J. H. *Bookman's Guide to America*. Scarecrow Press, Metuchen, New Jersey; Bailey Bros, London (1971).
Highet, G. *People, Places and Books*. Oxford University Press (1953).
Imlay, Gilbert. *Topographical Description of the Western Territory of North America*. Facsimile of 3rd edition, 1797. Kelley, Clifton, New Jersey (1970).
Lewis, Samuel. *Topographical Dictionary of Ireland*. Irish Culture and History Society: Kennikat Press, Port Washington, New York; Bailey Bros, London (1970).
Manwaring, G. E. *Bibliography of British Naval History*. Conway Maritime Press, London (1970).
Parry, J. H. *Trade and Dominion: the European Oversea Empires in the Eighteenth Century*. History of Civilisation Series: Weidenfeld and Nicolson, London (1971).
Penrose, Boris. *Travel and Discovery in the Renaissance 1420–1620*. Harvard University Press (1960).
Sabin, Joseph (ed.). *Dictionary of Books Relating to America*. Scarecrow Press, Metuchen, New Jersey; Bailey Bros, London (1968).
Sibley, M. M. *Travellers in Texas 1761–1860*. University of Texas Press, Austin and London (1967).
Seymour Smith, F. *Bibliography of Herts County: Periodicals and Translations*. Andre Deutsch, London (1964).
Seymour Smith, F. *Bibliography in the Bookshop*. Andre Deutsch, London (1964).
Smith, L. T. (ed.). *The Itinerary of John Leland in or about the years 1535–1543*. Centaur Press, London (1964).
Thornton, Mary L. (ed.). *A Bibliography of North Carolina 1589–1956*. Greenwood Press, Westport (1973).

Tooley, R. V. *Collector's Guide to Maps of the African Continent and South Africa.* Carta Press, London (1969).

Tooley, R. V. *Maps and Mapmakers.* Batsford, London (1949, revised with additional bibliography 1970).

Winsor, Justin (ed.). *Narrative and Critical History of America.* 8 volumes. Boston (1884–89).

Wagner, Harry R. *The Spanish Southwest, 1542–1794: An Annotated Bibliography.* Berkeley, California (1924).

Wood, G. Arnold. *The Discovery of Australia.* Macmillan, London (1922).

Wykes, Alan. *A Miscellany of English Travel Writing. 1700–1914 Abroad.* Macdonald, London (1973).

Children's Books

Barry, F. V. *A Century of Children's Books,* London and New York 1923.

Besterman, T. *A World Bibliography of Bibliographies,* see under 'Children' in volume 1, Lausanne 1966.

Colby, J. P. *The Children's Book Field,* New York 1952.

Crouch, M. *Treasure Seekers and Borrowers; Children's Books in Britain 1900 to 1960,* London 1962.

Darton, F. J. H. *Children's Books in England, Five Centuries of Social Life,* Cambridge 1958.

de Vries, L. *Little Wide-Awake, an anthology of Victorian Children's Books and Periodicals,* 1967.

Ernest, E. *A Kate Greenaway Treasury,* 1967.

Eyre, F. *20th Century Children's Books,* London 1952 and Boston 1953.

Green, R. L. *Tellers of Tales; Children's Books and their Authors from 1800 to 1964,* London 1965.

Hazard, P. *Books, Children and Men,* Boston 1944. (Contains much information on books in other languages.)

Hill, R. and Bondeli, E. *Children's Books from Foreign Languages,* New York 1937.

Lines, K. M. *Four to Fourteen, a Select List of Contemporary Children's Literature,* London and Toronto 1950.

Mahony, B. E. and others *Illustrators of Children's Books 1744 to 1945,* Boston 1947. (A supplementary volume edited by R. Viguers covering the period 1945 to 1956 was published in 1958.)

Meigs, C. and others *A Critical History of Children's Literature,* New York 1953.

Nineteenth-century Fiction

Flower, D. S. *Century of Best Sellers.* (1934).

Griest, G. L. *Mudie's Circulating Library and the Victorian Novel.* David and Charles, Newton Abbot (1970).

Sadlier, M. *Excursions in Victorian Bibliography.* Dawsons Pall Mall, London (1922).

Sadlier, M. *XIX Century Fiction; a Bibliographical Record.* 2 volumes. Constable, London (1951).

Summers, M. *A Gothic Bibliography.* Fortune Press, London (1969).

Modern First Editions

Armitage, C. and Clark, N. *Bibliography of the Works of Louis Macneice.* Kaye and Ward, London (1973).

Ehrsam, Theodore G. *Bibliography of Josef Conrad.* Scarecrow Press, Metuchen, New Jersey; Bailey Bros, London (1969).

Myers, Robin (ed.). *Handlist of Books and Periodicals on British Book Design since the War.* Galley Club: Collins, London (1967).

Stott, Raymond Toole. *Bibliography of Works of Somerset Maugham.* Kaye and Ward, London (1973).

Woolf, Cecil (ed.). *Bibliography of Frederick Rolfe, Baron Corvo.* Soho Bibliographies, Hart-Davis, London (1972).

Index